COME AS
YOU AREN'T!

Also by Norine Dresser

Multicultural Manners: Essential Rules of Etiquette for the 21st Century

I Felt Like I Was from Another Planet: Writing from Personal Experience

Our Own Stories: Readings for Cross-cultural Communication

Our Own Journeys: Readings for Cross-cultural Communication

American Vampires: Fans, Victims & Practitioners

To Judy — Thanks for your interest in my work.

COME AS YOU AREN'T!

Feeling at Home with Multicultural Celebrations

Norine Dresser

Norine Dresser

M. Evans
Lanham • New York • Boulder • Toronto • Oxford

Copyright © 1999, 2006 by Norine Dresser
First M. Evans edition 2006

This M. Evans paperback edition of *Come as You Aren't!* is an original publication. It is published by arrangement with the author.

Portions of Part Two of this book appeared in *Multicultural Celebrations*, published by Three Rivers Press, a Division of Random House, Inc.

Published by M. Evans
An imprint of The Rowman & Littlefield Publishing Group, Inc.
4501 Forbes Boulevard, Suite 200, Lanham, Maryland 20706

Distributed by NATIONAL BOOK NETWORK

Library of Congress Cataloging-in-Publication Data
Dresser, Norine.
    Come as you aren't! : feeling at home with multicultural celebrations
Norine Dresser.
        p. cm.
Includes bibliographical references and index.
1. Etiquette—United States. 2. Holidays. 3. Multiculturalism—United States. I. Title.
BJ1824.D74 2005
395—dc22   2005012049

ISBN-10: 1-59077-093-5
ISBN-13: 978-1-59077-093-1

☉™ The paper used in this publication meets the minimum requirements of American National Standard for Information Sciences—Permanence of Paper for Printed Library Materials, ANSI/NISO Z39.48-1992.

Manufactured in the United States of America.

For Harold.
Despite 54 years of marriage, you still ask,
"But will it last?"

CONTENTS

ACKNOWLEDGMENTS

My favorite part of writing is the research. Hunting for data on the computer or digging through volumes at the library is captivating. However, what exhilarates me most is that candid moment when a human being opens up to me. The names that follow are those I spoke with who energized me by providing information, sharing customs, or leading me to others. You spurred me on to completion of this project. Thank you for your generous contributions.

Victor Agbo; Shahriar Ahmed; Chris Aihara, Director of Community Programs, Japanese American Cultural Community Center; Kristine Alvarez; Barry J. Ancelet, Ph.D; Ruth E. Andersen, Ph.D.; Lenny Arkans; Lynn Ballin; Robin Baltic; George Bamber; David and Marge Barg; Debbie Bellon, Armine Berberian; Ramaa Bharadvaj; Bruce T. Bliatout, Ph.D.; Nancy Blumstein, M.D.; Rebecca Blustein; Rabbi Daniel Bouskila, Sephardic Temple Tifereth Israel; Ann Bradley; Ann Brenoff, Dwan Bridges, Ph.D.; Mogus and Dereju Brook; Vanessa Brown; Heather Bryan; Marvin Call, M.D.; Norma E. Cantú, Ph.D.; Rabbi Carie Carter, Park Slope Jewish Center; Señora Berta Castillo de Torres; Suellen Cheng, Curator, Chinese American Museum; Soo-Young Chin, Ph.D.; Tenzing Chonden, Friends of Tibet; Diane Cohen; Carolyn Cole, Project Director, Shades of L.A.; Jeanne Córdova; Mrs. Dawa; Minister Deb; Luisa Del Giudice, Ph.D.; Ann Del Signore; Kieran Devane; James R. Dow, Ph.D.; Yossi Edelstein, M.D.; Rabbi Lisa Edwards, Congregation Beth Chayim Chadashim; Lucy Eisen; Claire Farrer, Ph.D.; Joseph F. Fennelly, M.D.; Heng Foong, Project Director, Pacific

Island Asian Language Services; Terry L. Garlock, Million Gebreyesus; Clarice Gillis; Mary Georges; Mikka Gutierrez; Alan Hedman, Ph.D.; Kimberly Hemmingson; Kimberly Hughes; Debbie Henderson, Friends of Children from China; Lin and Merrit Humphrey; Gianna E. Israel; Athina Kenekeo; Mary Mom Keo; Anne Marie Khalsa, M.D.; Margaret Kim; Sojin Kim, Ph.D.; Mark Kingsdorf, Queen of Hearts Wedding Consultants; Julie Kirkpatrick; Pastor David L. Kreuger-Duncan, Northwest Community Church, Las Vegas; Tracey Kumer-Moore; Rev. Masao Kodani, Senshin Buddhist Temple; Sokunthear Kong; Provost Donald B. Kraybill, Ph.D., Messiah College; Cecilia Ledezma; Pat Luce, Director, Samoan Affairs Central Region; Ellen Mark, Levy Sephardic Library; Quinn McDonald; Riem Men, Southeast Asian Health Project; Doug Metz, Mortuary Science, Cerritos Community College; Teferi Michael; Ann Milton; Chanida Mumanachit, Tourism Authority of Thailand; Louis Negrete, Ph.D.; John B. Niazi; Richard J. Nitti, Executive Director, Neighborhood House, Inc.; Clarice W. Nuhi; Jon Olson, Ph.D.; Natalie Olson; Tracie Owens; Jane Ka'ala Pang, Hawaiian Civic Club; Nina Phan; Florence Pou, Samoan Community Center; Ruth Polan; Harihar Rao; Reverend Tonyia Rawls, Unity Fellowship of Christ Church; Cheryl Revkin, D.C.: Robert A. Ringler, Ph.D.; Donna Devera Rojas; Eddard Romero; Rebecca Rona, Together; Saint Sophia Cathedral, Los Angeles; Arpi Sarafian, Ph.D; Jeannie Shade, R.N.; Amir Sharafi; Nancy K. Shimamoto, Hispanic & Asian Marketing Communication Research, Inc.; Venerable Kong Sophan Wat Khmer Temple, Los Angeles; Sherry Skramstad; Connie Spittler; Hany Takla, President, St. Shenouda The Archimandrite Coptic Society; Father Tom Stehle; Theresa Sterling; Rabbi Stephen Stern, Arden Heights Boulevard Jewish Center and Congregation Etz Chaim; Frances Tally, Ph.D., UCLA Archive of Popular Belief and Superstition; Judith Terzi; Waraporn Tiaprasith; Barre Toelken, Ph.D.; María Torres; Chue Vang; Veronica Vera, Miss Vera's Finishing School for Boys Who Want to Be Girls; Bibian Vosgien; Mary G. Wentz; Anne G. Wilcoxen, Ph.D., Director, Center for Cultural Fluency, Mount St. Mary's College; Marshall Wong, Los Angeles County Department of Human Relations; Patchara and Vibul Wonprasat, Thai Community Arts and Cultural Center; Jack Yaffe; Gerald D. Yoshitomi, Ph.D.; Jeanne Youngson, Ph.D.; Mai Xiong; Arina Zahid; Fahimeh Zand.

Hats off to the reference desk staffs at the Glendale and Pasadena Public Libraries, who attentively and enthusiastically answered my countless phone queries. My appreciation also goes to Mary MacGregor Villareal, Ph.D., who did a bang-up job of early research.

I wish to acknowledge my dear friends. First are those who pondered with me throughout the process and answered urgent questions: Janice Garey; Rachel Spector; Jan Steward; Lucia Van Ruiten; Dolores Wong. Next come my eagle-eyed cronies who gave the manuscript thoughtful readings and helped me solved dilemmas: Virginia Crane; Marilyn Elkins, Ph.D.; Montserrat Fontes. I'm blessed to have such loyal and talented friends. You are *amigas fantásticas!*

My New York team was invaluable as well—agent *consigliere* Sheree Bykofsky and especially editor PJ Dempsey, my guiding light and good friend, who believed in me and enlivened the writing process by sending me daily doses of e-mail humor.

A special note of thanks to my long time buddy Julie Benton Siegel, self-proclaimed "Winner of the Nobel Puns Prize," for her contributions of the titles *Come As You Aren't!*, *Ethnice-ities*, and *The Rites and Wrongs of Multicultural Celebrations*. Nonetheless, I regret scuttling her provocative interfaith marriage title: *When Hansel Met Shtetl: A Mixed Marriage Mishigas*.

Finally, I recognize my outstanding family who constantly supply me with leads and support: my children, Mark, Andrea, Amy; my favorite daughter-in-law, Carol; grandkids, Leila Sharafi, Zach and Avi Berk, Isa Del Signore Dresser; plus Mickey Shapiro, the best of brothers.

I offer all of you my gratitude and love.

INTRODUCTION

Come As You Aren't! spotlights celebrations and their potential to unite or divide, particularly when celebrants literally and figuratively come from different places. The goal of *Come As You Aren't!* is to help us enjoy harmony during life affirming rituals.

When I was growing up, "Come as You Are!" parties were popular pre-teen girls' events. In my neighborhood, they worked this way: A friend would phone early in the morning and casually ask, "What are you wearing?" and after I described what was often matching two-piece, pastel printed cotton pajamas and curlers, my friend would jubilantly command, "Come as You Are!" That meant that I, and other guests, had to show up at an appointed time for a party wearing the clothes we had on at the time of the call.

Incredibly, this type of party still goes on, but it has evolved technologically. Now, the guest-of-honor, or her mother, may awaken the girl and, armed with a video camera, record the startled response to the shouted "Come as You Are!" invitation. Then the girl is taken to the honoree's home where other sleepy guests have gathered in their pajamas, which may be a tank top with boxer shorts or a tee-shirt with pajama bottoms, to share a special breakfast and a rollicking video of the awakenings. The major point *was* and *is* surprise.

In contrast, *Come As You Aren't!* intends to prevent unnecessary surprises. My goal is **no surprises**. I want you to know what to expect and what's expected of you. The book prepares readers so that they can enjoy unfamiliar events to their fullest. Guests invited to weddings, funerals, and celebrations of people from different ethnicities, religions, sexual orientations, and cultures need to know what to expect and what is appropriate or inappropriate behavior.

Whether you are a new member of a multiracial/interfaith family, the father of a same-sex bride, the mother of an adopted daughter from China, *Come As You Aren't!* helps mixed families avoid social pitfalls at holidays and rituals for birth, coming of age, marriage, death. It gives tips on appropriate behavior when attending a variety of unfamiliar ethnic and religious life-cycle events.

Who Will Benefit From Reading This Book?

1. Couples already in, or who are contemplating, interfaith and multiracial marriages

They will learn how others have solved their holiday and rites-of-passage dilemmas. Clergy, couples, and families offer their points of view.

2. Families of interfaith and multiracial couples

Experts, secular and religious, counsel about the effects of withholding emotional support. Families will better understand the pain this creates for their loved ones.

3. Families who have adopted, or are contemplating adopting, children from other races within and outside the United States

Families who have successfully adopted children share their methods for integrating the children into already existing family groups. Prospective adoptive parents will learn to implement rituals to help new family members feel that they belong.

4. Members of the Gay/Lesbian/Bisexual/Transgender (GLBT) communities

In this section the clergy and other experts offer support and advice to this community. These advisors encourage GLBT members by revealing how supportive members of the straight community can be.

5. Families of GLBT community members

They will gain greater perspective on what a difficult path GLBT persons travel. Clergy and other experts offer suggestions for accepting them as bona fide family members, particularly through participation at holidays and rites of passage.

6. The clergy and other professionals who perform interfaith and same-sex marriages

Come As You Aren't! suggests ideas for meaningful ceremonies as well as recommendations for resolving pre-nuptial angst.

7. Marriage and family counselors

For those marriage and family counselors seeking assistance, other experts offer ideas for helping couples resolve family conflicts during holidays and rites of passage.

8. Guests invited to unfamiliar rites of passage

The book provides handy dos and don'ts of what to say, give, wear, and act. Guests will know what to expect when they attend such events.

9. Anyone seeking information about the celebrations of their neighbors, co-workers, acquaintances, and clients

* * *

Because the gay marriages of 2004 have polarized the nation and interfaith, multiracial families and adoptions have become an increasing part of the social landscape, Part One of this book is devoted to our new cultural diversity. As aptly described in *Vanity Fair* magazine by social commentator James Wolcott, "The country is evolving into a multi-racial, multi-ethnic, multi-faith, omnisexual creamy rainbow swirl." *Come As You Aren't* recognizes this evolution and places it front and center of the book.

Part Two focuses on our old cultural diversity—differences based on religion and ethnicity. It makes an ideal resource for a deeper understanding of Part One.

Part One, Embracing our New Cultural Diversity, focuses on the creative ways people cope with conflicts that may arise during ceremonial occasions involving family or friends with differing religious, racial, or sexual orientations. How do we reconcile the differences? How can we experience more harmonious and pleasurable celebrations?

Chapter One shows how interfaith couples, especially Jews and Christians, negotiate the December dilemma of competing Christmas Hanukkah celebrations. It describes innovative ways to represent both faiths at weddings, coming-of-age ceremonies, *bar* and *bas mitzvahs*, and funerals. It reflects the views of grandparents, who may be more reticent to embrace new ideas. Clergy and other experts offer strategies for helping everyone make creative accommodations.

Chapter Two focuses on multiracial families and how they reconcile differences during rites of passage and holidays. Some give up certain customs to achieve family harmony. Some combine customs and others find ways to help grandparents cope with these changes. Additionally, parents of children adopted from other races within and outside the United States describe how they integrate their children's birth culture into existing family traditions.

Chapter Three describes rites of passage and holidays as celebrated by the Gay Lesbian Bisexual Transgender (GLBT) communities. GLBT community members share their experiences and report on the pain they have suffered or the support they have received—for example, a person of differing sexual orientation may be excluded from holiday activities, and their family members may boycott GLBT activities. Clergy give advice and offer suggestions to conflicted parents. In addition, this part describes innovative rituals.

Chapters One, Two, and Three are integrated to emphasize that these communities are all a part of the fabric of our diverse American culture and should be recognized as such. *Come as You Aren't!* is a commentary on, and an exaltation of, our heterogeneous society, honoring American culture for nurturing diversity. The book also pays tribute to the participants' creativity and use of humor.

I have gathered the information from scholarly and popular publications, the internet, and personal interviews. Generally, when I use both first and last names of people, those are their real names. Citing people by one name only usually means that I have changed names to maintain privacy. At the end of the book, I have included a bibliography and resource section for further reference.

Part Two, "Ethnice-ities: The Rites and Wrongs of Multicultural Celebrations" describes a variety of ethnicities and religions, such as Chinese, Japanese, Filipino, Catholic, and Muslim. I've divided the rites discussed in "Ethnice-ities" into Birth, Coming of Age Rituals, Marriage, and Death—the major passages in individuals' lives.

To make this section user-friendly, I have placed guidelines at the top of each entry. I suggest what (and what not) to wear, say, do, and give.

It provides a handy how-to guide. More background information and description are provided in the text that follows.

A note of caution: When referring to people's traditions I am not referring to fixed laws of science. Variations in folklore are the rule, not the exception. Traditions diverge within the same ethnic or religious group. For example, some people open their presents on Christmas Eve while others open them on Christmas morning. Neither is right or wrong. Therefore, if you are of a particular ethnicity and your customs are not the same as what you read in this book, do not be alarmed. Other members of your ethnic group may mirror these practices. That is the nature of folklore.

How Do We Benefit From Celebrations?

Since I am a folklorist, I view human behavior through the lens of my training and background. Thus I see a need for celebrations—creating commonalities helps us flourish. Holidays and life-cycle events—birth, coming-of-age, marriage, and death—can all be precarious. We find ourselves thrown off balance when these events upset the status quo. For example, consider how unsettling it is to have a new child, whether through birth or adoption. In spite of the anticipated happiness, a new child requires financial, spatial, physical, and emotional alterations. Most rites of passage entail these adjustments. Consequently, at these important times, family and friends observe appropriate customs to help people cope with the changes.

While celebrations are ideally joyous times, they can also have a downside. Holidays and rites of passage can open old wounds of family disharmony. Overspending on gifts can put a strain on the budget as well as the psyche. Emotional pain can ensue if people are separated from their families. If families have recently suffered the loss of a loved one, that loss seems more acute at these times. Media images of warm and fuzzy families may leave people feeling deprived because they are not enjoying their family.

Although skeptics might dismiss life cycle celebrations as frivolous occasions, they have important functions. They allow for "conspicuous consumption," a term anthropologists and folklorists use to label the material aspects of the celebrations, which commonly are displays of the hosts' extravagance. Through these activities, wealth circulates within the community. Honorees receive useful goods; shopkeepers profit; community employment increases to accommodate the needs of the event.

Beyond material considerations, celebrations give us a break from our workday routines. They force us to take time out from the mundane to savor precious moments. Some encourage fantasy, playfulness, creativity, and joy; some evoke laughter, goose bumps, tears, and sighs. Celebrations surrounding life cycle transitions, in particular, cause us to take inventory of who is still among us, and who is no longer here. Celebrations cause us to stop and reflect on where we are in life. Perhaps that is what makes tears spring to our eyes at these events—the awareness of our own life journey, its beginning and its approaching end.

These celebrations give us something to look forward to; they buoy us and can even lengthen our lives. The ninety-fifth birthday celebration of Harry Asimow in Venice, California, offers an excellent example. After being incarcerated in a Russian prison for inciting revolutionary activities while serving in the czar's army, he was released and fled to the United States, where he became a union organizer in the sheet metal industry. Following retirement, he took adult education classes and began writing poetry and essays. Later, he helped found the first senior citizens center in Southern California and in his eighties became actively involved in the Israel Levin Senior Center.

Each year, Harry's devoted family prepared a large birthday party for him at this Venice center, where he always gave a speech. However, by the time he reached his ninety-fifth birthday, Harry was quite frail. Still he insisted that he attend the party and read a speech containing an important message: He was leaving money for five more birthday parties to be celebrated in his honor, whether he was there or not.

For this special occasion, 150 friends, relatives, and center members attended. Part of the time, Harry rested backstage on a cot using the oxygen that his family had provided. After lunch, Harry mustered all his strength and gave his speech. After receiving many accolades, he sat down at the table, folded his hands, and died. While many of those who attended believed that the angel of death had waited until after Harry's speech to take him, others might say that Harry's anticipation of the celebration and the honor he was about to receive from family and friends sustained his life.

Harry's story is unique in its particulars, yet celebrations can extend lives for others as well. Like Harry, we hold on so that we might live to witness significant events—a graduation, a wedding, a birth.

We need symbolic action to draw us together and keep us going. That's what celebrations do. They make us feel that we belong. This feeling comes through the creation of *communitas*—a feeling of oneness. When friends and family come together to sing "Happy Birthday," to toast the bride and groom, or to bid a final farewell to a loved one, they demonstrate that happiness and grief can be shared. These symbolic moments are communal hugs.

I have written this book from a folklorist's perspective because folklorists often examine rites of passage, customs, beliefs, ceremonies and holidays in order to understand human behavior and culture. This research has been my vocation and avocation for over thirty years, lecturing at California State University, Los Angeles, delivering papers at academic folklore meetings, talking before organizations, publishing books and articles, and writing an eight-year-running newspaper column for the *Los Angeles Times*.

Personally, my avid interest in "other peoples'" customs and rituals is so strong that my Iranian Muslim *ex*-son-in-law invited me to his second marriage so I could photograph his Persian wedding traditions for my slide collection.

Multicultural explorations are not just scholarly interests. I attended a workshop on "Mixed Marriages" and asked my husband to accompany me. As an icebreaker, the leader divided participants into dyads to share stories about any mixed marriages they knew. My husband drew me aside and whispered, "Do we know any?" Sarcastically, I responded, "How about your three children and their mates? Your brother-in-law? Your niece? Your nephew? You want more?" While at first I was annoyed that he forgot, later it dawned on me that he was so accepting of our multicultural family that he didn't think of them as being anything other than "our family." And we take pride in our grandchildren who are Jewish, part Italian, part Iranian Muslim.

In addition to personal and professional interests, I have been attracted to this study because life cycle celebrations provide comfort by giving people responsibilities to tackle during unsettling times—"Don't just stand there. Do something." These celebrations bind us to our communities; they furnish creative outlets for the human spirit. They allow us to express our emotions nonverbally. Celebrations, whether they elicit laughter or tears, confirm spirituality and authenticate life.

(PART ONE)

EMBRACING OUR NEW
CULTURAL DIVERSITY

Interfaith, Multiracial, Adoptive Families
Gays, Lesbians, Transgenders

Whereas most people think of ethnic and religious differences when speaking about diversity, in this book I have expanded the diversity concept to include mixed families—interfaith and multicultural families, families with transracial adopted children, as well as the gay, lesbian, bisexual, and transgender communities. This more accurately reflects American society in the twenty-first century. Not that these added communities haven't always been here, but they have not always been as visible.

1. Interfaith Families

According to interfaith minister Susanna Stefanachi Macomb, over forty percent of marriage-age Catholics wed outside the Church; three in ten Mormons are now in interfaith marriages; one in three Episcopalians and one in four Lutherans marry outside their churches. The Greek Orthodox Archdiocese of America reports that two-thirds of its marriages are interfaith; and four in ten Muslims choose non-Muslim spouses. The intermarriage rate approaches sixty percent for Buddhists, who are the fastest growing Eastern religion in the United States.

In the past, Jewish/Christian unions were the most discussed in print and at the pulpit. Catholic born journalist Cokie Roberts and her Jewish journalist husband, Steve Roberts, are a well-known example. In their book *From This Day Forward* they detail the joys and challenges of their interfaith family, especially during holidays and rites of passage.

2. Multiracial Families

An article in *Adoptive Parents* claims that, by the year 2020, approximately one-half of all marriages will be bicultural or biracial. Golf champion

Tiger Woods' father is one-half African American, one-quarter Native American, and one-quarter Chinese, and his mother is half-Thai, one-quarter Chinese, and one-quarter white. In October 2004, Tiger wed Swedish model Elin Nordegren.

Adoptions create other kinds of multiracial families. Sometimes parents adopt children of different races from within the country. Other parents seek to adopt children internationally. In 2002, film star Angelina Jolie received a great deal of publicity when she adopted her son, Maddox, from Cambodia. Not to be overlooked are the five million non-celebrity Americans who have opened up their hearts and homes to abandoned or needy children from inside and outside the United States.

3. Gay/lesbian/bisexual/transgender Communities

Since the flurry of Gay/Lesbian weddings in 2004, there has been a greater awareness among the general population of Gay/Lesbian couples enacting marriage rites. The *New Yorker* magazine cover by Mark Ulriksen (March 15, 2004) whimsically depicts the situation: A female customer trying on a wedding dress and veil looks shocked when she sees a bearded male customer trying on an identical gown and headpiece.

Today we applaud high-profile gay entertainers such as Ellen DeGeneres and Harvey Fierstein for their talents, and their sexual orientation is a non-issue. This doesn't mean that prejudice in the entertainment industry or elsewhere doesn't exist. It merely reflects the baby steps that the public is beginning to take in considering sexual orientation irrelevant.

[1]

CELEBRATIONS IN
INTERFAITH FAMILIES

Our multicultural nation provides constant opportunities for people to meet others from different faiths. Christians and Jews regularly interact at work, school, and play. Other religions intermingle as well. A Lutheran reporter interviews a Catholic musician. A Muslim engineer works on a project with a Presbyterian coworker. Such casual relationships open the door to friendship, possibly romance, maybe even marriage. A 2001 American Religion Identification Survey indicated that 22 percent of U.S. households were interfaith, amounting to twenty-eight million adults.

In an interfaith marriage, major life events or transitions can involve more emotion, more difficult decisions, and more opportunities to "work things out" than such moments in a single faith marriage. Challenges arise as the couple struggles to accommodate one another's customs, symbols and belief systems, and maintain harmony between themselves, their children, and their respective families.

Problems can arise beginning with the wedding, a major rite of passage, followed by the arrival of children and finally, death. Religions and cultural customs cluster around these ceremonial moments, and when the customs of one family differ from those of the other family, negotiations must take place. Religious holidays, too, may require mediation.

While some interfaith couples might think that their conflicts and compromises are unique, from a societal perspective such problems are widespread. Most interfaith couples share similar dilemmas, and their responses to disagreements can be innovative as well as instructive to other couples who find themselves struggling to reconcile deep seated beliefs as they plan special occasions.

For many years I have interviewed interfaith couples and their families and discussed issues associated with multicultural celebrations with experts. With this experience in mind, I offer suggestions and examples for ameliorating conflicts that naturally arise when couples have different religious backgrounds yet desire to celebrate their unions and build harmonious families.

RITES OF PASSAGE

"Religious urges surface most visibly three times in life: when people get hatched, when they get matched, and when they're dispatched."
—Rabbi Shimon L. Berris

How do couples from different religions meet the challenges presented by their differing faiths?

For any interfaith couple, the most critical moments in their lives are likely to involve their own union, the birth of their children, the death of a loved one. In each rite of passage, critical decisions usually have to be settled with a good deal of discussion and planning. Four major questions generally arise when preparing for a marriage.

Who will officiate at the ceremony?
Where will the ceremony take place?
How can each partner's religious tradition be honored?
What is the role of the parents?

Marriage

Books and organizations which address the oppositions of interfaith marriages seem to focus most frequently on Christian/Jewish unions. Indeed, marriages between Christians and Jews have increased dramatically. Before 1970 only 13 percent of Jewish marriages were interfaith. Since 1996, 47 percent of all Jewish marriages involve a non-Jewish spouse. That phenomenon will no doubt continue, so the first question is, who will perform the ceremony?

Who will officiate seems an easy question to answer on the face of it. But this decision may require more investigation, discussion, and settlement than a couple might expect. When an interfaith couple is planning their wedding, the first step to take is to talk to clergy from both faiths to see if they would be willing to officiate together. While logic dictates that religious leaders from both sides be present, that logic is faulty. Clergy representing one faith may be prohibited from performing rituals in another house of worship. For example, some rabbis will not officiate in a chapel containing Christian symbols but exceptions do exist.

I attended a Catholic/Jewish wedding in a Catholic church where a rabbi was present. He was the rabbi from the groom's family's temple and travelled across the country to attend the ceremony. Essentially, the wedding turned out to be a Catholic service with only minor participation from the rabbi, who, when the ceremony concluded, was quickly whisked back to his home town safe from scrutiny from his own congregation.

If the designated clergy persons refuse to perform a service together, select just one of them or look for an alternative.

Interfaithclergynetwork.com is a great source for alternative clergy. It is an organization of 75 rabbis, priests, and ministers who, because they are retired, have no congregations to object when they perform ceremonies with clergy from other faiths. I found this organization on the internet. They specialize in interfaith weddings, obviously, particularly in the northeastern United States. But there are many other sources—just Google "interfaith clergy," and you will discover over 32,000 entries.

Just last year I attended a Christian/Jewish wedding of a former neighbor officiated by Robert Ringler, Ph.D., a non-denominational minister and humanist counselor for the American Humanist Association. He began officiating at interfaith marriages more than twenty years ago while working at UCLA because the university-affiliated rabbis, priests, and ministers were often prevented by the rules of their faith from performing interfaith marriages or were uncomfortable officiating at them. Marrying couples of all faiths has now become a full-time occupation for Ringler, and as of October 2004, he had married over 9,000 couples through his Bel-Air Wedding Ceremonies organization.

Ringler encourages his couples to create their own ceremonies, thus demonstrating their uniqueness. He shows them over fifty different ceremonies from his library so they can see more options and personalize their ceremony. Sometimes they request humor. For example: "Love is understanding. He understands that she has to go shopping every week. She understands that he has to play basketball."

Ringler's outlook is broad. If the bride is pregnant, after pronouncing the couple husband and wife, he addresses the fetus. "If you're listening, here are some special vows your mom and dad have just for you." He recites these vows and has the couple repeat them, uniting the family.

When children from a previous marriage are present, he has the family say vows promising to look out for each other, through good and bad times, to share lives and dreams with love and respect. To their children they vow to always love them and give them wings to fly.

Because Rabbi Carie Carter, of the Park Slope Jewish Center in Brooklyn, belongs to the Jewish Conservative movement, she may only marry Jewish couples, yet often one person in the couple may be a converted Jew. Obviously that person's family is from another faith. Under these circumstances, she suggests having the non-Jewish family learn about each step of the ritual beforehand. "It's more fulfilling to them if they have a sense of what's going on," she claims. That will make the ceremony more enjoyable for them and they will participate more willingly.

At Carter's temple a non-Jewish person can offer a blessing or read a poem. For example, the Jewish parents may say the Hebrew version of "May God bless you and keep you," and the non-Jewish parents will say it in English. Her only caution is that the non-Jewish family members not invoke the name of Jesus. Certain blessings have to be Jewish. It wouldn't make sense for non-Jews to give them.

As an interfaith couple begins wedding plans, it is essential they do not take the agreement about clergy for granted. Direct inquiry, lots of discussion and careful arbitration may require a good deal of time and a good many decisions. So start planning early, and be open to creative compromises on who will officiate your marriage ceremony.

The second question an interfaith couple will need to address as they plan their wedding is where will the ceremony be held? This may seem a relatively simple question at first glance. But once more, celebrating an interfaith union is not allowed in some places of worship—investigate early.

If a traditional house of worship is not an option, look for an alternative setting.

Some couples may be tempted to elope just to avoid the conflicts. But you needn't run off to Vegas and be escorted down the aisle by a look-alike Elvis, or go to a zoo, or get married at the bottom of the sea in your scuba diving outfits. You can still select a beautiful setting that is spiritual yet secular, and one that reflects your sensibilities.

Seek a religiously neutral environment: home, banquet hall, hotel, country club, or park. Nonetheless, once you've found the perfect setting more issues can arise. Your traditions and your partner's traditions may not mesh or perhaps even conflict. Then you're back to the same options. If you choose one set over the other, conflicts are certain.

Incorporate customs from both religious traditions.

At the wedding reception for an Italian Catholic groom and Greek Orthodox bride, the music focused on line dances á la Zorba, the Greek. The exasperated groom's mother loudly complained, "When we gonna do the tarantella?"

Blending customs during the ritual is the most common solution. For the union of Christian and Jew, symbols of each faith might be incorporated into the setting or the ceremony. For Christian representation, during the ceremony, couples can light a unity candle. Jewish elements may include the breaking of the glass and/or standing under a wedding *chupah* (canopy). At the reception, there can be a Christian blessing of the meal and the traditional Jewish dancing of the *hora* and performing of the chair dance.

The important thing to remember as you plan is that inclusiveness is the goal. "Don't let anybody feel left out," recommends Tracey Kumer-Moore of Your Las Vegas Wedding Concierge. Kumer-Moore is an established wedding planner in Las Vegas, and when I interviewed her, she was adamant about including both families. "They will have a really cool experience and learn something."

Of course, not leaving anyone out applies to all weddings, even when both families are of the same nationality or religion. During the 1980s I attended a wedding where both the groom and bride's families were involved with performing folk music. At the reception, the bride's family was front and center onstage singing, while the groom's side was only nominally called on to perform. This upset the groom's family and friends. Feelings were hurt and discontent was expressed. No one would have considered religious prejudice in this situation. Nonetheless, when religious differences occur, interpreting the motivations for being left out might erroneously be labeled as prejudice and get the marriage off to a bad start.

Often parents initially resist the blending of traditions, such as honoring both the Old and New Testaments. Consider that the families may be uninformed about the new in-law's religion and ritual requirements for marriage. Try and dissipate their anxieties by telling them exactly what will take place. Don't assume that they know much about religious customs other than their own, or they may think they know what your rituals are and what they mean but may be misinformed.

Expect parents to be initially less than enthusiastic about your wedding plans.

Parents may try to impose their own preferences and emphasize their traditions more than the other traditions, and although each of you may wish to respect your own family, remember that this ceremony represents the beginning of your new life together and that your faiths must be represented in the way you find most suitable. It is the beginning of your new life together that must be equally represented. Above all, remember that it is *your* wedding, not your parents'. For any couple the wedding ceremony, who officiates, where it occurs and how it represents them becomes a symbol of their union and establishes the foundation of their future lives together.

Parents must remind themselves that their role is to be positive and supportive.

The wedding and marriage should focus on what the couple desires. Don't manipulate your children in the name of love to get your own way: "If you really love us, you'll let Father Tom perform the ceremony." Even if you suspect that the marriage will ultimately not work out, try not to interfere with the wedding plans by insisting on your faith's dominance. Neither should you try to scuttle the marriage. Your intentions may be good, but the results may boomerang and place a distance between you and your child that could last a lifetime.

What if your child's future mate insists you participate in a custom that absolutely goes against your principles? You are perfectly within your rights to abstain. That's what Marvin did at the Jewish/Scottish Christian ceremony for his daughter. Although the wedding couple blended some customs, playing bagpipes and stomping on the glass, Marvin refused to wear a kilt.

With interfaith weddings, choices mostly boil down to his, hers, or a blending of the two. Yet despite the extreme planning and focus on details, weddings last less than a day. The marriage, not the wedding, should be the focus. What follows the wedding festivities requires even more conciliation and compromise, especially with the arrival of children. Adding children to a couple's relationship dynamics guarantees that new issues must be tackled.

Arrival of Children

It is common knowledge that the arrival of a child can bring all kinds of new stresses and conflicts to the lives of any couple. Even though my husband and I are both Jewish, we faced family conflict hours after our son was born. According to our tradition, he would be circumcised. My mother assumed that we would have a traditional *Brit Milah* (ritual circumcision) performed by a *mohel* (see Birth, p. 127). She was unaware that my husband had witnessed a mishap at a relative's ritual circumcision and was adamantly opposed to anyone performing the procedure other than a surgeon. I was in my hospital bed, on the phone with my mom and in tears, when the doctor entered the room. When he saw me crying, he remarked, "I know what that's about." Despite my parents' pressure, I stood by my husband's decision.

In an interfaith family, birth traditions bring even more layers of complexity to decision making. Whether a circumcision is to be performed by a *mohel* or a surgeon or not at all is a conflict that surfaces within the first days of a child's life. Naturally, the prudent thing to do is to discuss and resolve these kinds of issues before the child arrives, but this is an ideal rarely achieved.

> Begin discussing circumcision long before the child arrives. Don't leave the conversation until after the child is born or assume that you're going to have a girl.

Before a child is born, especially the first one, most couples cannot fully fathom the emotional responses that lie ahead. Birth rituals, ostensibly joyous occasions, can bring about painful deliberations. While circumcision presents one type of early issue, naming and baptizing the child are other potential sources of conflict.

> Other issues must also be addressed before delivery, such as naming and baptism.

A Japanese/Mexican/Catholic woman married a Jew and they were expecting a baby boy. The maternal grandparents assumed that the baby would be named "Junior" in typical Mexican/Catholic tradition. These grandparents had difficulty accepting the Ashkenazi (of Eastern European heritage) Jewish tradition that prohibits naming babies after living persons because it is thought that to do so places that person at risk of death.

Additionally, the Irish Catholic side of the family might not be thrilled with Jewish names like Hymie or Rachel. The Jewish side may be equally disturbed by names such as Christopher or Mary.

Baptism is an obligation for some Christians but not others. In one family, a Lutheran mother and Catholic father elected not to baptize the child at all to avoid strong reactions from their respective families. That seemed the simplest solution to them. Elsewhere, a Jewish mother could not comprehend her future Catholic's son-in-law's insistence on a baptism for the baby. He explained that after death the baby would remain in limbo without this ritual, an obscure concept to his mother-in-law. Her first words were, after hearing this, "Don't invite me." Later she decided that if it meant that much to her son-in-law she would participate, but she couldn't handle telling her own mother about it. The Jewish great-grandmother would have been inconsolable at the thought of a baptized great-grandchild.

Nan Meyer, another Jewish grandmother, revealed that despite her smiles her heart broke while attending her grandchild's baptism. She avoided taking pictures in front of the cross and refrained from reacting when the Christian grandfather claimed, "At least now the baby has a decent religion." She reconciled herself with the knowledge that the baby was healthy, beautiful, blessed by God, and loved by both sides of the family. Meyer's response and attitude are admirable because she placed the welfare of the baby and the baby's parents above her own emotions.

The children of interfaith marriages have conflicts as well. A Catholic mother and Jewish father are rearing their daughter as a Jew. Despite the respect shown for both religions, the daughter felt that she was somewhat alienated from her mother. One day she wistfully admitted, "Mommy, I wish you were Jewish."

But both sides must maintain a sense of humor in order to overcome the smaller conflicts. A Jewish father had misgivings when his Catholic wife wanted to pull their daughter out of Hebrew School early so that she might march in the St. Patrick's Day Parade. This same student couldn't understand why her parents didn't allow her to wear her "Our Holy Name Savior Swim Team" sweatshirt to Hebrew School. In the book *What To Do When You're Dating a Jew*, a Catholic/Jewish couple revealed their answer to those who asked how they were raising their children, "Very guilty."

My mother-in-law once told me, "With babies you have small problems, but when the babies get older, the problems get bigger." That applies to interfaith families as well. The Buddhist wife of a Christian husband told me that they were fine together before they had a child and even when their son was a baby, but now that he was older conflicts have surfaced. Her Buddhist background had taught her that when school was out, her son should continue learning. Her husband believed that during school vacations their son should "kick back" or take golf lessons, just the way he had been raised. How did these parents resolve their differences? They divided their son's summer. Half the time he continued his studies, the other half he "kicked back" and took golf lessons.

Coming-of-Age

Coming-of-age ceremonially marks the moment when children become adults and profess membership in a particular faith. In the United States, when and where such a celebration takes place will be dictated by the religious affiliation of the family. If Mexican-Catholic, girls have *quinceañera* celebrations at fifteen; if Catholic, both boys and girls have confirmation ceremonies during their high school years; if Jewish, *bar/bas mitzvahs* take place at age thirteen; if Protestant, confirmations take place during the early teens. In one interfaith family, Heidi, the mom, was a Catholic who converted to Judaism. She and her husband both wanted their children to be raised Jewish and have bar and bat mitzvahs. The children claimed it was unfair. Their mom never had to go through the rigorous training to learn Hebrew and read from the Torah. Why should they? To counter their complaints, Heidi began *bas mitzvah* preparation, learned Hebrew, and had her own *bas mitzvah* much to the amazement of her children, her Catholic parents, and siblings.

BAR/BAS MITZVAH

> Involve the non-Jewish side of the family as much as you can and as much as they are willing.

During coming-of-age rituals, involvement of the non-Jewish parent and the non-Jewish side of the family varies according to the stance of the particular rabbi and their branch of Judaism. At a *bas mitzvah* at the Park Slope Jewish Center in Brooklyn, the father was Jewish and the mother Italian Catholic, and Rabbi Carie Carter ensured that non-Jewish family members were included in the ceremony. The maternal Catholic aunt and uncle came to the *bimah* (stage) to read the "Prayer for Our Country," and the Catholic mother gave a speech from her heart that brought tears to the congregation.

What happens when people of other faiths adopt your customs? This should be regarded as honoring, not insulting, your traditions.

FAUX MITZVAH

> If you are Jewish, don't misunderstand or be offended when non-Jews adopt your traditions. Understand that it is part of a natural cultural process.

Although faux *mitzvahs* are not a blending of customs within sets of interfaith families, they reflect a larger principle—the adopting and adapting of appealing customs from outside one's own religious community. In anthropological terms, the process of incorporating others' traditions into yours is called diffusion and is one way to explain how customs spread from culture to culture. Faux *mitzvahs* parallel the behavior of other non-Jews who are attracted to Jewish customs. Examples include Madonna's adopting the Jewish name of Esther and wearing the famous red string, a custom of Kabbalists (a mystical form of Judaism). These strings are tied with seven knots, blessed in Bethlehem at Rachel's Tomb, and worn on the left wrist to keep away evil. Red strings became so popular in 2004 that for a while Target Department stores were selling them for $29.99. Other celebrities, such as Demi Moore, Britney Spears, and Paris Hilton are also known to sport these strings.

Similarly, faux mitzvahs are celebrations for non-Jewish thirteen-year-old boys and girls who have attended real *bar/bas mitzvahs* and would like the same kind of celebratory event as their Jewish friends. Generally, it is children who wish to adopt the mitzvah celebration. They see something appealing in being feted in an elaborate way to mark their entrance into adulthood, particularly since American culture offers no ritual coming of age celebration other than the debutante's "Coming Out" party or the Latina's *quinceañera.*

In faux *mitzvahs*, some rabbis see the beauty of one culture admiring and appreciating the traditions of the Jews. More commonly, rabbis deplore these events, complaining that they merely copy the celebratory aspects without religious obligation. They worry that the depth and meaning of the tradition of *bar/bas mitzvahs* will be stripped away.

Whether approved or disapproved, the faux *mitzvah* trend is growing. Hart to Hart, a party company in Woodland Hills, California organized three faux mitzvahs in 2001, a dozen in 2003, and scheduled more for 2004. Daniel Rose of Montville, New Jersey, says he did two in 2001 and seven or eight in 2003. New York Rhythm Entertainment booked about a dozen in the past two years and none before that.

According to Barbara Mahany of *The Chicago Tribune,* "It's a scene seen in heavily Jewish areas, where Gentiles are just trying to keep up with the, er, Cohens. But it's also popping up in places where there are very few Jews." Could this be labeled "culture envy"?

Death

Death elicits conflict unless interfaith couples have clearly made decisions in advance. To avoid unwarranted interference from your mate's family, try to discuss openly and thoughtfully how each of you feels regarding end-of-life issues such as health directives and disposal of the body. Forms for living wills are available on the internet. Advanced health directives that officially appoint someone to carry out your wishes if you are incapacitated are available from physicians and health care organizations.

> Even as a young married couple, make decisions in advance. It is much easier to talk about these issues when you and your spouse are young and in good health. Make pre-need arrangements if possible.

Because intermarriage has become increasingly common, formerly religiously segregated cemeteries have made accommodations to please families. The policy on interfaith burial grounds differs according to cemetery. For example, at one Jewish cemetery in New York, interfaith families have a special area set aside for them. At Mt. Sinai Cemetery outside of Los Angeles, their policy is, "We don't break up families." When the non-Jewish spouse dies, he/she may be buried next to the Jewish spouse. However, no non-Jewish clergy person may officiate, nor is the family required to have a rabbi. Instead, the bereaved may appoint a family spokesperson to lead the service.

Hillside Cemetery, a Jewish cemetery in Los Angeles, will not split up married couples. If the Christian family members desire a Christian service for the deceased, it can be held at a church away from the burial grounds, but no non-Jewish clergy can preside over the concluding service at the burial grounds. There can be no cross or Christian symbols on the stones, and Hillside will not bury the Christian parents of the Christian spouse on the grounds.

Regarding Catholic cemeteries allowing non-Catholics to be buried alongside their spouses, the Catholic Archdiocese in each American city across the country determines policies on burial of interfaith family members. As long as one spouse is either a baptized or practicing Catholic, the non-Catholic spouse may be buried with her/him.

Interfaith couples need to inform their families so that they know what memorial customs they prefer. Put your desires in writing.

Generally, Catholics have a Mass said for the soul of the departed, while Jews may have trees planted in Israel. Both may choose to have donations made to their favorite charity. Jews also light a memorial candle (*Yahrzeit)* at home each year at the death anniversary, based on the Hebrew calendar. The couple needs to come to terms with what kind of death rites each desires and to express their wishes in writing if possible. At the same time, be aware that those desires might change as one ages. Often there is a pull towards the religion of birth as one moves closer to the end of life.

While there are many general books available regarding death topics, it was refreshing to discover *Kaddish for Grandpa in Jesus' Name Amen,* a children's book that helps them cope with death rituals in an interfaith family. The presence of this book demonstrates how interfaith customs impact the entire family.

In this story, five-year-old Emily tries to cope with the death of her beloved paternal Christian grandfather, who read and sang to her as she was growing up. Emily's mother is Jewish and her father is a converted Jew, so Emily first attends a funeral service in her father's family church. Later, when they return home, her father gathers other Jewish friends together in their living room to say Kaddish, the Jewish prayer for the dead, which Emily also witnesses. Both families honored Grandpa according to each tradition. Nonetheless, at the end of the book, the five-year-old puts everything together from her perspective, uttering the title and last line of the book, "My kaddish for Grandpa in Jesus' name amen."

Author Renée Garfinkle criticizes this book and its underlying philosophy for falling into what she calls, "The Homogenization Trap." To Garfinkle, saying Kaddish in Jesus' name is ". . . anathema to both Judaism and Christianity. It is exactly what each religion fears—the fusion of ideas that skews their respective messages in the name of tolerance."

Religious purists, like Garfinkle may be offended, but this criticism is but another example of denying the reality of interfaith families. In the book the child merely interprets and melds both traditions in an effort to respect her cherished grandfather. The last lines describe the process. "It wasn't the Christian way and it wasn't the Jewish way. It was just my way. My kaddish for Grandpa in Jesus' name amen."

When interfaith tragedies occur, blending customs as Emily does can be a way of uniting bereaved families.

COMMUNAL DEATH MEMORIAL

After a particularly painful death or large tragedy, people may feel the need to gather and grieve together. Communal death memorial ceremonies serve such a purpose, particularly when the victims have been by struck down by hate, racism, and violence. One physical example of this is the memorial built commemorating the tragedy of the 1995 Oklahoma City bombing of the Alfred P. Murrah Building— 168 empty glass and granite chairs representing each life lost. Another is the planned memorial for the victims of the Twin Towers disaster on September 11, 2001, in New York City.

Community interfaith symbolic memorials work as well to bring healing, as exemplified by the memorial for Joseph Ileto.

On August 10, 1999, white supremacist Buford O. Furrow Jr. entered the North Valley Jewish Community Center of Granada Hills near Los Angeles and fired more than seventy shots from a submachine gun at the Jews in his path. Three boys between the ages of five and six, a sixteen-year-old girl and a sixty-eight-year-old woman all survived but were seriously injured physically and emotionally.

Furrow fled the scene in a stolen car and an hour later, noticed a thirty-nine-year-old Filipino postal worker at a mailbox on his route. Furrow stopped his car and asked Ileto if he would mail a letter for him. After Ileto agreed, Furrow pulled a pistol from his back pocket and shot him nine times. His reason? Because Ileto was a non-white "target of opportunity," he said. His rationale for the shooting at the Jewish Community Center was that he wanted to send a wake-up call to America to kill Jews.

Two years later, U.S. District Judge Nora M. Manella sentenced Furrow to two consecutive life sentences without the possibility of parole, plus an additional 110 years. In pronouncing sentence, the judge said that Furrow's deeds were a "stark and brutal reminder that bigotry is alive, if not well, in America."

Nothing can be done to bring back the life of Ileto or heal the wounds of the other victims. However, on August 10, 2004, exactly five years to the date of Furrow's lethal rampage, a memorial service took place. On the program, the letters of Joseph's name capitalized on the community's hopes for the future:

J OIN

O UR

S TRUGGLE

E DUCATE

P REVENT

H ATE

Held at the stunning Catholic Cathedral of Our Lady of the Angels in downtown Los Angeles, the memorial service began with a procession of costumed Korean Americans. The Rt. Reverend Alexei Smith of the Archdiocese of Los Angeles welcomed the guests. The UCLA Filipino chorus sang *"Malayo Pa"* (We're Still Far). Dr. Cecil "Chip" Murray from the First African Methodist Episcopal Church led a prayer, followed by a reading from the Jewish scriptures by Rabbi Harold Schulweis. More interfaith pronouncements and blessings came from Thai Buddhist Monks, Sikhs, a Gospel choir, and a Muslim prayer offered by a representative from the Islamic Center of Southern California. The brother of Ileto brought a message from the family, followed by a final moment of silence, a closing prayer and a reception.

The event was an appropriate tribute and healing activity. It exemplified the reality that tragedies promoted by hate can be transcended by the acceptance of ethnic and religious differences and respect for all human beings.

HOLIDAYS

The decisions we make when marking the occasions of major rites of passage—birth, coming-of-age, and death—are critical decisions, often once in a lifetime decisions. You have but one opportunity to decide about the wedding, the circumcision, the funeral. In contrast, holidays allow flexibility, whether celebrated in interfaith or same faith families. Decisions about holidays are often most critical when the family includes members of both Jewish and Christian traditions, yet families can experiment. They can alternate customs from year to year; they can adapt and modify, or even omit some.

Jewish-born Natalie, a psychologist, married Jon, a nondenominational Christian professor. Natalie describes how their Passover Seders have evolved over the years. As a child, her family had traditional, joyous, song-filled Seders. Sometimes they celebrated at the homes of other Orthodox family members whose long seders were solemn and without any singing. After she married Jon in the 1970s, they had a hippie Seder and ate French onion soup with a bread crust, breaking the Passover taboo of no raised dough. Years later, they had an academic Seder where they read relevant articles until midnight. The next year they participated in a feminist Seder, celebrating that women were generally responsible for the Exodus, for Judaism, and just about everything else. Another Passover they took part in a desert Seder where the family room was converted into a tent and all guests sat on pillows on the floor and acted out the plagues, a colorful part of the Passover story. Finally, in her post-menopausal years with all nuclear family members now deceased, Natalie merely notes the date, buys a box of matzos, remembers her early Seders, and cries a little.

The December Dilemma
for Christians and Jews

Overheard conversation between two brothers, nine and twelve, who attend Hebrew school. Both parents are Jewish but now are divorced. The father has remarried a Christian; the mother has remarried a Jew. Older boy: "When I grow up, I'm going to celebrate Christmas and Hanukkah."

Younger boy: "Not me. When I'm eighteen, I'm just going to celebrate Hanukkah—unless I marry a Christian."

When an excited young Jewish woman brought home her breathtakingly handsome Catholic boyfriend to announce their engagement, the first thing her mother asked was, "But what about the Christmas tree? This surprised everyone, especially the mother herself, who considered herself non-religious. It was an emotionally reflexive response.

These are just two examples that illustrate some of the problems that confront interfaith marriages at holiday time. In a 2001 study by the American Jewish Committee, of 127 interfaith couples interviewed, 82 percent reported Christian activities of some sort in their homes, mainly at Christmas and Easter. The purpose of the study was to reveal the dynamics of mixed marriage homes. The American Jewish Committee concluded that ultimately, Judaism would yield to the majority culture. In 2003, children in Jewish/Christian households numbered 750,000. Less than one-third were raised as Jews. A full half of them learned nothing of their Jewish legacy. By the year 2005, an estimated two-thirds of Jewish marriages involved a non-Jew. These estimates are not limited to the United States. The trend extends to France, Germany, Eastern Europe, and Latin America.

December has always posed problems for Jews because they feel segregated during the onslaught of advertising and Christmas activities. This accounts for "The December Dilemma." How can anything compete with the aroma of evergreen trees and the beauty of Christmas tree ornaments?

Personally, I'll never forget the thrill when I was twelve and our new neighbors, the Englands, invited me to help trim their Christmas tree, a custom forbidden in my Jewish home. Nonetheless, my parents allowed me to help our neighbors, and I savored the activities—the baking of holiday cookies, the placing of shiny ornaments on the fragrant tree branches, and the stringing of popcorn and cranberries.

Jewish parents everywhere struggle to make Hanukkah as attractive as Christmas. Despite the shiny dreidels, blue and white lights and streamers, gold and silver Stars of David, and Hanukkah decorated Oreos, it's difficult to compete with Christmas. And it shouldn't compete because Hanukkah is only a minor Jewish holiday. Still Jewish children crave something comparable. Many Jews wrestle with the issue of Christmas trees, sometimes having them but calling them Hanukkah bushes. Despite the name, it's still a Christmas tree and this symbol often raises the toughest questions for interfaith couples.

> When deciding whether or not to have a tree, recognize that it's not a lifetime decision. Each year experiment until you find out what's comfortable for you, your mate, and your children.

Should We Have a Tree or Not?
Is the Tree a Religious or Secular Symbol?
What Does It Mean When a Jew Has a Christmas Tree?

For many Jews, the Christmas tree question causes a knee-jerk response. For instance, the Christian girlfriend of a Jewish physician wanted to have a Christmas tree. He agreed, but with conditions. "Only in July," he said. Needless to say, they broke up.

The Christmas tree causes even more angst in interfaith families who must deal with the input and emotions from extended family members. Some Jews see the Christmas tree strictly as a symbol of Christianity, and for them it would be a betrayal of their own faith to have one in their home. It boosts the feeling of alienation in a primarily Christian country. Not so for the Christian side for whom the tree may primarily represent family nostalgia. So how can this conflict be eased?

> Creative compromise brings the most satisfaction.

Despite most mainstream rabbis believing that parents should raise their children in one faith or the other to avoid confusion, in reality many families observe Hanukkah in the home if the children are being raised Jewish and Christmas at the homes of relatives or friends. Stories from interfaith families who have solved their December dilemmas illustrate how satisfying creative compromises can be.

One possibility is to have symbols of both Hanukkah and Christmas in the home at the same time, such as a menorah and the tree. Some couples decorate the tree with Hanukkah symbols, such as dreidels and Stars of David. Other couples may decorate only their doors and mantles with branches and lights. One mother of an interfaith couple told me that the first time she entered her children's home during the holidays and unexpectedly saw the Christmas tree she gasped. Then her son handed her a pair of cardboard sunglasses. When she looked at the tree through the sunglasses, the lights converted into Stars of David.

A Jewish mother and a Catholic father visit the maternal aunt's house for Hanukkah to eat latkes and foil-covered chocolate Hanukkah *gelt* (Yiddish for money) and to accept gifts for the children. They light the menorah every night, and the mother reads the Hanukkah story to their son. They also have a small decorated Christmas tree and follow the father's tradition of leaving milk and cookies on Christmas Eve for Santa, who delivers a few gifts. On Christmas Day, they go to the husband's family to open gifts. Their child has accepted both celebrations, understanding that "My mom's Jewish and my dad's Catholic."

Another family puts a Christmas tree with colored lights and ornaments in one room and in the other room, a menorah, a Star of David candle and a Happy Hanukkah wall hanging. Their holiday party features eating potato latkes and trimming the tree with an exchange of songs and gifts.

Some families may have Christmas trees but no nativity scenes. One Jewish father purchased only Israeli-made Christmas gifts for his children, and as a further joke signed the card to his twenty-year-old son "Santa" but wrote it phonetically in Hebrew letters.

A Los Angeles extended family comprised of Mexicans, Jews, Italians ,and atheists customized their observance of Hanukkah. They no longer serve the traditional brisket as the main course. Instead they have burritos, tacos, enchiladas, latkes with salsa, Corona beer, and a piñata shaped like a dreidel filled with Hanukkah gelt. They start the party on a weekend during the eight-day Hanukkah holiday and light menorahs, including one brought from Germany by the grandfather of one of the participants. After the candles are lit they exchange gifts.

> Avoid sending holiday cards that emphasize
> the religious aspects of the season.
> Select more secular themes.

At the website www.Chrismukkah.com, the interfaith owners wish friends and family "Merry Mazel Tov" and have produced a line of cards that combine symbols: a menorah with candy canes in place of candles; a snowman with a yarmulke on its head; a Christmas tree draped with dreidels; Santa preparing latkes. In 2002, American Greetings, the second largest producer of greeting cards in the U.S., offered ten different cards that mixed Christmas and Hanukkah imagery. And the use of the word Chrismukkah is becoming accepted by those in mixed families as well.

But not everyone accepts this. Protesting the term Chrismukkah, the president of the Catholic League for Religious and Civil Rights and two rabbis signed a letter of complaint to the Jewish newspaper *Forward*. "Copying the tradition of another faith and calling it by another name is a form of shameful plagiarism we cannot condone. Frankly, those who seek to synthesize our spiritual conditions might be well intended, but they are hurting both of us simultaneously. We Jews and Christians respect one another, realizing that there is a time to be separate and a time to be together. We see each other as separate spiritual brothers and sisters who will work together to better the human family."

While both organizations have the right to protest the Chrismukkah combination, I think they miss the point. Using the term Chrismukkah is not an act of plagiarism. Instead, it supplies a coping mechanism utilizing humor to confront an emotional issue. By acknowledging both religions, interfaith couples are trying to keep their families whole.

Beyond the tree, other sources of conflict exist, for example, Santa Claus. If you are a Jewish parent, it is hard to resist having your child's picture taken with Santa over at the mall, but Alan Katz, a professional Santa Claus who is a Jew, has no problem with the December holiday dilemma. "I don't have to be Christian to believe in the joy you see in a child's eyes when they [sic] first meet Santa. That goes beyond religion." Katz calls himself the "Kosher Claus, a Santa with more chutzpah than ho, ho, ho." He draws on Jewish shtick when he performs, especially for those who request his Kosher Claus. In addition to the red suit, he may wear a prayer shawl and a yarmulke or a top hat and coat often worn by Hasidic Jews.

Katz calls the holiday "Hanamas" and sings appropriate songs: "The First Ba-gel," "Rudolph the Hasidic Reindeer." The star he places on the tree is either a picture of Jerry Seinfeld or Barbra Streisand. A resident of Long Beach, California, where he regularly performs at shopping malls during December, his regular job is as a chauffeur for a limousine company. Katz's Santa Claus role began while he was working as a loan officer for an escrow company. The company's regular Santa wasn't available so they asked Katz to step in, provided him with a red suit, and the rest is Katz Claus history.

**Accept that this is a Judeo-Christian nation and there is
a precedent for acknowledging both faiths.**

In "Born-Again President—White House Hanukkah," Dennis Prager, a former college lecturer in Jewish history, observes that Jews have been involved with the U.S. Government since the beginning of this country. In fact, many of the founders studied Hebrew; Thomas Jefferson wanted the Seal of the United States to depict the Jew's exodus from Egypt; Yale University's insignia is in Hebrew; a verse from the Torah (Leviticus) is inscribed on the Liberty Bell; a rabbi attended George Washington's inauguration—the list of pro-Jewish expressions in U.S. history is endless. But perhaps most telling is the fact that although there have been any number of Christian countries and there are many secular ones today, it is the U.S. that calls itself Judeo Christian.

Prager was one of 200 Jews invited to the George W. Bush White House in December 2004 to celebrate Hanukkah in a room that contained both a menorah and a Christmas tree. Other invitees included rabbis from ultra-Orthodox to Reform congregations to ultra-secular Jews. If the current White House administration with its Conservative residents can celebrate Judeo-Christian traditions in the same room, then certainly this can become a model for solving the December Dilemma.

**Above all else, successful interfaith
partners must possess a sense of humor.**

In a mixed Christian/Jewish home, when the parents were out of cookies to leave with a glass of milk for Santa, the Jewish mom recommended leaving a plate of matzos.

A Catholic mother, who had promised her Jewish husband to raise their child Jewish, ran out of Hanukkah gifts for the required eight days of gifts and gave her daughter an Advent calendar on the last night.

While these creative solutions satisfy children and parents, grandparents are likely to be more traditional and thus more upset with interfaith celebrations. They can either try to soothe the situation and give everyone an opportunity to enjoy the holiday fully, or consciously or not, stir up emotions.

GUIDELINES FOR GRANDPARENTS

Establish alliances with the other
set of grandparents before the birth.

Don't confuse family problems with interfaith problems. If strained feelings exist between you, attempt to smooth things over, even before the baby arrives. Become allies, even if you are the ones who must reach out first. It will be worth it.

Honor the faiths of both families by including the other
grandparents in your holiday.

If they are Christian and you are Jewish, accept their holiday invitations to their home and inside houses of worship. If the event takes place inside a Catholic church, for example, you won't be expected to kneel or approach the priest to take Communion, or do anything that is against your religious rules. While you might feel awkward at first, subsequent visits will seem easier because you'll now know what to do. Just follow the cues of the rest of the congregation.

If they are Jewish and you are Christian and they invite you to a home Seder, go and participate. The Passover Seder is the re-telling of the Jews' exodus from Egypt and its universal theme of freedom from bondage will not contradict New Testament beliefs. If you are invited to a temple occasion, they will tell you whether head coverings are required for men and whether or not men sit separately from women. Your grandchildren will benefit from seeing both sides united at these significant family occasions.

Remember that the welfare of your grandchildren comes first.

Children should not be punished because their parents have different faiths—religious conflicts are harmful. They negate spirituality and teach bigotry. Instead of thinking about the families' differences, think of your grandchildren as being blessed by having such a rich background that will better equip them for living in a multicultural world.

Respect the decisions that your children
make about their children's religious upbringing.

Above all, don't interfere. At the same time, don't neglect exposing your customs to your grandchildren. That is your role. Tell them stories about their heritage; teach them to enjoy ethnic foods. Explain the backgrounds of holidays—become their learning source.

Even if you live far from one another, you can still keep in contact by phone, e-mail, or snail mail. You can send pictures by cell phone and encourage them to do the same. You can photograph Seders, Purim carnivals celebrating the rescue of the Jews of Persia from Haman's plot to exterminate them, and family get-togethers. You can mail them holiday food treats.

Some grandparents have no problems with intermarriage and handle interfaith grandchildren with grace. A good example is Evelyn Maxwell, a United Methodist grandmother of two interfaith grandchildren. She gives the children and their parents (her daughter converted to Judaism) December gifts wrapped in blue instead of red and green. She and her husband still have a Christmas tree but have eliminated the crèche. Their daughter gave them a menorah, and the children light Hanukkah candles at their Methodist grandparents' home.

Mrs. Del, an Italian Catholic, has also easily slipped into the role of grandparent of a half-Jewish grandchild. Her daughter, son-in-law, and granddaughter celebrate Hanukkah at home with Jewish friends and family, but at Christmas they visit Mrs. Del and the rest of her family, where they celebrate Christmas. This solution has worked out well. Mrs. Del also enters into the interfaith spirit by giving her granddaughter Hanukkah gifts as well as a Hanukkah Gingerbread House decorated with Jewish stars, dreidels, and figures of Maccabees, purchased from a Rhode Island grocery chain.

Mrs. Del is lucky that she can find such an interfaith artifact, but that has become a growing reality. It is increasingly common to merge holiday customs, especially with the growing interfaith market. For example, in a Jewish online catalog, one may purchase a Hanukkah Piñata. Stores and catalogs sell Christmas stockings adorned with Stars of David, and Christmas lights are available in blue and silver Hanukkah colors. As time passes, expect more innovations in merchandise.

Because December has been a time of heightened Jewish/Christian ceremonial conflict, Rabbi Harold Schulweis has dubbed the Jewish response "Santa Klaustraphobia." Despite his diagnosis, an article in the Jewish *Forward* estimates that Jewish anxiety about Christmas revelry is waning and that Christmas is gaining a new multicultural appeal. The *Forward* cites Barbra Streisand's releasing a second Christmas album;

Robert Rand's book about Jewish celebrations of Christmas at a Skokie, Illinois, high school; and Judith Shulevitz's statement in the *New York Times* that the American Christmas is no longer a religious celebration, but is now a secular blessing of homes, children, families, and communities. In sum, the article says that the December Dilemma has lost its sting.

Steven Bayme, director of Jewish Communal Affairs at the American Jewish Committee concurs. He says that today Jews are less anxious about Christmas because it has become so quintessentially American. Bayme believes this indicates how comfortable Jews are in American society.

But we must be realistic. Given the overall divorce rate, same faith families as well as mixed families don't all live happily ever after. For example, a Jewish woman who married a Catholic man and had two children early on in the marriage sent out a holiday greeting card where all four family members were dressed in red. On the next holiday card, the father was wearing a Santa's hat, the children were dressed in red, and the mother was dressed in blue.

After the divorce, the holiday card showed the two children seated with a menorah between them, implying that she and her children no longer observed Christian traditions and had now returned to their Jewish heritage.

The December Dilemma for Muslims

RAMADAN

While the December Dilemma is primarily associated with Christians and Jews, now that the United States has a large and growing Muslim population (approximately five million) Muslim children also feel the lure of Christmas. Ramadan, Muslim's most holy time, sometimes falls during December, which may bring conflict to their homes, not specifically due to intermarriage but because they are living in a largely Christian culture.

Some Muslims feel the Christmas tree is a sign of their Americanization. Indeed, in Mission Viejo, California, a community with a large population of Iranians, on one street the house with the most Christmas decorations on the block belongs to an Iranian Muslim family. In that same interfaith community one December, one intersection displayed a Menorah on one corner, Ramadan symbols on a second corner, and Santa Claus and a Christmas tree on the third and fourth corners.

When Ramadan falls during the December holiday season, as it did in both 1999 and 2000, Muslim children tend to feel left out. They want to know why they too can't have a tree and lights. Even though it is not part of the Ramadan tradition, one Muslim family, immigrants from Jordan, adapted Christian symbols to their Ramadan observance and decorated their apartment with green, white, and gold crepe paper and glittery placards of sayings from the *Qur'an* (Koran). They gave gifts to their children, to be unwrapped on *Eid al-Fitr*, also called *iftar*, the three day celebration marking the end of the month of fasting, prayer, and good deeds.

To reduce interfaith tensions educate the outside community about your customs and share your celebrations with friends of other faiths.

Since 9/11, community organizations across the country have tried to lessen religious tensions through interfaith celebrations. Some have opened up Ramadan celebrations, in particular *Eid al-Fitr*, to other members of the community, attempting to demystify and educate the non-Muslim world about Islam.

Ramadan, the holiest time of Islamic worship, begins according to the lunar calendar and requires Muslims to abstain from drink, food, smoking, and sex from dawn to sunset each day. After sunset, they break the daily fast with *iftar*, a meal often begun by eating dates and drinking water or milk. It is a time to eat and relax with family and friends.

In Portland, Oregon, the *iftar* celebration has become a multicultural/ interfaith potluck event. After September 11, 2001, Neighborhood House, a one-hundred-year-old social service agency in Portland, reached out to their local Muslim communities. Anxiety reigned high at that time, especially among some women who feared leaving their homes because people taunted them for their religious attire. Apprehensive families kept their children home from school because they didn't know what might happen to them.

Neighborhood House Executive Director, Rick Nitti, discovered that most Oregonians knew little about Islam, so he and his staff created an interfaith *iftar* end of Ramadan fast in conjunction with the Islamic Society of Greater Portland. Approximately 15,000 Muslims live in Portland, originating from ten different countries including Somalia, Bangladesh, Afghanistan, and Iraq. The two organizations brought together leaders of the Abrahamic faiths, those who teach that Abraham was the father of Isaac, leader of the Hebrews, and Ishmael, leader of the Muslims. Religious leaders from the Jewish, Christian, Muslim, and Sikh communities convened. They wished to promote dialogue and understanding between Muslims and the majority community. The first year they drew 300 attendees for the potluck *iftar* dinner and dialogue. People sat at tables together, chatted, ate, and learned about each other.

Shahriar Ahmed, a Portland participant originally from Bangladesh, calls 9/11 a cancer and believes that the Portland interfaith *iftar* is a magnificent story because it demonstrates that Christians, Muslims, and Jews recognize their common humanity. The 2004 *iftar* celebration brought together even more participants than the first year, half Muslim, half non-Muslim. Ahmed believes the big turnout occurred because they all were feeling anguish and pain and were looking for some semblance of hope in the midst of the Iraqi war. Participant Harriet Cooke asked, "Can you imagine what the world would be like if we kept making potlucks for each other?"

Easter/Passover

A Christian/Jewish couple solves their Easter egg hunt dilemma by hiding only chocolate eggs which the Jewish chocoholic can't resist.

Because the Passover seder was originally the Last Supper, Christians can easily accept it. Indeed, many different groups of people celebrate Passover, as I discovered one semester while teaching an anthropology course at a private college. When the students turned in their papers describing an unfamiliar ritual they had attended, I was surprised at the variety of Passovers they had observed—and this was at the Worldwide Church of God, among Quakers, with a militant feminist group. After my initial surprise, I realized how that made sense since Passover celebrates freedom from oppression, a theme that everyone can appreciate and relate to.

In contrast, Jews respond differently to Easter, since they are often blamed for the crucifixion, even by some church clergy, with a history of pogroms as a result of that blame. In addition, Jews do not believe in the resurrection of Jesus. These elements often make Easter a time of discomfort for Jews. Despite these barriers, there are ways to mediate the differences.

> Since Easter and Passover are connected in time and in history, use their commonalities as a basis for celebration.

For interfaith couples, besides having a Seder, pertinent to both holidays, families can emphasize the beauty of spring and renewal, and the common symbol of eggs eaten during the Seder as well as decorated and hidden during Easter egg hunts. Buddhism is applicable to the holiday as well. Lynn, a Buddhist, easily accepts her Jewish husband's Passover. She sees it as the "cleaning out of old energies to bring in the newness of beauty."

Finally, to add to the evidence of the connectedness of the two holidays, Gilda Berger offers semantic references of the relationship of Easter to Judaism. The name for Easter in several languages comes from *Pesach*, the Hebrew word for Passover; in Spanish, it is *Pascua,* and in French, it is *Pâques.*

An interfaith couple marrying in today's multicultural world may find their lives easier in many ways than interfaith couples of only a few decades ago. Despite this, they will still have many challenges and many emotion-laden decisions to make about celebrating the major events of their lives together. In the next chapter, mixed marriages become more complicated by adding features of differing races and ethnicities.

[2]

CELEBRATIONS IN
MULTIRACIAL FAMILIES

While interfaith families have religious differences to resolve, multiracial families may have the additional complications of physical and color differences. Let's face it, ours is a color conscious society. Just ask any person of color who, while in an exclusive neighborhood, has been stopped by the police and questioned just because of his or her skin tone. Similarly, when the white member of a multiracial couple introduces the non-white beloved to the family, the family may at first respond as if that other person were trespassing. The reverse happens as well; the family of the person of color may react negatively when the white person is introduced to the family. These negative reactions often result from lack of personal experience with those of a different race. Under most circumstances the passage of time bonds the families, and after a while the color issue fades.

Later, just as in all families, complications ensue with the arrival of children.

This chapter deals with multiracial families formed through marriage and adoption. The examples highlight the ability of people to convert potential culture collisions into healthy flourishing families. My sources include interviews with multiracial couples and families, adoption agencies, adoptive parents and adopted children, as well as printed resources listed in the back of this book.

Are you a Hapa (Half-Hawaiian)?
Afroasian (African American Asian)?
Jamaicanese? (Jamaican Japanese)
Eurasiacan? (European Asian Mexican)
Jewban (Cuban Jew)? Amerithai (American Thai)?
Korgentinian (Korean Argentinian)?
Thaimericano (Thai American)?
Japino (Japanese Filipino)? Mestizo?
VietFrançais (Vietnamese French)?
JewBu (Jewish-Buddhist)? HinJew (Hindu-Jewish)?
Blaxican? (Black Mexican) Mexirican (Mexican Puerto
Rican)? Jewpanese (Jewish Japanese)?

Social commentator Richard Rodriguez calls the above labels inaccurate because they confuse ethnicity, race, and culture. Nevertheless, people identify themselves by these sometimes humorous names that illustrate the many combinations of ethnicities and races that exist today in the United States.

Marriages across racial lines have more than doubled in the last twenty years to about one and a half million. Nearly seven million Americans identified themselves as members of more than one race in the 2000 Census. There are almost 400,000 white/black marriages. More than 100,000 biracial babies have been born every year since 1989 resulting in more than one million first-generation biracial children across racial and ethnic groups: black/white, Japanese/white, racially mixed Native Americans, Hispanic mixes, and other Asian American mixes.

For the first time, the 2000 census allowed people to check more than one box for race. The San Francisco Bay area's mixed race population more than doubled the national average. California and the San Francisco Bay area led the nation for interracial couples (four to five percent), second only to Hawaii, where twenty-one percent of children are of mixed race.

In a telephone survey of 2,002 people conducted in late 2003 by the Gallup Organization for the AARP and the Leadership Conference on Civil Rights, seventy percent of whites said they approved of marriage between whites and blacks. Eighty percent of blacks and 77 percent of Hispanics said they generally approved of interracial marriage.

A large majority of white respondents—66 percent—said they would not object if their own child or grandchild married someone of another race. One of the most unexpected results came when polltakers asked participants to consider the prediction that by 2050 the majority of Americans would be nonwhite. Only about 13 percent of each group said this would be a bad thing. Most Americans said it simply wouldn't matter.

When such unions take place, the first hurdles occur when planning the wedding. Yet many multiracial/multiethnic families (who are often interfaith at the same time) appear to rejoice in their differences and proudly display them at their first joint ritual appearance.

Marriage

Cultural dissimilarities have the power to enhance lives and enliven wedding ceremonies. Display them; don't hide them.

A woman rabbi officiated at the marriage of a Senegalese groom and a Jewish bride. Her sermon focused on international peace and understanding. The Muslim brother of the groom held up one end of the *chupah* (wedding canopy), while a relative of the bride held the other end. The bride wore a white satin dress, amply cut to cover her five months–pregnant figure. At midnight, Senegalese drummers began drumming and African dancing commenced.

A Jewish groom and Bengali bride had two ceremonies. At the first one, a rabbi officiated—the bride wore a traditional white gown; the groom wore a tuxedo. Bengali style set the theme for the second ceremony—she wore an embroidered skirt suit, completely covered with jewelry and henna designs on her face and hands; he wore a white brocade suit.

At one Jewish/Chinese mixed wedding, the Chinese bride brought Chinese pork-less dumplings to the reception. At the wedding of a Jewish groom and a Colombian Catholic bride, the couple was married under a *chupah* (wedding canopy) crocheted by the groom's grandmother, and before the groom stepped on the glass, a Jewish wedding reminder that pain exists elsewhere, he counted, *"Uno, dos, tres."*

At a HinJew (Hindu/Jewish) wedding, the Indian groom's sister sang a song in Oriya, an Indian language, and the Jewish bride's friend sang songs in Hebrew. In accord with Indian tradition, the couple exchanged sweets during the ceremony and concluded with the Jewish breaking of the glass.

An Iranian/Muslim groom and Chinese/Buddhist bride bowed to respect their ancestors. Guests rubbed sugar cones above the couples' heads for a sweet life as prescribed by Persian tradition (see Marriage/Iranian, p. 198). The wedding featured classic Chinese music and Persian popular music. While the mannerisms and affect of the Chinese and Iranian guests were different, overriding the differences were the similarities in cultural beliefs—respect for family, education, integrity, and success.

An Italian groom and Puerto Rican bride danced to salsa music, ate Jordan almonds and empanadas and drank sangría. When the brother of the groom went up to make a toast, the DJ played the theme music from the movie *The Godfather*, and the brother walked as if he were an old man.

A Buddhist/Thai bride and her Catholic/Jewish groom flew to Thailand to purchase elaborate matching Thai costumes—a demonstration that one can marry someone from another culture in the United States and not forget one's own background.

A Scottish groom and his Chinese bride read Scottish and Chinese poems during their wedding ceremony and had "Double Happiness" signs projected on a fabric screen at the reception. At another reception for a Latino groom and Anglo bride, they served ceviche shooters as appetizers, had a mariachi band play for the ceremony, and asked the officiant to speak important parts of the ceremony in both Spanish and English.

Compromise is the key.

Prior to the wedding of Andrew Marshall and Judy Chia Hui Hsu, the groom's mother asked Judy where she planned to register for her list of preferred gifts. Judy said she didn't plan to register anywhere because it was customary to give money at Chinese weddings. After Andy's mom told Judy that in Jewish tradition guests more commonly gave household gifts pre-selected by the couple and listed at designated stores, the bride-to-be acquiesced and registered.

Their wedding invitation was blended, too. It was bicultural and bilingual. They enclosed a standard wedding invitation in English on white paper along with an invitation in Chinese printed on red paper, for good luck.

Upon arrival, guests signed both a standard guest book as well as a red satin wall hanging with words literally translated as "Honored Guest Sign Name." An embroidered dragon on one side, representing the male, and a phoenix on the opposite side, representing the female, adorned the hanging. It also featured Chinese Double Happiness characters, always present at Chinese weddings. True to tradition, some of the Chinese guests gave Chinese money-filled red envelopes to the couple's representative who also had them sign the guest register.

Judy's mother wore a traditional silk *cheongsam* dress embellished with purple flowering plum branches; the bride wore a traditional American white wedding gown; and the bridesmaids dressed in pink, an auspicious Chinese color. Many of the female guests wore red or pink, again symbolizing wishes for the couple's happiness and good luck. To represent Jewish culture, a simple *chupah* sheltered the bridal couple, and the groom stepped on the glass at the closing of the ceremony causing Jewish guests to shout "Mazel Tov!" Before the meal, an elderly Jewish male blessed the bread in a Hebrew prayer. They had pink rose petals on the table, and during the reception, when guests clinked their water/wine glasses with eating utensils, the bride and groom kissed.

To fascinate and edify wedding guests and family members, provide cultural information on the customs they will be observing and the backgrounds of the wedding party members.

That's what happened at the Inoue/Shneer nuptials. They produced a printed program that revealed the Chinese, Persian, and Vietnamese backgrounds of the bridal party. The booklet also described the other blended traditional elements of the wedding they were observing: the Ketubah, the Jewish marriage contract, the Chinese Double Happiness symbol. They combined the Japanese sharing of three cups of sake with the Jewish partaking of wine by sharing three cups of wine with the parents, Matron of Honor, Best Man and Officiant. Creating something new with the passing of rings, they let the rings pass through the hands of each of the groom's attendants before reaching the fingers of the bride and groom. This represented the impact the groom's best man and groomsmen had had on his life.

Hosts placed a Maneki Neko, a Japanese welcoming charm in the shape of a cat with an uplifted paw for good luck and fortune, on each reception table. The couple had favor bags with two red foil-wrapped candies, a Chinese tradition, and origami Japanese cranes symbolizing longevity, prosperity, and peace. They also included the chair dance, a Jewish tradition, and Chinese red roses, the symbol of happiness and ultimate joy.

Five Case Studies of Successful Multiracial Unions

Moving away from weddings, I would like to present a few examples of how multiracial couples may steer their way around potentially stormy aspects of marriage. The following examples highlight the pliability of the marriage partners. They have made thoughtful decisions leading to stable healthy multiracial families. They demonstrate how American culture is becoming transformed into a thriving multicultural society.

WHITE CHRISTIAN WITH NATIVE AMERICAN HOPI

Mixed-race couples are fortunate when families on both sides welcome them. When Dr. Allen, a Protestant physician, fell in love with Kaya, a Hopi nurse he met while working at a Native American Hospital in Arizona, her parents accepted their relationship because the Hopi, in general, are very understanding when a Hopi marries a non-Hopi. They take in the outsider and try to make him/her feel part of the family. Dr. Allen's family accepted the union as well, although initially, he could detect some unspoken resistance. However, later in their relationship, Allen's mother confided to Kaya that she was her favorite daughter-in-law. After more than forty years of marriage, both husband and wife feel comfortable in each others' worlds.

Remain open-minded. Don't believe that your way is superior to your mate's way. Accept that it is merely different.

They had a small wedding in a Protestant Church away from the reservation. Upon their return, Kaya's aunt and grandmother performed a traditional Hopi marriage custom. They washed the couple's hair in a yucca mix, then intertwined their hair as a symbol of unity, just one small aspect of traditional Hopi weddings, which ordinarily last from ten to fourteen days. Despite their own small Christian ceremony, when one of Kaya's relatives plans a Hopi wedding, the Allens try to participate in food preparation and attend as many days as possible.

Learn about your spouse's upbringing.
Try and incorporate these traditions
into the lives of the next generation.

Hopis usually give their babies their Indian name when they are twenty days old. All of the Allen children and eight grandchildren went through the Hopi naming ceremony that traditionally occurs early in the morning. The women, usually clan relatives, bathe the baby and then smear corn meal on its skin. They move an ear of corn back and forth over the baby's chest as they bestow the baby's Hopi name. Then they take the infant outdoors, and as the sun rises they present the baby to the sun and offer a prayer.

The Allen family celebrates Christmas and Easter, and this has never presented any conflict since many Hopi also celebrate Christian rituals. The Allen family also participates in the annual Kachina dance, a significant religious ceremony. For the Hopi, who live on a reservation on the First, Second, and Third Mesas in northern Arizona, Kachinas represent the spirit essence of everything in nature, acting as intermediaries between mortals and the Hopi gods. The Kachina dances take place annually from January to July, and the Hopi consider them sacred. At Kachina sacred dance ceremonies in July, Hopi men dress in colorful costumes and wear masks representing birds, beasts, and monsters; men adorn themselves with symbols of clouds, rain or rainbows. In the past, Kaya sprinkled corn meal on the shoulders of the dancers, but she now limits her participation to providing food for the dancers.

The doctor and his wife try to attend as many dances as they can, and their daughters and grandchildren drive out to the reservation and attend when they are able, usually in the summer. The entire Allen family attends the annual Kachina dance, also called the Niman Festival. When their children and grandchildren were small, the Kachina dancers presented them with traditional gifts given to all Hopi children up to the age of ten: baskets, plaques, and carved Kachina dolls for girls; rattles, bows and arrows for boys.

Social dances take place after the Kachina dance season has ended. Butterfly dances occur in August and September. Teenage girls pick a partner and thirty or forty couples dance in the plaza for two days. One of the Allen daughters took part in this when she was in high school. One-day basket dances take place in November. This celebrates the end of harvest where anything extra is redistributed to help through the hard winter. Many of the older women take part, but the Allens only observe.

> Don't say anything derogatory about your partner's cultural background. Put yourself in that person's place and think about how you'd feel hearing your mate make a slur about your culture.

I once worked with a young Australian woman who casually called an older Anglo office worker, "You dirty old woman you!" The older woman recoiled, so the Aussie quickly objected, "But that's just an Australianism!" The older woman remained steadfast in being insulted. She invoked, "The spoken word is something that can never be retracted." She was correct. Once something dreadful has slipped out of your mouth, it echoes in your own ears. That's why mates in mixed marriages have to be extremely cautious about never saying anything negative about the other's culture; those words will come back to haunt them. This is a rule that the Allen's have seriously applied.

JEWISH AMERICAN WITH AFRICAN AMERICAN CHRISTIAN

A common interracial union occurs between Jewish American and African Americans. Nancy G. Brown serves as an excellent resource for this group. She is the president of the Association of Multiethnic Americans (MASC), the organization responsible for changing the 2000 Census allowing Americans to claim more than one ethnicity. Brown is Jewish with a European ancestry and her husband is African American with a Methodist background. They have been married for twenty-seven years and have two daughters, ages twenty-four and nineteen.

Celebrate and learn about each other's rituals.

The Browns gave their girls a Jewish education and background; both had a *bas mitzvah* (see Coming of Age/Jewish, p. 163). Their daughters have had more Jewish training than their mother received in her own childhood. Their father has participated in all of the Jewish life cycle events as well as the holidays. He feels comfortable attending their synagogue. Equally, when the Browns visit the husband's family out of town, they attend church as a complete family. Locally, they participate in Kwanzaa at home or go to a celebration nearby.

The Browns have also integrated their food habits. They eat pork, and barbecued ribs are the husband's signature dish. They make corn bread and latkes, eat black-eyed peas on New Year's Day, and enjoy collard greens as well as lox and bagels.

Each member of the couple should discuss what's important to that individual.

Christmas presents a slight ambivalence for Nancy in terms of the tree. Sometimes they have had one. Sometimes not. Obtaining a dog inadvertently solved the dilemma; fearful that it might eat the ornaments, they opted to give up the tree. Nancy says her husband has been very generous in tolerating her ambivalence about the tree.

In the previous examples, both partners were born in this country and even with racial differences they had American culture in common. These next case studies feature one American-born partner with someone born elsewhere, compounding issues.

AFRICAN AMERICAN CHRISTIAN WITH SENEGALESE MUSLIM

Even when both members have the same African heritage, their cultures and religions can still create significant national differences. African American Lucinda, a Christian, married Amadou, a Senegalese Muslim. This was not only an interfaith union but an international marriage with conflicts between African and African American traditions.

Rites of passage evoke strong feelings of what is wrong and what is right about how they should be carried out. Negotiation and compromise are the only workable solutions for bringing satisfaction.

The Senegalese keep pregnancies secret as long as possible, so when Lucinda became pregnant, Amadou did not want her to tell anyone. Additionally, Amadou opposed Lucinda's American co-workers hosting a baby shower for Lucinda. Under protest by Lucinda, who was anxious to be ready for the baby, Amadou only allowed her to bring a crib into the house during the last month of pregnancy, lest they jinx the birth. This custom of delaying preparation for the baby is grounded in a social reality.

Senegalese fear acknowledging pregnancy because of the high infant mortality rate in Africa. This fear also affects child-raising methods. Parents try not to say anything negative to their children. They let their religion and their community—in this situation, the Wolof—dictate rules of behavior. Parents show only love and happiness toward children because they do not know whether their offspring will survive into adulthood.

When one of Amadou's and Lucinda's Senegalese friends had a baby, Lucinda was shocked. She had no awareness of the pregnancy, not only because no mention had been made of it but also because Senegalese clothing made it easy to camouflage the body. In addition, the pregnant friend had been exceptionally reluctant to talk about her pregnancy because she had previously lost two children.

When Lucinda and Amadou's daughter was seven days old, they had a baby naming ceremony. Amadou merely told Lucinda that a few friends were coming over, but Lucinda became suspicious when he asked her if they could find a hall. Because he never revealed plans, she was unprepared when over 150 people showed up at a local gymnasium to which they had been given access. Her husband had contacted other Senegalese people living in New York, as well as Ohio, Rhode Island, and New Jersey! Lucinda became overwhelmed seeing so many people, many of whom she had never met.

At the ceremony, the couple successfully mediated one major compromise. In Senegalese tradition, on the seventh day they shave both boy and girl babies' heads with a straight-edge razor. They believe the hair is impure due to its journey through the birth canal. In contrast, African Americans don't touch the baby's hair until the child is one year old. They don't want to tamper with the baby's head because the scalp and skull are sensitive.

Lucinda prevailed. They did not shave the baby's head. Nonetheless, in compliance with Senegalese custom, a Senegalese woman held the baby wrapped in a Senegalese printed cloth, said a prayer over the baby, and then blew over the baby's face. She then walked around the room to each person, who in turn, blew over the baby and said prayers: "You will grow to be a Muslim." "Respect your family." "May you have good health and prosperity." Lucinda and her co-workers, all in the health field, were aghast at all these strangers blowing their germs into the baby's face. Lucinda didn't stop them, and the baby suffered no ill effects.

If possible, visit your spouse's country before you get married. Spend time with your partner's family and friends and pay attention to the roles of the men and women in the society.

Another difference became apparent while visiting Senegal—Lucinda observed that the women do everything. They are completely in charge of household responsibilities. While courting in the United States, Amadou, like all people during courting, was on his best behavior. He cooked and he cleaned. After marriage, Amadou reverted to the more traditional Senegalese male role customs. At the same time, when something was broken, he didn't expect Lucinda to fix it as he would have in Africa, yet he wouldn't fix it himself either. Instead, he paid someone else to do it.

Learn as much as you can about your loved one's country regarding relationships to the environment and natural resources.

When Lucinda planted flowers at their home in the United States, Amadou and his Senegalese friends wanted to know why she planted flowers and not vegetables. To them, flowers were a waste of time and resources.

Educate your own family as you learn about your spouse's differences. Point out any wrong assumptions your family members may have about your spouse to avoid their inadvertently stirring up trouble.

Most of Lucinda's family and friends knew little about Africa other than what they had seen in movies or on television. Few had first-hand experience with Africans. They asked Amadou embarrassing questions:

Did they have buildings in Africa? How many wives did he have in Africa? Was he marrying Lucinda just to stay in the country? (They were unaware that he already had a green card.) Family and friends assumed that what they heard about one African nation and ethnic group applied to all African nations and ethnicities, such as voodoo, body piercing, and female genital mutilation. Misinformation led to more misconceptions. They also assumed that by marrying Amadou, Lucinda would convert to Islam, cover up her body and act subservient.

By educating her family and friends regarding her husband's culture and religion, Lucinda was able to increase their support. By opening the doors of communication and interaction, her friends and family ceased misinterpreting unfamiliar actions of her spouse, his friends, and family.

If possible, draw up a prenuptial agreement, or at least talk about future issues.

Lucinda discovered some Senegalese customs that were difficult for her to accept, such as a man being able to have as many as four wives. In Senegalese culture, a son is the one who carries the father's name. Consequently, if a first wife does not have a son, a man may take a second wife. Since Lucinda and Amadou have two daughters, Lucinda made it clear to her husband that taking a second wife was both unacceptable and unlawful in this country. Dealing with his friends' opinions about this often led to difficulties.

Expect some resentment from your spouse's friends and family who were also born abroad.

Amadou's friends think Lucinda has too much freedom, and they are afraid she will inspire insubordination among their wives. When Lucinda travels alone as part of her job, some of the other wives aspire to more independence for themselves. Still others become jealous or consider her a bad wife. While at first Amadou took pride in his wife's independence, his friends' criticisms affected him negatively.

Despite Amadou's flourishing American business and his externally seeming to fit into American culture, Lucinda cautions that around other Senegalese, he returns to his traditional values and reactions. This makes it difficult for Lucinda because it is as if he regresses and the progress they've made in living together amicably for over twelve years and his acceptance of her as an independent woman is gone.

> While you may have trouble accepting your partner's customs, your partner may have equal difficulty in accepting your customs. Set priorities on what's most important to each of you.

Lucinda and Amadou encountered a major conflict over funerals. In Africa, Senegalese Muslims bury their dead within twenty-four hours; family members wash the body immediately after death and afterward the casket is closed and remains closed so that one never sees the face of the dead.

Amadou attended his first African American funeral when Lucinda's godfather died. Amadou suffered nightmares for days afterward because he was unprepared for the open casket, the wake, the screaming and falling out (sudden collapse). He now refuses to attend any more African American funerals and will not allow his children to attend. Like most Senegalese, Amadou and other Africans living in this country desire to be buried in their place of birth. Commonly, when a Senegalese dies in the United States, the community raises money to help him or her accomplish this desire.

Amadou and Lucinda have navigated many bumps in their journey as a unified family. Their success attests to their love and commitment to each other. What follows is an example of another African and American successful union. This time the combination is Jewish American and African Yoruban. The Yoruba are from Nigeria and have rich traditions that have spread to Brazil and the Caribbean and have influenced the Santería and Candomblé religions.

JEWISH AMERICAN WITH AFRICAN YORUBAN

Couples combining backgrounds of Jewish American with African Yourban might appear to have less in common than couples of African American and African ethnicities, but not necessarily. The sixteen-year marriage of Carole Zeitlin to Ayo Adefemi, an African musician and drummer, demonstrates great harmony in their union.

Carole, a New York Jewish girl, and Ayo, a Yoruba from Nigeria, fell in love. When she became pregnant, her parents responded according to old-fashioned Jewish tradition. When a daughter has a child out of wedlock, and/or if children marry non-Jews, the parents consider them dead and all relations are severed. Turned away by her family, Carole totally embraced the Yoruba culture just as Ayo's family embraced her.

If your family rejects you, don't fight it. Focus on the love and care you receive from your partner's family.

Ayo's family was ecstatic about the forthcoming baby. In accordance with Yoruba tradition, his sister, a physician and Minister of Population Control in Nigeria, flew to New York to take over household responsibilities for forty days after the baby was born. Carole and Ayo called the baby Louis. Ayo and Carole also had to marry because Yoruban customs decree that Ayo's sister would never be able to marry until he married first.

Ayo's sister took care of all the wedding arrangements including the food and Carole's outfit. An African American opera singer, who is also a minister, officiated. Over one hundred guests danced to the Drums of Passion in joyous celebration.

Jewish and Yoruban traditions have similarities. Both practice circumcision, but Carole had a doctor circumcise Louis rather than a traditional *babalawo* (Yoruban medicine man). Both cultures have naming ceremonies, as well. The Jewish naming ceremony is often a simple religious ceremony held at home. Not so for Yoruban naming practices.

Be prepared for cultural surprises.

On the baby's seventh day, some Yorubas brought the new family to a church in Brooklyn. They took the baby from Carole because a Yoruban mother can't go into the sanctuary until forty days have passed. Carole waited outside for over four hours only seeing her son every hour or so when he was brought out for a feeding. Finally, the celebrants allowed her in for the purpose of announcing his name: "Congratulations on your son, David Victor." Carole was stunned. His birth certificate read Louis Alexander Adelaja Adedotu Zeitlin Adeyemi. Despite this, the Yorubas told her that they had done a reading, and in a trance-state one of the elders discovered that Baby Louis was a reincarnation of King David and that he would be victorious, thus accounting for his name, David Victor.

Carole subsequently learned that the Yoruba believe a child belongs to everyone, so anyone can name him. She began receiving letters and gifts from Yoruban friends and family and each referred to him by a different name.

Baba Olatunji, a world-famous African drummer and close friend, called him Bandele, meaning, "he's the one who will follow me home." Olatunji has included a composition called "Bandele" on one of his recordings.

Research the culture you're marrying into.

Carole completely immersed herself in African culture. She wore African clothing, cooked African food, and was initiated into the Ifa religion (the basis of Santería). She and Ayo created Yoruba House in Los Angeles, an oasis of African drum and dance. It attracted people from all over the world to drum or dance for hours. They taught seven classes a week, and every month they celebrated the full moon and the new moon as well as the changing of the seasons and the birthdays of the *orishas* (the lesser gods in the *Ifa* religion). Yoruba House demonstrated unity through music and Carole called it a dance temple. But on September 3, 2001, Yoruba House burned down, and although a neighbor had seen someone on the roof prior to the blaze, arson was never proven because authorities turned their attention elsewhere after September 11. Carole and Ayo suspected that not all of the neighbors approved of their interracial family and the activities that took place at Yoruba House. The couple believe that one or more of these persons set the fire that completely destroyed Yoruba House.

Their son, Louis, had always been an integral part of Yoruba House; his first words were *gun go-do*, the sounds of a basic African rhythm. Carole and Ayo raised him to share everything as African children so. According to his mom, he doesn't have a "mine" attitude. To him all children are his brothers. Once when he called another child his "brother" and the other child retorted, "I'm not your brother," Carole consoled Louis: "He's your brother but doesn't know it."

Even though Louis and Carole were completely inculcated into the Yoruba culture, Carole eventually felt the tug of her Judaism.

Don't negate your own culture.

As Carole became absorbed in Yoruban tradition, she realized the value of her own Jewish culture. She had reconciled with her mother and joined a multiracial temple, B'nai Charim, where Louis had a *bar mitzvah*. Ayo stood beside him on the *bimah* (stage) and blessed his son in Yoruba. Carole's mom was impressed. "He speaks Hebrew very well."

Now that she has rediscovered her own roots, Carole observes the Jewish Sabbath and other Jewish holidays. Louis has become a star high school athlete and also participated in the Maccabee Games, a sports competition for Jewish athletes from sixteen different countries. Ayo and Carole's son has flourished in his multiracial home. Carole is proud of what she and Ayo have created.

> Look for the gifts from around the world
> and use them in your life to enrich your
> own and that of your family.

Carole concludes, "If you never get out, and you just marry someone from down the street, you're missing so much."

Carole and Ayo represent an excellent example of an American marrying an African, both having different religions, and how successful multiracial families can be.

Now here is an example of what may occur when both partners have been born in different places overseas, are of different ethnicities and religions and raise their family in the United States. What follows is from the point of view of one of their daughters.

FILIPINO CATHOLIC WITH JAPANESE SHINTO

After World War II, Donna's mother, Tomiko, met Lino, a Filipino in the U.S. Merchant Marines, at a Dance Club during his stopover at a military base in her home town, Okinawa, Japan. Although most Filipinos were anti-Japanese because of the brutal Japanese occupation of the Philippine Islands, that didn't deter the couples' love for each other. When they met, Tomiko, like most Japanese, believed in Shintoism, while Lino had been raised a Roman Catholic. Today, Lino has rejected Catholic practices, but Tomiko primarily continues her religion by praying to her ancestors. Consequently, religion has played a negligible role in their family.

> Don't overlook the power of the media to influence traditions.

Tomiko and Lino and their four children moved from military base to military base in the United States, and finally settled in California. When Donna was growing up, she and her siblings watched a lot of television where all lead characters were white. She and her siblings assumed they would eventually marry whites, not because they were racist, as some people suggested, but because the TV presented that as the norm.

As anticipated, Donna's two sisters married white men, one of them Jewish, and Donna married a Cuban, who grew up Catholic but became a Seventh Day Adventist in the United States. Donna and her husband have not given religious training to either of their two children, but Donna has strong feelings about maintaining one of her mother's traditions.

For cultural continuity, select at least one tradition that you can pass along to your children.

As youngsters, Japanese relatives gave Donna and her siblings New Year's envelopes decorated with red borders and cranes. Donna's mother taught the children to say, "*akemashite omedeto gozimasi.*" ("When I open this, I'll thank you for whatever it contains.") Donna has discontinued that practice for her own children because she claims they receive too many gifts for Christmas. They also no longer eat the sweet rice traditionally served on New Year's. Donna maintains no Cuban family traditions because her husband has not held on to any, nor does he desire to do so. The only thing he remembers and likes are some Cuban foods, like *flan* and *ropa vieja*, that Donna willingly prepares.

Donna is committed to maintaining and passing on her mother's most important Japanese cultural traditions: Making sukiyaki on New Year's Eve and on New Year's Day preparing ozoni, a soup made of clear fish broth with pork, fish cakes, mochi, green onions, and mushrooms. Donna is the only one of her siblings to do so. She feels strongly about this.

The preceding examples of multiracial families demonstrate five different variations, but the combinations are infinite, with each family succeeding through imagination and practical decision-making. On the other hand, grandparents sometimes have difficulty accepting their children's multiracial decisions. Some may even be embarrassed when their grandchildren have the racial characteristics of the other family. That's what happened to one Korean grandfather who had to continually explain that the Anglo toddler at his side was his biological grandson.

Guidelines for Grandparents

Grandparents sometimes have difficulty in coping with religious differences in their children's new families. When children marry into a different race, some grandparents struggle even more with acceptance—but not Grammy Terri.

Terri came from Arkansas and was raised as a Methodist. After she married her husband, also a Methodist from the South, they became Unitarians and raised their children in that faith. Later, their daughter, Blair, met and fell in love with a black man from the Virgin Islands, who had been raised in a Catholic orphanage. In California, at the age of thirty-eight, he captivated the hearts of a Jewish family who legally adopted him. When he and Blair had a daughter, the young couple agreed to raise their child Jewish. Later, after the couple separated, Blair, who had in the meantime converted to Judaism, and her daughter, moved in with Grammy Terri. Blair, her daughter, and the girl's father are currently preparing for *bas/bar mitzvahs*. Grammy has supported these plans.

Respect your children's decision regarding traditions they choose, but that doesn't mean you have to totally negate your own customs.

Grammy honors her daughter's religious decisions, especially since her daughter and granddaughter now live with her. Nonetheless, she is not going to give up all her own traditions either. Grammy still hangs Christmas stockings and puts up a Christmas tree, mainly to display the family collection of ornaments, which from Grammy's point of view is an important way to pass on family stories to her granddaughter. As they place the ornaments on the tree, they talk about who made it and where they lived. Terri presents her grandchild with only one big present, but Blair gives her child one gift for each of the eight nights of Hanukkah, so both practices are upheld

Treat the changes lightly. Being avid about anything makes it more difficult to adjust.

On Passover, Blair prepares a *seder* (ritual feast with no leavened bread) and Grammy helps with that. They invite Grammy's friends, mostly non-Jews who love participating in, what for them is, an exotic ceremony. Grammy says that as a result of her daughter's and granddaughter's conversions, she has lost Christmas and Easter and the big meals that accompany these holidays. Yet, she consents to these changes.

Have a sense of humor about changes and conflicts.

What Terri misses most is not being able to prepare Easter baskets for the family. With great humor she assesses the situation, "I gave up Easter baskets for latkes." Terri has graciously accepted her new interfaith and interracial family. In contrast, Blair's father, who is divorced from Grammy, is now a Mormon. Although he loves his daughter and granddaughter, he would prefer that they would become Mormons and tries, when he can, to anoint his granddaughter and offer blessings upon her. He is reticent about accepting Blair's own path.

Just as Grammy Terri has welcomed family transformations, so too have Pearl and Lou. Married for fifty-nine years, they came from mixed families of Catholics and Jews but have rejected organized religion. Pearl credits her membership in the Ethical Culture Society for nurturing her humanistic attitudes that have shaped her colorful multiracial family. They have three children, two adopted Indian granddaughters, two half-Chileno grandsons, and two half-Japanese granddaughters who enjoy lighting Hanukkah candles.

Even if you do not belong to a religious institution, encourage home celebrations as a way of passing on cultural traditions.

Despite a lack of institutionalized religion, Pearl and Lou celebrate religious holidays at home, with different children taking on responsibilities for holiday dinners such as Christmas, Easter and Thanksgiving. Pearl chooses to make the Passover Seder.

Pearl takes pride in what she and Lou have created. "What does all this mixing, this tiramisu of family mean to a grandparent? Lou and I come from families full of Jews and Catholics, a few Protestants in the mix. With great interest I watch the children to see how they incorporate the aesthetics of ceremonials into their own experiences."

Pearl adds, "We are such a talking bunch that the greatest pleasure for me has been the talking around the ceremonials. Christmas seems not to have any religious connotation—it has been so secularized here, but Thanksgiving and Passover—ah, there you have grand occasions for intermingling and participating; the Passover, for example, always opens into a discussion of modern diasporas. And Thanksgiving is another. I think this year there will be reflections on the Sudan desperation."

Pearl and Lou appear to be ideal grandparents, welcoming the variety of religions and races that their children have brought into their family. But, what happens when the interracial/interfaith marriage fails? Grandparents can either jump into the rift or remove themselves from the battleground and maintain a safe haven for the grandchildren.

HOW SHOULD GRANDPARENTS RESPOND WHEN THE CHILDREN DIVORCE?

Remain respectful of the other family's race and religion. Don't blame the failure of the marriage on it.

Grandparents of children from failed multiracial and interfaith marriages shouldn't automatically blame the failure of the marriage on the other family's ethnicity. That might not have been the cause of the breakup at all. Nonetheless, culture conflicts might have contributed to the dissolution, yet there is nothing you can do about that. Saying "I told you so," is fruitless. It is in the grandchild's best interest to remain respectful of the other family. Even if you are not overt about resenting the other family's race and/or religion, grandchildren will pick up on your negativity and apply that hostility to themselves.

Each family must try not to feel threatened when the child participates in religious and ethnic practices of the other family.

This situation can be avoided if early on in the marriage, each family respected the customs of the other family. A Jewish maternal grandmother asked her Persian half-Muslim granddaughter if she went to the mosque or used a prayer rug at home in her father's home. When the grandmother noted how defensive the child became while answering, she stopped asking those questions altogether. The child was not responsible for her conflicted homes. Why add to her emotional burdens?

Try to let celebrations be emotionally unblemished by the past.

At grandchildrens' rites of passage, both sides will come together. This can be a time of angst for the children if they know that Mom's family and Dad's family won't talk to each other, won't sit next to each other, won't celebrate with each other.

When the grandfather heard his wife inviting the parents of their ex-son-in-law for lunch to celebrate their granddaughter's graduation from elementary school, the grandfather was incredulous. His wife explained, "It's not about the graduation. It's about the wedding."

The wife understood that peaceful coexistence had to be established early during the divorce so that future celebrations could be enjoyed by all, especially the grandchild.

Families must try to forget former bitterness and put the welfare of their grandchildren first.

A grandchild from a failed marriage told her maternal grandfather, "I'm so glad you and my Dad get along." And why shouldn't they? Despite an initially traumatic divorce, both parties realized that they shared this beautiful child in common. To emotionally harm her in any way would have negated all the love they had for her.

Certain issues arise immediately in multiracial couples when they have children. But what about multiracial families who come about as the result of adopting children from other races and other countries and incorporating these children into their existing families?

Adoptions

According to the 2000 Census, one and a half million children in America under the age of eighteen joined their families through adoptions, representing 2 percent of all children in the United States. In the United States today, a total of five million people have been adopted. More than 100,000 children are adopted each year. Adopting children from outside the nation is called a transnational, transcultural, or transracial adoption. Before 1989, nearly all transnational adoptions consisted of children from Latin American or Asian countries. At that time most Westerners adopted Korean children.

American attitudes toward adoptions have changed dramatically since the early twentieth century when "she's adopted" was a whispered confidence. No longer. The anguish of adopted children wondering about who and where their parents are has diminished with the phenomenon of open adoption, where the birth mother may not only choose the adoptive parents but also maintain ties through the years. Open adoptions have found great favor in the United States.

But long waits and bureaucratic difficulties in adopting inside the United States can cause parents to look overseas to find babies. After the fall of Nicolae Ceausescu in Romania in 1989 and an American television show exposed the plight of their orphaned children, a surge in Romanian adoptions followed. Between 100,000 and 300,000 children had been warehoused in Romanian orphanages. Most had experienced severe emotional and physical deprivation. United States families adopted 2,594 of these children in 1991. Several years later, adoptions from Russia began. In 1998, there were 15,774 adoptions from Romania and Russia. Russian adoptions were more frequent because of health problems with Romanian children such as malnutrition, infectious diseases, growth and developmental impairment. Moreover, adoption became a source of easy money for shady dealers who were selling babies, so Romania temporarily ceased adoptions. The decrease in Romanian adoptions, a decline from 621 in 1997 to 406 in 1998, was accompanied by increased adoptions from Russia.

Large-scale adoptions of children from China by American families began in 1992, when the Chinese government passed a law authorizing international adoption. Because the Chinese government encourages families to have no more than one child, and the Chinese prefer boys, most of these children are girls. In 2000, the number of children from China who were adopted amounted to 5,053, with similar numbers in 2001 and 2002. In 2003, the numbers increased to 6,859.

Help the child appreciate his/her cultural traditions.

In the past, transracial adoptions emphasized assimilation, but today adoptive families attempt to embrace the cultures of their adopted children. Children are entitled to acknowledge their birth ethnicity. Denying them this access has lasting repercussions as children begin to probe the "Who am I?" question. Yet attempts to provide cultural identity may sometimes boomerang.

Accept that some children may reject their birth culture traditions.

In the 1970s Sharon and her husband Rob were raising two children adopted from Korea. Many of the international students and faculty in their Ann Arbor, Michigan, university town sent their children to Korean Saturday school for cultural enrichment. With amusement, Sharon reminisces about the time she enrolled her nine-year-old daughter and six-year-old son. To the children's dismay, the school placed them in gender-specific activities: calligraphy for the girls, *tae kwon do* for the boys. But Sharon had raised her children with less rigid gender roles. Her daughter wanted to learn *tae kwon do* and her son wanted to learn calligraphy. The school denied the children's desires, so the children refused to attend.

One of the best methods of acknowledging adopted children's ethnicity is through the celebration of their holidays and the customs related to their heritage. Yet not all adoptive parents are in accord with this practice. A minority of parents believe that the children are American and should be treated no differently than birth children.

One adoptive family, in which the mother was raised as a traditional Christian and the father is half Jewish but identifies with Buddhism, adopted two children from Korea and one from China. They acknowledge no Asian holidays or traditions, yet they consider themselves a multicultural family. They celebrate Hanukkah and Christmas, but to this family the tree and Santa are not about the birth of Christ. They talk about it historically.

These parents are very open with their children. They asked their eleven-year-old from Korea if he wanted to learn the Korean language. He answered, "Why would I want to learn Korean? I'm American and I'm having enough troubles with English."

The parents strongly believe that there are many different paths to truth and loving kindness. Buddhist philosophy seems to guide them, and they try to walk through life with the goal of being decent people.

WHITE PARENTS AND CHINESE CHILDREN

The more current thinking, especially from those adopting children from China, is that adopted children benefit by remaining tied to their birth country traditions. This philosophy guides Margo and her husband Dan who adopted Fay from China at fifteen months into their existing family of two biological sons. Margo and her husband belong to the organization, Friends with Children From China (FCC).

On September 11, 2004, this family invited me to attend their Chinese Moon Festival, sponsored by the Southern California branch of FCC, representing 500 families. The Chinese Moon Festival, observed annually in Chinatown, pays homage to the circle of life. The juxtaposition of the memory of what happened on 9/11, three years before, with the joyous scene I witnessed is indelible in my mind with over one hundred family members, including forty Chinese daughters and their siblings, had the best time together. I was charmed by one youngster who tugged at my sleeve and asked, "Are you waiting to get a kid, too?"

Families ate foods in the shape of a circle: pizza, cookies, cupcakes, grapes, donut holes, rice cakes, and sliced orange rounds. The children made fans gluing popsicle sticks to red paper plates and decorated them with stickers of multiracial children's faces; they colored pages with round Happy Moon Festival drawings; they dipped different sized hoops into wading tubs full of bubble solutions, launching big iridescent bubbles into the air with delighted screams.

For educational and emotional support, join organizations of other adoptive parents.

Friends with Children from China (FCC) commit themselves to ensuring that their daughters recognize and embrace their Chinese heritage as well as become integrated into American life and their particular family's religious heritage. They meet monthly for meetings offering Chinese-related family activities as well as educational workshops for the parents. Many of the children attend Chinese schools or take classes in traditional dance. FCC provides comfort and safety for adoptive parents who offer support to one another with helping their children feel secure in their homes and in the new country.

By belonging to FCC, the children benefit in developing bonds with others like themselves. Eight-and-a half-year-old Fay told me that FCC was "like a cushion." She had many friends there who shared her same experience of being adopted, being Chinese, living with Caucasian parents and sometimes Caucasian siblings, and living in the United States.

Adoptive parents need to take an active role in their children's schools.

FCC parents actively participate in their children's classrooms as volunteers to serve as resources on Chinese culture and adoption. For example, sometimes challenges arise when teachers ask children to bring baby pictures from home or ask them to draw a family tree.

Chinese New Year provides an excellent opportunity for sharing Chinese culture in schools. In Fay's school, Margo brings bubble wrap to spread on the floor. Then the students jump all over it, popping the bubbles to emulate the sound of fireworks, an integral part of Chinese New Year celebrations. Who could resist such joy?

Jane Jeong Trenka, an adult adoptee from South Korea, disapproves of the ways that FCC and other families of Chinese adoptees emphasize Chinese culture. She criticizes their attempt to identify the child with "this weird exo-tourism grasping at cultural tchotchkes, taking stuff out of its context." She claims that these parents' efforts to give Chinese culture back to their daughters are wasted, for the children can never be Chinese again.

Teach children how to deal with questions from strangers; they are not obligated to answer. They can refer the questioner to the parents.

The FCC invites experts in the field of transracial adoptions to give them advice on how best to strengthen cultural identity. An important name in this field is Jane Brown, MSW, who has eight children, five of them adopted. She is well-known for her playshops—activities to help adopted children explore in a group setting what it means to have been adopted. Margo has embraced her counsel. When Fay feels uncomfortable about a question such as "How come you don't look like your Mom?" Fay may say, "Why don't you ask my mom?" or "Why don't you ask your mom?" Or she might say, "I look like my biological mom."

Many adoptive parents become activists who work to promote more understanding of transracial adoption, such as the Garlocks, of Georgia, who adopted their children, Melanie and Kristin, from China in 1998 and 2002. Terry Garlock's book about the experience, *Sisters Redeem Their Grumpy Dad*, reveals how the girls brought them great happiness. Garlock is committed to helping his daughters adjust.

Start telling children their adoption story when they are very young. It's better to plant the ideas in their minds rather than wait for them to start the conversation.

When Melanie was two years old, her dad created a power point presentation about her adoption. The story explains that in China they love children, but the government says they may only have one child per family. Parents prefer boys because they help their families financially when they grow up, while girls must leave their birth families when they marry. Garlock emphasizes many positive aspects of Chinese culture and stresses that Melanie must always honor her birth parents, that adoption is a wonderful thing, and that he, Julie, Melanie, and Kristin are a "forever family."

During her first year in the family, Melanie wanted to watch her story every day. That lasted for a year. Now she only requests seeing it about once a year. Garlock claims that starting this storytelling process at age two builds pride in adoption and that, eventually, the child becomes convinced that her new family will never go away. He feels that the illustrated adoption story provides a way for parents to start the conversation about some uncomfortable topics, especially abandonment.

Garlock assumed that by repeating Melanie's adoption story he had cleared up misconceptions about adoption. He learned otherwise when one day he discovered that Melanie thought all children had two sets of parents.

Melanie asked her dad to do a power point presentation for her school about Chinese New Year. Dad spent endless hours putting the presentation together, and the school appreciated it. He followed up with another power point presentation on the Chinese Moon Festival that he offered to send free to teachers on the AIM (Adoption International Mission) China list serve. "Be careful what you wish for," he told me. As a result of his offer, one hundred teachers requested CDs. Undaunted by the work and inspired by the results, he next plans to do a presentation on the Dragon Boat Festival.

Although the Garlocks purchased some paintings while in China picking up Melanie, Terry said they are not trying to become Chinese. For example, they don't cook Chinese food. Terry emphatically declares that his daughters are American, born in China, and with a lifetime link to Chinese culture.

Associate with other families with adopted children from the same background as yours.

This family has connected with other families who have adopted Chinese daughters and they get together for social activities, both on Chinese holidays and at other times for cultural field trips together, such as museums. The children and parents have formed lifetime connections with one another.

Both parents have Christian backgrounds but observe no religious affiliations. They celebrate a secular Christmas, and Easter means the Easter bunny and chocolate eggs. Their other milestones are birthdays and Halloween. They don't celebrate Gotcha Day (see Multiracial Families / Gotcha Day, p. 87.) because Terry dislikes the term. To him, it emphasizes that the child is different. He feels that celebrating birthdays is sufficient.

Just as the Garlocks have dedicated themselves to disseminating information about transracial adoptions and assisting adoptive families, so too has Hemlata Momaya, founder and director of the *Bal Jagat* ("children's world" in Hindi) Adoption Agency, in existence for over twenty years and located in Chatsworth, California. Momaya comes from India and has supervised the adoption of over 2,000 children. Currently, most adoptees come from Russia and China.

Momaya told me that overseas orphanages give the child some symbolic token when they hand them over to the adoptive parents. In India they place something sweet in the child's mouth and affix a *bindi*, a red dot in the middle of the forehead. In China, they may dress the child in red, and when the worker hands over the baby they will give it a coin in a red envelope to wish the child good luck for the rest of her life.

Let children socialize with other multiracial adoptive families.

What is special about Momaya's agency is the ongoing personal attention she gives to her families, sponsoring get-togethers on a regular basis. "When you bring the families together, they see 200 children of all kinds and looks and realize that they're not the only ones who are adopted."

Her agency sponsors picnics and observes ethnic celebrations of the children's home countries. They have celebrated Romanian Dancing Day; for Chinese New Year, they gave the children red envelopes with lucky coins; for Divali, a Hindu Festival of lights, they put henna tattoos (*mehndi*) on the children's hands and wrapped the girls in saris; at Christmas, they hold two parties, one in Los Angeles County, another in San Diego County.

I attended their 2004 Christmas holiday party, where the children participated by reciting poems and singing songs and visiting with Santa. It was a joyous multiracial event with adoptees from India, China, Romania, Guatemala, the Ukraine and Moldova.

Allow the children to explore their birth culture, but don't forcefeed it if they resist. Accept their individual attitudes.

One adoptive mom discussed the difference between her two daughters. The younger one more or less rejects Chinese culture—she wants to be like everybody else in the United States. When her mom adopted her at age six, she only knew a few Chinese songs, yet ironically, she excelled at dancing the Macarena. In contrast, her older sister is at ease with Chinese traditions. Her mother notes the differences and accepts them rather than pressuring her daughters.

Momaya has become a kind of super mother for the children adopted through her agency. One of the Indian adoptees was convinced that she was his birth mother because of her looks and her love. He repeatedly asked, "Are you sure you're not my mom?" She finally convinced him that she was not, and that while she loved him, she also loved all children. She believes, "Every child needs a roof and family. Adoption is a gift of life."

WHITE PARENTS AND BLACK CHILDREN

Jana Wolff, author of *Secret Thoughts of an Adoptive Mother* states that "Adopting interracially is like donning a permanent sandwich board that advertises your adoption (and your infertility too)." Woolf, who is Jewish, adopted an African American son. She says that he's different by being adopted, by being Jewish, by living in Hawaii, and by having a Hebrew name. She worries that she's contributed to making life more difficult for her child.

She recognizes the difficulties with whites raising blacks, even the small detail of knowing how to take care of her son's hair. She has had to learn that the method for washing her own hair does not work for her son.

Here are some suggestions made by Pact, An Adoption Alliance. They address the issue of white parents dealing with the appropriate method of black hair maintenance. They claim that hair is a significant adoption concern in building African American racial identity.

To maintain moisture, wash your child's hair every week or two. Hair should be brushed daily to avoid matting.

Use hair products that remoisturize and are designed for African Americans.

Use close cuts for boys and allow girls' hair to grow long and tie or braid.

To avoid ashy, excessively dry, or flaky skin, use natural lotions containing cocoa butter.

WHITE PARENTS AND EAST INDIAN CHILDREN

Help adopted children develop a strong sense of self-identification by exposing them to their own cultural and religious traditions for as long as they desire.

About 600 Indian children are adopted in the United States every year, and most of these adoptees' families try to introduce the children's heritage into their homes in some way. In one household, the son takes lessons in classical *kathak* Indian dance. Although his adoptive family is Mormon and he is being raised as a Christian, the family has visited both Hindu and Jain temples and the boy can identify the many Indian Gods. He claims, "When I grow up, I want to marry a brown girl and have brown babies."

When dark-skinned, Indian-born Benjamin Mahadev was three, he took his white American mom's drivers license picture and colored it because he wanted her to look like him. In another home with four adopted Indian daughters, one of the girls exclaimed, "Mom, you must be sad because you will never be Indian." Her mom, who frequently travels to India, joked, "Before, I was an Italian American. Now I am an Italian Bengali American."

Rosalie and her husband, both white, adopted two toddlers from India, one now nineteen and the other twenty. Rosalie became so immersed in Indian culture, especially when the children were small, that she used to tell people that she was American and East Indian. Now she claims she is also part Latina because she works in an all Latina school in a large Mexican American neighborhood and has become bilingual in Spanish.

When their daughters were small, she put them in a private school with other Indian children. They learned about Indian foods and manners, and learned to take off their shoes when visiting Indian households. At home they made Indian foods and observed some Indian holidays. They stopped most of this at age eight when their interests broadened. Later, when their oldest daughter attended UCLA and became interested in dating, another Indian coed warned her that because she was adopted she would probably never find an Indian husband. Since the caste system is so strongly embedded in socialization, not knowing who her real parents are would be an impediment to an Indian marriage.

WHITE PARENTS AND NEPALESE CHILDREN

When six-year-old Sita, newly adopted by California white parents, discovered that she had been drinking cow's milk, she was outraged. She was born in Nepal where cows are holy and eating beef and drinking cow's milk is a major taboo. After her traumatic discovery, each morning she suspiciously queried her father as he filled up her glass. "Is this cow's milk?"

> Be cognizant of deep-rooted cultural beliefs of the adopted child, such as food taboos that might cause great conflict and plant a breach between parents and child.

Sita had been abandoned on the streets of Kathmandu as a toddler and subsequently lived in an orphanage, so her new parents were more concerned about her nutrition and rebuilding her health than cultural issues. Thus, they avoided telling her the truth for quite a long while. Instead, Dad told her he was pouring "house milk," an acceptable Nepalese combination of buffalo milk and cow's milk. At the same time, when her parents fed her beef, they told her it was buff (buffalo) or chicken. Although they had regrets about deceiving her, her parents believed that Sita's health was top priority. They planned to deal with the issue later on, yet they never anticipated the depth of the child's initial reaction.

> Ask adoptive parents about their preferences regarding gifts for their children.

One recommendation would be to choose dolls that resemble the child. If the child is not white, it is preferable that the doll be of color too. Select books with that same color sensitivity, and make sure you confer with the parents before you make your purchase.

Sita's parents were adamant about not wanting to turn their daughter into a "material girl." At the same time, friends and family were eager to bring gifts for Sita. The parents cautioned, "Bear in mind that this is all too big, too many, too much for her, and we want to keep her away from consumerism as much as possible." They printed out a list of gift recommendations for friends:

1. **If you really want to help Sita, send a contribution for her college education.**

2. **If you want to give her something more personal, look for anything educational: books, videos, DVDs, and educational software.**

3. **Tax-deductible checks to a charity in Nepal will be appreciated.**

4. **Warning: ABSOLUTELY NO BARBIES.**

Coincidentally, I was present when Sita received her first Barbie from a former neighbor who was unaware of the desires of Sita's parents. Interestingly enough, Sita wasn't much interested in Barbie or in any other dolls. Ironically, she expressed interest in having her mom dress in sexy clothes and wear high heels—for Mom to become Barbie.

Sita's mom possesses a great sense of humor and told me how surprised she was when her Nepalese daughter came home from school and sang the first American song she had learned, "Oh Hanukkah, Oh Hanukkah!"

JEWISH PARENTS AND CHINESE CHILDREN

Jewish American families have joined their Christian counterparts in adopting transracial children from China. Shelley Kapnek Rosenberg claims that these children need information about Jewish traditions as well as encouragement and assistance in integrating them into their personal identities. She warns that if parents fail to teach Judaism to their multicultural adopted children, the children may question their connection to Judaism and may assume that, because of their different cultural heritage, they are not welcome in the Jewish community.

Naming ceremonies can acknowledge multiple heritages.

Since names signal origin, a child may have his birth name, honoring the birth culture; an American name, indicating entry into one new culture; and a Hebrew name, symbolizing inclusion in a second new culture. Rosenberg suggests that if the child if from China, parents can display a red cloth embroidered with a good luck symbol or integrate foods, stories, and poems from the child's native culture.

Other Jewish adoptive parents may incorporate customs from their child's heritage into the practice of Judaism. They might research how Jews in their child's birth country celebrate their Judaism and include specific customs into their own celebration.

Marilyn Kress, a single adoptive Jewish mother, describes her Chinese daughter's literal immersion into Jewish culture by means of Kress' own father wearing a Great Wall of China T-shirt, carrying his granddaughter into the *mikveh* (ritual bath) and dunking newly-named Zoë the required three times for conversion to Judaism.

Kress has since emphasized her daughter's dual heritage by decorating the child's room with Chinese arts and crafts, celebrating Chinese festivals as well as three New Year's: American, Jewish, Chinese. They eat ethnic foods and light Sabbath candles. Zoë goes to Jewish day school as well as Mandarin language school.

Ann, a Jewish woman, and Vic, an unaffiliated Christian man, have been married for five years. In 2003, Sophie, a five-and-a-half-year-old Chinese girl, rounded out their family. The family is very active in Jewish Families with Chinese Children.

Let the child learn Jewish values.

Ann is rearing Sophie as a Jew, so she had to be officially converted by being immersed in a ritual bath (*mikveh*) with appropriate prayers and blessings. Because the conversion process requires total immersion, Vic quipped to Ann that Sophie will always remember "the day my mother tried to drown me."

Ann teaches her daughter values by telling her Old Testament Bible stories. They have no Christmas tree, but they celebrate Christmas when they visit Vic's adult children where the celebration is strictly secular. Since Ann's favorite holiday is Passover, she wants Sophie to have a Seder. At Hanukkah, Sophie herself reacted negatively to all the presents. "Mama, I've had enough." Sophie is happiest when other children are running around the house, when there is food and happy chaos.

Let children learn the Chinese language and become bicultural. Let them know and love China.

The parents are clear in their desire for Sophie to maintain ties to her Chinese culture as well as her new Jewish affiliations. They observe Chinese

New Year and Jewish New Year. They have hired a Mandarin tutor for her and have enrolled her in a Jewish day school. They are trying to keep her surrounded by diversity. They observe *Shabbat* (Sabbath) with the lighting of candles on Friday nights and attending temple. At other times, they visit Chinatown. Paradoxically, Sophie's favorite restaurant in Chinatown is Thai.

As the preceding examples have shown, adopting children from outside the United States brings pleasure and opposition. Frictions and enjoyment multiply in homes where adopted children come from a variety of races.

ADOPTED SIBLINGS OF DIFFERENT RACES

As important as it is for adoptive families to maintain connections to their children's birth cultures, families with adopted children from differing cultures must find ways to bond their siblings together. Celebrations can serve as bonding events.

Expose your children to each of their siblings' cultures. Attend their different houses of worship.

One Native American mother with a Jewish husband and adopted children of many faiths and colors tells how she has incorporated multicultural celebrations into their lives. They attend Native American powwows and other Native American ceremonies, where the spiritual leader welcomes all the children. To honor their African American children they worship in African American churches. They attend *bar mitzvahs* of friends, and with their most recent adoptee, of Lutheran background, the family attended a *lutefisk* dinner at a local Lutheran church.

This mom exalts in her multiracial family. "Never did I dream I would ever be so involved in so many different cultures. They enhance our lives so much. I am so thankful that these doors have opened to us through adoption."

Rituals help families reinforce their unity. One ritual in particular, has become popular with adoptive families. Called Gotcha Day, it ceremonially acknowledges the new family member.

GOTCHA DAY
ADOPTION DAY CELEBRATIONS

Similar to a birthday, Gotcha Day pays tribute to the date when the child was physically and officially placed in the loving arms of waiting new parents. It frequently commemorates the day on which the parents traveled to a foreign orphanage to take possession of their child. For the child, it reinforces how important he/she is to the rest of their new family. For the parents, it recognizes the major task they have undertaken in creating a home for the child.

Gotcha Day represents the human need to ritualize significant moments where no ritual had existed before. It demonstrates the power of rituals to unite.

The website http://www.adopting.org/Olderchild/gotchaday.html offers the following advice:

> There is no one "right" day to select as your adoption day. It might be the first time you and your child met, the day you went to court, the day your child got home, or the day the adoption was finalized. The idea is to celebrate the special aspects of how your family was created and/or expanded.

Parents and children can be as imaginative as they like because there are no fixed rules for celebrating Gotcha Day—anything, from the child's wearing of a crown or the lighting of candles, to honoring both sets of parents or the sending of packages to the child's orphanage, is possible. The internet is filled with suggestions for and by adoptive parents to make these events memorable. Here are some parents' ideas for celebrating their children's Gotcha Days:

1. A parent grateful for her Indian daughter gave a well to a small village in India, providing them with clean drinking water.

2. A single Mom and her Chinese daughter go outdoors and the daughter tells her Mom what she wishes her birthparents knew about her. They then release balloons and express the hope that the balloons will carry the information to the birth family.

3. "We always call it our 'Family Birthday' and celebrate it like a birthday, excluding presents. We go out to eat together or do something together."

4. "We don't celebrate on Gotcha Day, but on the Chinese Moon Festival, my Chinese daughter and I go out at night and look at the moon and talk about her birthparents being able to see the same moon. We tell the moon to let her birthparents know that she is alive and well in the United States and to thank them for letting us become a family."

An FCC mom shared her celebration of Gotcha Day in her family of one adopted Chinese daughter and two younger white biological children. They brew Jasmine tea, purchased in China, in a teapot that has decals of black dragons on it. The heat of the brewing tea turns the dragons red. When the tea is cool enough to drink, they turn black and the mom pours it into Chinese small tea cups to accompany their Chinese take-out meal.

Gotcha Day pays tribute to the reconfigurations of multiracial families as the result of adoption. The next chapter focuses on diversity in sexuality and gender assignment and the role of celebrations in the lives of GLBT (Gay/Lesbian/Bisexual/Transgender) community members. When GLBTs celebrate their rites of passage and holidays, repercussions from family and community are often severe. Nonetheless, it's time for Americans to accept that they are a not-to-be-overlooked part of our new cultural diversity.

[3]

CELEBRATIONS IN THE GLBT
(gay/lesbian/bisexual/transgender)
COMMUNITIES

When considering diversity, most people automatically think about racial, ethnic, and religious differences. They tend to ignore another form of multiculturalism—sexual diversity. While this segment of our culture has always been here, the majority have kept a low profile. That has changed and the GLBT population has become a more visible part of American culture, whether in politics (New Jersey Governor James McGreevey), entertainment (Elton John), business (David Geffen), sports (Billie Jean King), or any other work category. According to the U.S. 2000 Census Data, the Gay/Lesbian population over the age of eighteen numbers 209,128,094. Although GLBT communities refer to gay, lesbian, bisexual, and transgender, I will not be addressing bisexual ceremonies in this section because bisexuals can theoretically participate in gay, lesbian, or straight celebrations. On the other hand, since the ceremonial needs for transgenders are unique, I have devoted a special section to them at the end of this chapter.

Just as I have begun the preceding sections on the new diversity with rites of passage and marriage, in particular, I will continue that pattern because chronologically it makes sense: first the union between two individuals, followed by the arrival of children, and eventually death.

RITES OF PASSAGE

Same-Sex Marriage (also known as Unions, Partners-in-Life Vows and Commitment Ceremonies)

Partners need pre-marital counseling.

Reverend Tonyia Rawls heads the Unity Fellowship of Christ Church in Charlotte, North Carolina, that serves 160 members. In 2005, the church celebrated its fourth anniversary with the distinction of being the first congregation of African American GLBT members in the Bible Belt. This is an achievement because of the great antipathy toward the GLBT community in most African American churches. Many ministers preach that AIDS is God's curse on homosexuals; some refuse to bury African Americans with AIDS; even others deny hospital visits to AIDS patients.

When couples come to Rawls for pre-marriage counseling, she explains that there is a precedent within the African American community regarding non-traditional wedding ceremonies. Indeed they are common for African Americans. During slavery, the United States considered African Americans property, so the slaves couldn't have ceremonies like those of their masters. That's why they devised other ways to recognize the sanctity of their unions, such as "Jumping the Broom" (see Marriage/African American, p. 179.).

Before Rawls will agree to pre-marriage counseling of GLBT couples, certain criteria must be met: The couple must have been together for at least one year,. They must meet for three sessions before the union, and both parties must agree on important issues such as views on children. If children are included as part of the marriage plan, they must straighten out these disagreements during counseling because gay/lesbian weddings have no legal recourse.

The couple must understand what is sacred and significant for each other. She counsels that a wedding is a public acknowledgment of something that has already happened in their hearts. Valid reasons for desiring a wedding follow:

1. To offer up to God the relationship that it might be blessed.

2. To pledge their dedication to each other before God and/or witnesses.

3. To present their blessed love to the community who can now recognize them as one.

Talk to your parents.

Tell them what the ceremony represents to you, what this relationship means to you as a person, and what it would mean to have them participate in your wedding. If you have gay/lesbian friends who have also had ceremonies, put your parents in touch with their parents. This may ease their anxiety.

Don't wait until the wedding to introduce your future spouse to your parents.

Make sure you have already established a relationship between your partner and parents before the ceremony. The event will go more smoothly that way. The fewer the surprises the better.

Parents need pre-marriage counseling, too.

In Los Angeles, Rabbi Lisa Edwards presides over Congregation Beth Chayim Chadashim (BCC), the first Gay/Lesbian synagogue. Begun in 1972, it now serves 180 families. Rabbi Edwards has clear suggestions for parents facing the challenge of a wedding/commitment ceremony for their gay/lesbian offspring.

With their children's permission, parents should call or meet with the person who will be officiating.

In a way, the ceremony is a "coming out" for the parents of a gay/lesbian couple. The more information parents have about the ceremony ahead of time, the better off they'll be. If they have the time to think about it ahead of time, the more they can explore their feelings. When Rabbi Edwards has the opportunity to meet with parents before the ceremony, she asks them about their expectations and their fears. Often people worry that the event will be embarrassing in some way. Instead, she reminds parents that everyone who will be present loves the wedding couple.

Sometimes the rabbi asks parents to visualize the event and discuss what they are picturing. Sometimes they are nervous about seeing two brides in bridal gowns, or one bride in a tuxedo. Parents are less concerned about two grooms in tuxedos. Creating a mental picture ahead of time helps them. Anything that brings in reality rather than imagination will help

Edwards observes that parents change during the wedding. They come into the sanctuary scared stiff and unsmiling, but when they join in the company of those who love the couple and see their children happy, they "get it." They realize, "Oh, what was I so afraid of?"

She says that sometimes the wedding couple fears their parents' response to the ceremony so much, they actually hope they will turn down the invitation. She believes couples don't really want their parents to refuse. In fact, couples truly hope their parents will attend and share their joy.

Parents need to ask their children what they would like from them at the ceremony.

Edwards advises parents that their children may simply request their presence at the event or to just smile during the ceremony. Children may ask them to participate in the ceremony, as parents do at heterosexual wedding ceremonies. They may ask, "Will you walk me down the aisle? Will you read something? Will you offer a blessing and a toast afterward?"

Parents must realize that it is not their life, but their child's life to live.

When Reverend Rawls deals with families of the couple, she emphasizes love. She believes that, even while rejecting their children in the name of God, their rejection comes from the parents' fear and shame around some of their own issues. Parents also have concerns as to what life will be like for their offspring. Regardless, they must focus on the love they have for their children, who suffer greatly without their nurturing and support.

It is especially important for parents and couples to talk beforehand when the wedding is interfaith/interracial AND same-sex.

Parents of a child marrying a same-sex partner may experience an extra sense of loss because that child is also marrying outside his or her faith or culture. Jewish parents might say, "Not bad enough that she's marrying a woman, but she's marrying a Christian, too!" If that couple marries in a synagogue, the Christian side of the family may assume that the non-Jewish partner is leaving his/her own religion which then implies their leaving their family of origin as well.

Rabbi Edwards says that with interfaith/interracial and same sex unions it is even more important for parents and the couple to communicate. She advocates that parents talk to their children, children to their parents, and the wedding couple to each other.

Numerous websites on the internet describe Jewish wedding ceremonies written for non-Jews. These can serve as models for ceremonies that would not be offensive to the non-Jewish partner and family.

Sometimes, the couple takes turns explaining to the non-Jewish guests the meaning of the different symbols used: the blessing over the wine, the wedding canopy, the rings, the *ketubah*, the stomping on the glass (see Marriage/Jewish, p. 202). Rabbi Edwards also does some explaining as she officiates, but she takes care not to over-explain. That would detract from the ceremony.

Wedding couples must be empathetic to their nuclear families.

Couples must be empathetic to their nuclear families who now must also journey out of the closet. Often couples have a fantasy that they'll tell mom and it'll be great, but perhaps they didn't have an easy time coming out of the closet themselves. It might have taken years, so why expect their parents' journey to be any easier?

At the ceremony, don't seat families according to the customary his side, her side.

Reverend David L. Krueger-Duncan, known as Pastor Dave, presides over the Northwest Community Church in Las Vegas. Pastor Dave, formerly a Lutheran minister, officiates at weddings, gay and straight, at his small congregation of eighty that is affiliated with the United Church of Christ, known for its social justice philosophy. This denomination considers itself open and affirming to all. Pastor Dave's openness to officiating at same-sex weddings has brought repercussions. Originally, their small congregation met in a public school. Then one Tuesday, without cause, they received notice that they couldn't return to the premises on the following Sunday. He assumes that the school gave no reason for ousting them because it may be illegal to say it was due to his performing gay/lesbian weddings. No problem. His congregation now meets in a building located in a business park, across the street from the school.

At Pastor Dave's church, homosexual weddings tend to be smaller than heterosexual ones because they don't ordinarily have three generations showing up. Usually the family of one of the partners declines the invitation. Maybe one partner will have some family support, but typically both don't. That's why he's against seating wedding guests by sides, so that the lack of support won't appear obvious.

In his marriage philosophy statement, available on his website, Pastor Dave avers, "May God bless the love of couples!"

Don't obsess about the wedding kiss.

Dear Abby: I need advice. A former co-worker has invited me to her wedding. It's between her and her girlfriend. If I go, I'll have to take my four-year-old son because I don't have a sitter. Part of me thinks I should go and take him because they're a nice couple who have been together for seven years. They love each other, and it would be good for my son to learn that it's OK to be different. However, the other part of me thinks, "How am I going to answer the inevitable question, 'Mummy, why is that girl kissing the other girl?'" I know I could answer it with, "Because they love each other," but I think it's a bit of a leap for a four-year-old. Should I go, or just send a gift and my best wishes? HELP! In Jacksonville, FLA.

This "Dear Abby" letter (July 25, 2004), reveals a concern of many GLBT wedding participants—how will they react to seeing two persons of the same sex kiss romantically?

Minister Deb, an ordained California official who specializes in gay/ lesbian weddings, confirms that "the kiss" sometimes presents a problem, especially in front of family members and straight friends. One Latino male couple, in deference to the presence of their grandmothers, hugged instead. Nonetheless, Minister Deb says that despite the worry, it's rare for the kiss to be eliminated. In her practice, only 5 percent have chosen not to kiss.

Pastor Dave is not concerned about "the kiss." Although the couple may feel squeamish or ill-at-ease about kissing in front of Grandma, he believes that couples underestimate the older generation. If older people, especially relatives, attend a gay/lesbian wedding, they know what to expect. He reminds the wedding couple that older family members are not made of porcelain. They've seen a lot of life, and "the kiss" should not be an issue.

Jim Weintraub, a photographer based in Long Beach, California recalls the first time he shot a gay wedding. He, too, was concerned about the kiss: "It was between these two gay priests, and the time was coming for their first kiss as married people. I honestly didn't know how I would react. Would I flinch? Would I freeze? This is a very tight shot and you get one chance at it, so I was very nervous. But when they kissed it was like their gender just disappeared—it didn't matter."

Dear Abby came to the same conclusion when answering HELP! in Jacksonville. She suggested that if the child asked why one person was kissing the other, the answer should be, "Because they love each other." She predicted that the child would probably be more interested in eating wedding cake and playing with other children than receiving an explanation or a lecture on tolerance.

Don't refer to a gay male or a female couple as husband and wife or bride and groom. Use the terms mate, spouse, newlywed, or partner.

For some people, same-sex weddings offer confusion over gender roles. Minister Deb tells of the wedding where one woman wore a wedding gown and her mate wore a tuxedo. Their wedding photographer kept referring to the woman in the tuxedo as the "groom." Deb had to correct him, reminding him that, despite the tuxedo, both of the women were "brides."

One male couple fretted over the wedding invitations. All their friends and family knew them as Phillip and Joel, but few realized that Joel was undergoing a sex change. By the time of the wedding he would have breasts. They wondered whether to print Phillip and Joel on the wedding invitation or Phillip and Joann, the name he would assume after the sex-change was complete. Minister Deb advised that they put Joann on the invitation to ameliorate the shock for guests when they saw him full-figured in his wedding gown.

At a Jewish gay wedding, a dilemma arose over which one of the male couple would stomp on the glass at the conclusion of the ceremony. Ordinarily, the groom performs this act. After the two grooms argued about who would do it, the loser conceded to let his partner be the one to stomp the glass.

The officiant should consider that some family and friends may feel uncomfortable about attending the ceremony.

Since most guests have never attended a gay/lesbian wedding, including members of the community themselves, they need to be reassured that nothing unpleasant will take place. Minister Deb uses humor to do this. She reminds guests that it is a "gay" wedding in the old-fashioned sense of the word, and she tries to add levity to relax the guests. For example, to relieve the tension, after the couple says their "I dos," she frequently responds with "Good answer!" She and her partner set a playful tone at their own wedding by reading a Dr. Seuss poem. When, Meryl Cohn, also known as Ms. Behavior, got married, she and her same-sex partner injected humor into the wedding vows as well. "I will always try to close the cupboard doors and put things back where they belong." Her spouse responded, "I may always leave my socks on the floor, but I promise to know how it affects you."

In contrast, Pastor Dave says nothing special to put the congregation at ease. He feels this would call attention to the couple and might be considered patronizing. Instead, he tries to exude a comfortable manner and assumes that the wedding guests will take their cues from him.

At the beginning of a ceremony, Reverend Rawls steps in front of the couple and addresses the congregation: "If all you want to know is if this marriage is going to happen and what people are wearing, you can leave now, but if you are here because you believe that this love should flourish, I welcome you to this ceremony."

She reminds the congregation that all couples go through ups and downs, and it is their job as friends and family to be supportive and help them stay together. She reminds the congregants that all of them are sharing in the vows, and that they are significant to the success of the union. She encourages family and friends to help the couple in the future.

So how do same-sex weddings differ from straight weddings? Sarah Benoit, sales representative for the San Francisco 2004 Same Love, Same Rights: Gay and Lesbian Wedding Expo, says that because no special traditions bind the GLBT community, a lighter feel prevails. Couples don't have to follow any conventions, so weddings may be more mischievous and can include humor with the music or with the costumes. Fashion designers for these events are likely to be more edgy, wild, and creative knowing they have fewer conventions to uphold. For example, the male wedding couple may have angel wings attached to their tuxedos or wear devil's horns.

SAMPLE WEDDING CEREMONIES
Some of the same admonitions apply to same sex weddings as to interfaith or multiracial celebrations.

To honor each partners' background, combine wedding traditions from both sides.

Just as interfaith weddings combine cultural symbols from both families into their weddings, so do same-sex couples. When Jeanne and Lynn had their Partnership Ceremony, they donned ceremonial robes over traditional wedding outfits of gown and tuxedo. Lynn's robe had African motifs representing her South African birth, and Jeanne's robe had Guatemalan designs tied to her Latino paternal heritage. They played South African praise songs by Ladysmith Black Mambazo.

Incorporate customs from other cultures.

During Jeanne and Lynn's ceremony they rang Tibetan bells and during the procession marched in to Pachabel's "Canon in D." Following Native American and Wiccan traditions, they blessed the elements and four directions, then participated in a Celtic handfast rite, where they clasped each other's hands to confirm their covenant of betrothal. Afterward, they tied a lover's knot, spoke their vows, exchanged rings, and marched out to the recessional.

Feel free to express your political views.

This wedding was an overt political statement about human and gender rights. An activist in the gay/lesbian movement, numerous guests acknowledged Jeanne for her contributions including folk singer Holly Near, who sang in honor of the couple and their commitment to each other.

At the reception, replicas of the couple dressed in their robes topped the wedding cake. The miniature couple stood beneath trees, Lynn's metaphor for women because trees, like women, nurture and reach to the heavens, their branches representing relationships. Each guest received a memento of their commitment and love in the form of a souvenir bookmark.

Be innovative. Same-sex celebrations can be as imaginative as the couple likes.

Couples may create new traditions, or mix and match customs from other religions and ethnicities. At an elegant private ceremony, Alexandra and Kathryn welcomed their guests with a description of their beliefs inscribed on their wedding program and an explanation of the multiple ritual motifs they had chosen. The celebrants blended customs and rites from many sources, incorporating what they liked and what seemed appropriate. They played music by Barbra Streisand and Sade; a priest gave blessings and led them in a guided meditation and closing benediction; a friend performed a Native American smudging with burning sage to carry prayers to heaven and purify the energy and to bless the four directions in honor of the four spheres of their lives: physical, emotional, mental, spiritual. The couple lit a unity candle, and under an arch created by seven strands of forty- to fifty-foot long helium-filled balloons, one for each color of the rainbow, they had a blessing of the rainbow wishes, a ritual of their own creation.

Before the ceremony, they requested that each guest go to a wishing table under the balloon rainbow archway and select two beads of different colors. Each person made a separate wish with each bead, one for themselves, one for the newlyweds, then placed the beads into a Native American wedding vase, later blessed by the priest. The newlyweds took home the beads and strung them together and hung them over an indoor ficus tree to honor the day, their families and friends. Finally, during the recessional, guests blew bubbles at the couple.

Weddings need not be realistic and/or fantastic.
The ceremonies can even be parodies of weddings
and still have a unifying effect.

CAR WEDDING

In 1994, when same-sex ceremonies were less commonplace, Carol and Vicki created a surrogate ceremony—and quite by accident. They had been together for a while, had purchased a home together in the state of Washington, and now had purchased two used cars that they wanted to put in both names on their insurance and car licenses. They went to a local sporting goods store and the person helping them was a very tall man, with his head nearly touching the ceiling. As he stood on a platform looking down at the couple while they signed both their names on the applications, Carol observed, "This feels like we're getting married." The man who knew nothing about their backgrounds joked around with them about it, and that was the genesis of their car wedding—uniting one 1986 Toyota Tercel Hatchback with a 1986 Nissan King Cab Pickup, both silvery blue.

Other friends had also recently purchased cars so they decided to have a wedding motorcade/caravan. Carol made dashboard ornaments for each vehicle—little copper wires in the shape of cars with netting and ribbons attached.

On a July afternoon, Carol and Vicki drove their two cars to a bridal shower (a carwash), then motorcaded to an appointed spot which ended at an overlook, where the other cars and friends had gathered for the car wedding. Their female officiant wore a headdress with fuzzy dice hanging from it, batman tights, and a silk kimono top. She attached an oil funnel over each breast.

During the vows, the couple's cars promised to be true to each other through rust and ice and sleet and snow. Then Carol and Vicki exchanged key rings, hooked them together, and became one. The couple crossed arms, turned on their windshield wipers, threw water at both cars at the same time, and cars and couple were joined in holy weldlock.

Afterwards, the entourage drove to a neighborhood park where friends sang appropriate song parodies, "On the Street Where You Park" and "Side by Side." Wedding cakes were shaped like the two cars with blue frosting to match the paint, and the gifts consisted of car accessories: oil, waterless car wash, windshield wiper fluid, shammy cloths, and steering wheel covers.

Carol admitted that the ritual did not make her feel married, yet she felt totally embraced by her community, both gay and straight. Their friends went the extra mile. "People were willing to go with us on this, our only attempt at making a statement about being joined, however ridiculous."

Once the wedding has occurred, there are some people who will ignore that fact and deny the union by ignoring the same-sex spouse. This puts a strain on the marriage.

When inviting GLBT persons to social occasions, don't exclude their spouses.

Ms. Behavior, Meryl Cohn, the author of *Ms. Behavior's Guide to Gay and Lesbian Etiquette*, finds that omitting partners from social invitations is common and hurtful. With tongue-in-cheek, she offers some rationales:

1. They don't know you have a lover;

2. They know you have a lover but were stricken with amnesia and "forgot" when they were sending out invitations;

3. They judge your relationship with your lover as less than meaningful;

4. They know you have a lover but are too cheap to invite him or her;

5. They are afraid you will create a big queer scene by pressing your bodies together on the dance floor;

6. They fear that you and your lover might have loud, uncontrollable sex in the bathroom or touch tongues at the table and cause the other guests to run screaming into the parking lot, taking their gifts;

7. They don't want you both fighting over the bouquet.

Cohn has some extra advice regarding the same-sex wedding ceremony. She expresses dismay at onlookers taking pictures of gay weddings occurring in public spaces. "It's definitely bad form to photograph groups of people marrying as if you're on a whale watch. That's a no."

While individuals may disapprove of same-sex marriages, businesses ignore the moral dilemmas and head for the profit. The U.S. Census 2000 projects that the spending power of gay Americans is expected to reach

$608 billion by the year 2007. Gay/lesbian wedding expos existed before the headlined 2004 same-sex commitment ceremonies. Since then, they have become more prominent with expos in Cambridge, Massachusetts; in Minneapolis, Minnesota; Las Vegas, Nevada; Orange County, California; and San Francisco, California. Like ordinary wedding expos, they market wares to prospective couples.

GAY/LESBIAN WEDDING EXPOS

Don't mock or turn away visitors to your booth.

Gay/lesbian wedding expos are the same as heterosexual wedding expos: photographers, florists, caterers, wedding cake specialists, jewelers, custom stationers, fashion designers, and realtors fill up a convention center to sell their services. At the 2004 Orange County Wedding Expo, organizer Minister Deb screened all vendors to make sure they were gay-friendly, that they wouldn't freak out if they saw two men holding hands approaching their booth. She and her staff held an orientation meeting for their vendors, teaching them how to market to this community.

Have same-sex samples of your work.

Couples visiting a photographer's booth will want to see photos displayed of same-sex couples, rather than heterosexual couples. The same applies to wedding cake specialists. They need to display same-sex cake toppers. The biggest turnoff for attendees is seeing no representation of the gay/lesbian community. This sends the message that vendors do not care about their clients and only want their dollars.

ARRIVAL OF CHILDREN

If same-sex weddings seem complicated, the arrival of children into a same-sex family brings new issues. Rituals incorporating children into same-sex families may be different than the same rituals observed in other families—but not necessarily. All parents from all backgrounds have the same desires for their children: to protect them, to bless them, and to celebrate them. It's just the method of impregnation that differs.

Ms. Behavior has examined the responses of parents to lesbian couples wanting to get pregnant via artificial insemination. Many confusing emotions surface. She talks about one mother who wanted her lesbian daughter to change her mind about artificial insemination, reminding her that she could still get married. "It's never too late. Then you can have a baby the *normal* way." According to Cohn, when the lesbian mother informs her mother that she is going to be grandmother, the grandmother-to-be looks like *she* is having morning sickness.

Rabbi Edwards says that the imminent arrival of children in the lives of a gay or lesbian couple causes a new worry for the future grandparents. Some wonder how two mothers or two fathers can successfully raise children. While the parents might have been happy at their children's wedding, they worry about their grandchildren growing up in a homophobic world. Such worry may also be a projection of parents' homophobia. Edwards encourages them to talk to other parents of gay/lesbian couples who also have children.

Consider various strategies for incorporating your child into your family.

BABY SHOWER FOR MALE PARENTS

Just as straight couples look forward to the arrival of a child and wish to ritualize that anticipation with baby showers, gay/lesbian couples have the same desires. Scott, forty-two, and Mike, forty, had been together three years when they decided they wanted a child. After investigating adoption and traditional surrogacy where the surrogate uses her own egg, they opted for in-vitro fertilization, using an anonymous screened egg donor. They selected Growing Generations, an agency that specializes in surrogacy and egg donations for same-sex couples and handles medical and legal aspects of the process. Both Scott and Mike provided sperm to fertilize eggs harvested from a donor from Sweden. An embryologist selected one of the fertilized eggs (they do not know whose sperm it was) and inserted it into the surrogate.

The surrogate, Jessica, was a Mexican American married woman, who had one adopted and three biological children of her own, and had previously been a surrogate mother for another couple. The agency presented Jessica with profiles of several couples desiring a surrogate mother, and she selected Scott and Mike.

One month before the baby arrived, the men hosted a baby shower in their own home. The invitation gave clues that it would be a light-hearted event. It showed outlines of two men and a baby dashing across a road hand-in-hand, in the style of the warning signs about illegal alien crossings posted near the California/Mexican border.

One hundred and twenty-five guests came, including Jessica, at that time, eight months pregnant. She brought her husband and three children. The hosts provided an ice cream bar and bounce house for other children in attendance. Adults dined on hummus, bruschetta, crackers, and spreads, a variety of salads and pasta salads, and satay chicken, and indulged in the ice cream bar as well.

There were no party games or toasts, nor did the expectant fathers open the gifts, believing that the party should be about circulating with friends and speaking to the surrogate mom. Because Scott and Mike want Jessica to be a part of their baby's life, they asked her and her husband to be the baby's godparents and invited them to visit every two months.

Don't call the surrogate the "mother."

One important misconception prevailed at this event. Most people incorrectly assumed that Jessica was the biological mother. She was only the biological enabler. Prejudice against Latinos subtly surfaced in comments, even moreso after the baby was born. Because his coloring reflected his Swedish maternal gene pool, people made surprised and almost-relieved comments about how light-complexioned he was.

Scott and Mike were with Jessica when she delivered the baby in a hospital located several hours away from their home. Mike held the baby, named George, while Scott cut the cord. The hospital provided a room for the two fathers to spend the night, and the next day they brought their beautiful healthy son home.

George, now three, calls Scott "Papa" and Mike "Daddy." Daddy was born Jewish but has no Jewish identity, while Papa was raised Christian celebrating the secular side of Christian holidays. Both men believe that if they want to raise a child with the freedom to choose its own religion later on, the child must first have some religious exposure. As a result, they have enrolled George in a Jewish preschool. George participates in a Tot *Shabbat* (Sabbath) every Friday, where they light candles, say the prayer, and then eat *challah* (egg bread). Both parents like the Sabbath tradition, believing that it's important to take time to appreciate life's bounties.

BABY'S ONE-MONTH PARTY (*MAN-YUE*)

When Stuart and Lance became parents of a baby boy through a surrogacy program, they celebrated their son's first month of life by honoring Lance's Chinese ancestry. They invited the family of origin, the family of choice, their neighbors, and colleagues to join them in dyeing eggs red and eating sticky rice symbolizing the abundance and fertility of a new life. Stuart's grandmother made Scottish shortbread cookies. They drank toasts to the baby's ethnicities with Elderflower, a traditional English drink.

> Don't ask, "What girl are you going to get to take care of the baby?"

This implies that male parents can't nurture children as well as females. Later, when the new dads brought their baby to Taiwan to introduce him to Chinese family members, they encountered prejudices regarding parenting. Female Taiwanese revealed their cynicism about the men's abilities to parent properly. Women kept telling them how to bottle feed and offered other unsolicited advice.

FAMILY BLESSING CEREMONY

Who are we to question the circumstances that have formed our lives? We have only to give thanks for the steps which have led us down the path that brought us together.

Thus began the family blessing invitation of Victor, thirty-nine, and Paulino, thirty-seven, who after four of nine years together had taken three children into their home with the intention of adoption. The children are siblings—a girl, now ten years old, and two boys, eight and twelve. On Friday, September 3, 2004, the family appeared in Children's Court of Los Angeles at 8:30 a.m. One hour later, the adoptions were finalized, and the parents and children returned home to prepare for an evening ritual to celebrate the creation of their family.

> Involve the children in the preparation from beginning to end.

Victor, who came up with the idea for the ceremony, feels strongly that the ceremony unified them. The incorporation of the children into their union created a powerful bond. He recommends that others include their children in the planning as well, and see if it doesn't do the same for them.

Held at a restaurant, the event resembled a wedding. Victor and Paulino and their sons wore tuxedos, their daughter wore a long powder blue dress. Victor walked down the aisle accompanied by his parents. Paulino's sister escorted him because their parents are deceased. Before an audience of 134 friends and relatives, Minister Pat Langlis, of the Metropolitan Community Church of West Hollywood, officiated in their unique commitment ceremony. The couple exchanged vows and rings in front of a burning candle dedicated to Christ; then they lit a unity candle. Afterward, the two fathers knelt before each child. Each father took one of their hands and made the following vows:

We believe that God brought you into our lives and that

we were meant to be a family.

We promise to keep you safe.

We promise to be loving.

We promise to be caring.

We promise to be understanding and supportive parents.

The children received white gold rings that had their first names engraved on them, punctuated by their birthstones, with 9/3/04 engraved on the inside. The fathers' rings, also of white gold and with 9/3/04 engraved on the inside, had nine diamonds, one for each year they had been together. Then the family of five lit a single family unity candle. Minister Pat concluded the service with, "We must remind ourselves that all it takes to create a family is love."

At a reception following the ceremony, a mariachi band played, honoring the Latino backgrounds of the couple, their children, and their families. In addition, they had a DJ, toasts to the couple and the family, and party favors consisting of nine chocolate kisses, six wrapped in silver foil, three wrapped in gold foil to represent the three children, and a total of nine to represent the couple's years together.

If you are going to register for gifts, register the children as well. Let them choose the kinds of objects they would like for their bedrooms.

Victor and Paulino registered at Target and Macy's. They also let the children pick out gifts for the dads with the assistance of a friend. (Of course, Victor and Paulino paid for them.) The children chose crosses for their dads, who promised to wear them for the rest of their lives.

* * *

Children bring happiness, but life's final rite of passage, death, brings sorrow under all circumstances, sometimes even more so in same-sex unions. When one of the partners dies, highly explosive issues may erupt if the birth family never recognized the life partner of the deceased. That is why it is so important early on to establish a solid foundation with your mate's entire family, just as a heterosexual spouse would do—that is, if they let you.

DEATH

Include reference to the partner of the deceased during the eulogy and in the obituary.

Death brings up particularly difficult issues for the gay or lesbian couple. Special efforts may need to be made to include recognition of the deceased person's life partner—they are often not mentioned in either the written obituary or in the eulogy and this is a very painful fact.

An online website tells of a gay physician in New York City attending countless funerals of gay men who died of AIDS where the principle mourners were biological family members. According to this physician, family members talked about the deceased as if his life ended at about the age of fourteen. According to the article, by only reclaiming the parts of the men's lives of which they approved, the families denied the relationship that was central to the grieving partner and to the man who died. Consequently, the funeral caused increased pain for the partner.

If the birth family excludes the life partner, create a private memorial tribute where the partnership and the person who has died can be honored.

Life partners can create more personalized ceremonies. As an example, a website describes a first death anniversary tribute to Kathy. Her partner, Doreen, invited their closest friends for hot fudge sundaes, Kathy's favorite dessert. The guests ate ice cream and told stories about Kathy.

Special memorial services and celebrations for those who die of AIDS have also been created. Guests are invited to look back on the life of the deceased and to celebrate it. They share stories, show videos, and display enlarged pictures to turn their mourning into something more positive. Some churches offer special prayer gatherings/services for those stricken with the condition. The Metropolitan Community Church performs these services, as do the Episcopal and Methodist churches.

According to Minister Langlis, especially in the past before drug therapy was so effective in prolonging life, AIDS funerals differed from ordinary funerals in the large numbers of young victims. If there has been a rift between the deceased and family of origin, mourners are more creative and more storytelling takes place at the service. In the event that the body has been cremated, the cremains may be shared between the blood family and the family of choice. Occasionally, loved ones package the cremains in individual containers and distribute them to the attendees, making the point that we are all connected.

THE AIDS MEMORIAL QUILT AND NAMES PROJECT

One of the most powerful contemporary death rituals in the GLBT community is the memorialization of AIDS victims through the AIDS Memorial Quilt and NAMES Project. On a plain or patterned fabric panel, mourners paint, embroider, spray paint, needlepoint, or appliqué their tributes. They may decorate the panel with pearls, rhinestones, sequins, feathers, or buttons.

Each panel contains the name of the deceased with birth and/or death dates. Words may be added, such as "His eye is on the sparrow" or "We love you." Some panel makers have attached photos of the deceased or included stuffed animals, keys, wedding rings or bows, cremains, Boy Scout merit badges, jockstraps, or condoms. Others have included visual representations through collage or needlework—pets, balloons, landscapes or moonscapes, or symbols of the person being memorialized—a piano keyboard or a chef's hat and a barbecue.

The concept for the AIDS quilt was sparked during a 1985 San Francisco candlelight march commemorating the city's one-thousandth AIDS death. Gay rights advocate Cleve Jones noted that the names of victims written on placards and taped to the side of a building resembled a patchwork quilt. This led to the establishment of the NAMES Project to celebrate the lives of those who had died of the disease.

The first part of the ritual is to create an individual quilt piece to memorialize a victim. The second part is the presentation of the visually moving massed quilts accompanied by the recitation of victims' names.

To display the massed quilts, officials lay out a big grid of walkways at a selected site. In the center of each grid square they place twelve-by-twelve-foot folded sections of the quilt, composed of eight three-by-six-foot panels stitched together. Dressed in white, teams of eight "unfolders" move through the layout to their assigned positions around a folded quilt section. They then join hands and stand in a tight circle around each folded section.

In choreographed movements, created in 1987 by Jack Caster, a NAMES Project volunteer, the unfolders begin a pattern called the lotus fold. Four unfolders reach in, take a corner of the folded quilt section and pull it back. After the first four persons step back, the second four reach in and unfold the next layer. Simulating the unfolding of a lotus, they repeat this act four times until each twelve-by-twelve-foot section is in full view. Then they lift the gloriously colored quilt section chest high as they make a quarter turn clockwise to set the fabric square in place on the ground. Folding teams are the only people allowed on the grounds until the quilts have been completely unfolded.

The introduction begins: "Welcome to the [name of location] display of the NAMES Project AIDS Memorial Quilt. The panels surrounding you were created by lovers, families, and friends to commemorate loved ones who have died of AIDS."

While listening to an appointed reader intone the names of thirty-two victims, the viewers surround the edges of the grid and join hands as officials unfold the quilt. Names of other sets of thirty-two continue to be read by a series of speakers for as long as it takes. Sometimes celebrities add their voices to the calling of names, such as actress Elizabeth Taylor, folk singer Arlo Guthrie, and Tipper Gore, wife of former Vice President Al Gore. More frequently, the readers are heartbroken parents, lovers, siblings, friends, or panel makers, and people with HIV and AIDS. When all of the quilts have been unfolded, family, friends, and spectators mill slowly around the memorial banners to pay their respects and weep. At the closing of the display, visitors once more circle the quilt, stand along its edge, and join hands as the appointed persons in white ceremonially refold it.

The first display of the AIDS Memorial Quilt was in Washington, D.C., in 1987 when 1,920 panels were shown. By 1996, the number of panels had exploded to just under 40,000, large enough to cover twenty-four football fields. As of February 1997, nine million people had visited it. The quilt has become a jolting reminder of the death toll. The United Nations Department of Economic and Social Affairs estimates that by 2002, the disease claimed twenty-two million lives worldwide. In the United States alone, the National Institutes of Health recorded 524,060 fatalities as of 2003.

The Washington, D.C., displays of October 1987, 1988, 1989, 1992, and 1996 are the only ones to have featured the entire quilt. Smaller traveling exhibits continue to be displayed, particularly in educational institutions. The Quilt, now consisting of over 48,000 individual panels made by relatives, friends or neighbors, was nominated for a Nobel Peace Prize in 1989 and is the largest community art project in the world. As stated by the official NAMES Project Foundation in Atlanta, Georgia, "The Quilt has redefined the tradition of quilt making in response to contemporary circumstances. A memorial, a tool for education, and a work of art, the Quilt is a unique creation, an uncommon and uplifting response to the tragic loss of human life." The NAMES Project has twenty-one chapters in the United States and more than forty affiliate organizations worldwide. The Quilt continues to grow.

HOLIDAYS

Many GLBTs feel unwelcome or even ostracized by their birth families, so they create new families with fellow GLBTs or other supportive straight people. They often spend Thanksgiving or Christmas with this new family as a way to avoid pain. Here are some rules for parents of GLBTs that apply to all holidays and celebrations.

Include life partners in family events.

GLBTs are still a part of your family, but rather than take for granted that a family member will or will not attend a holiday celebration, extend formal or informal invitations. Include references to your GLBT offspring and their mates in annual Christmas greeting letters and family photos.

> Don't forget to buy presents for your offspring's partner on gift occasions. Ask you child's advice about the partner's likes, dislikes, size, and color preferences.

Nothing will put a wedge in your relationship with your children more than hurting their mates by overlooking their presence in your child's life and excluding them.

Now I am going to cover the holidays of most relevance to the GLBT community: Halloween and Gay/Lesbian Pride Parades; transgender birthday parties; cross-dresser's graduations; and weddings.

HALLOWEEN

Joel Cruz of the Gay League of America in Chicago calls Halloween the "Gay High Holy Day." He sees Halloween celebrations as an extension of coming out of the closet because it allows participants to assume a new identity and liberates them from the restrictions of everyday life. He observes that costumes among GLBTs tend to veer away from the traditional monsters or homicidal maniacs and tend toward the more imaginative: two sailors each dressed as one-half of the Titanic or a girl dressed as a box of Chinese food. Costumes may also give GLBTs the opportunity to express outrageousness and push sexual boundaries, such as the elaborate drag queens and kings and leather daddies.

In "Out in the Mountains," an internet article, Terje Anderson echoes Cruz's view: "Halloween was meant to be a gay holiday. Living in a society where we are forced to hide, celebrating in costume somehow seems more appropriate—and safe. Halloween is ours—let's enjoy it for all it's worth."

Anderson recalls his first Halloween in a gay men's bar where he stared at dozens of Carmen Miranda, Judy Garland, and Diana Ross clones. In subsequent years he appeared as Jackie Kennedy in a pink dress and pillbox hat, as an Andrews Sister, as a Supreme, as a nun, and as a Freudian slip in lingerie wearing handcuffs for his "arrested development."

> Non-GLBTs need not be taken aback by Halloween's frenzy. The celebration is short-lived.

Gay Halloween celebrations provide a sense of community, especially vital for those who may have spent years in the closet. In *The Advocate,* writer Bruce Vilanch calls such celebrating "bigger than Gay Pride, because even self-conscious straight people can celebrate Halloween with us without fear . . . Halloween was the one night of the year when it was all right to wear a mask—a fun mask, as opposed to that protective mask most of us wore every day of our lives. That free, crazy, anything goes spirit that Puritan America kept chained in the basement was allowed to breathe free, if only for one night. It was intoxicating."

Non-GLBTs should be supportive of the revelry because in some places the holiday provides financial support for badly needed social services.

An event that began Halloween weekend in 1994 in New Orleans, Halloween's in New Orleans now attracts tens of thousands of gays and lesbians from around the nation each year. A small group of gay men started the tradition when they invited out-of-town friends to New Orleans for a costume party on the Saturday night of the Halloween weekend. In subsequent years they repeated the celebration and added new events. By 1987, the numbers of people attending had grown dramatically, and many within the group felt that this celebration could be used to raise money for the growing AIDS crisis.

The group formed a non-profit organization named Halloween's in New Orleans with Lazarus House as its beneficiary. Lazarus House is a New Orleans residential facility for men and women living with HIV/AIDS. It serves all people and does not discriminate on the basis of age, race, religion, gender, economic status, sexual orientation, or handicap. Since 1987, Halloween's in New Orleans events have generated contributions of over $3.5 million for Project Lazarus.

The Halloween's in New Orleans event has evolved into a celebrated gay circuit party weekend. It is considered to be THE gay and lesbian destination for Halloween. Nonstop partying lasts from midday on Thursday, with special events on each day, concluding with a Gospel Brunch on Sunday at the House of Blues. Each event raises funds for Lazarus House.

Bruce Gallassero, Vice-Chairman of Halloween's in New Orleans, Inc., says New Orleans is a perfect fit for this kind of Halloween celebration because of the city's fascination with things out of the ordinary—the supernatural, the magical. Usually, 5,000 attend the main event, the Saturday night costume party. Costumes are mandatory, yet they needn't be elaborate or costly. They can range from a simple jock strap to a full-blown Mardi Gras costume.

113

The organization chooses a theme each year which revelers can either follow or ignore. In 2004 it was "Freaks, Follies and Sideshows," evoking the Depression era. A stage adjacent to the dance floor allowed attendees to dance about the crowd and show off their costumes. Shortly after midnight, a choreographed show with forty costumed performers began onstage. Gallassero says that New Orleans is a very tolerant place, a city that celebrates diversity. "Lots of straights but not narrows come out to watch and see what gay people do."

In San Francisco in the early 1970s, men could be harassed for wearing women's clothes in public, even arrested. Halloween was the only day of the year when a man could safely go out in public wearing a dress. Many of the bars on Polk Street held costume contests. Drag Queens and their "male" escorts (usually in tuxedos) would rent limos and drive from bar to bar showing off their elaborate creations. The custom grew in popularity and people would gather outside bars and watch the exotic parade full of furs, rhinestones, feathers, and bearded brides. By the mid-seventies, the crowds became so large that the city closed the street to traffic. Because gay bashers and troublemakers caused the parade to be closed down, the parade switched to Castro Street where it has remained. Three hundred thousand revelers attended in 2003, despite several stabbings and other violence the year prior. The crowd hooted and howled at the ten-foot tall banana and a human wedding cake as well as the usual assortment of drag queens, leather-adorned S and M's, as well as the many dressed as popes and priests. In 2004, more than 200,000 viewed "Dykes on Bikes" leading the parade with some of the motorcycle-riding lesbians wearing veils.

Other notable Halloween parades take place in New York and West Hollywood and Chicago which calls its Halloween event Pumpkinhead and usually attracts 3,000 "guys and ghouls." Key West's Fantasy Fest, an annual ten-day bacchanal, attracts 80,000 revelers. It creates the world's longest traffic jam, since most of the only road leading to Key West has just two lanes.

* * *

Miss Veronica Vera, founder and director of Miss Vera's Finishing School for Boys Who Want to Be Girls in Greenwich Village, New York, calls Halloween the cross-dressers' national holiday because it gives them license to dress in women's clothes freely and safely. Miss Vera's suggestions work not only for those cross-dressing for Halloween but for cross-dressing in general (see GLBT/Cross-Dresser's Graduation, p. 120; GLBT/Fantasy Weddings, p. 121.).

1. Make a budget bosom by cutting the feet off a pair of pantyhose and stuffing the sacks with two pounds of birdseed to place in each cup of the brassiere. Knots at the tied-off ends of the stockings make perfect nipples.

2. Cover leg hair by wearing stockings or pantyhose over opaque flesh-colored tights.

3. Purchase wigs with curls because they're easier to handle. Anchor them with bobby pins attached to your real hair.

4. To extend sleeves and hide arm hair, cut off legs from pantyhose and make gauntlets.

5. Stand erect, shoulders back and down, buttocks tight, tits high.

6. Like ladies, swing your hips, not shoulders.

7. Hide five-o'clock shadow with red-brown lipstick before applying makeup.

8. Hide sideburns by attaching part of wig to face with eyelash glue.

9. Purchase large size women's shoes in major chains, such as Payless which carries sizes up to twelve-wide. Look in African American neighborhood shoe stores where they also carry larger sizes.

9. Use your head when using the head. When dressed as a lady, use the Ladies Room.

GAY/LESBIAN PRIDE PARADES

In spirit, Halloween parades are akin to the consciously more political gay pride parades. On June 27, 1969, at the Stonewall Inn, a gay and lesbian bar in New York's Greenwich Village, homosexual patrons fought back during a raid by agents of the New York Beverage Control Board and the New York City police. The Beverage Control Board was ostensibly looking for beverage law violations, and the NYPD hoped to arrest gays engaged in then-illegal homosexual acts. A riot by gays and lesbians ensued, followed by a protest that lasted three days. In July, activists circulated flyers calling for a "homosexual liberation meeting" with this call to arms: "DO YOU THINK HOMOSEXUALS ARE REVOLTING? YOU BET YOUR ASS WE ARE!"

Thus, the Gay Liberation Front was born to commemorate the Stonewall Rebellion. The Front's agenda included putting an end to police riots, protecting jobs for GLBT employees, repealing sodomy laws, and enacting local and national anti-discrimination laws. Decades later the Front still seeks justice and equality, and partnership rights for same sex couples. It offers a challenge to homophobia.

Despite the frivolity, non-GLBTs need to understand that the parades embody a serious political agenda.

Gay and Lesbian Pride Parades attempt to dispel the myths of homosexuality and gender identity and reduce homophobia, discrimination, and hate crimes against GLBT communities. Basically they are fighting for equal rights, legal marriage, and adoption rights. In 2004 alone, a total of eighty-three Gay Pride parades took place in the United States, Canada, and the United Kingdom.

The gay rights movement has three main beliefs: that gays should be proud of being gay; that sexual diversity is a gift; and that one's sexual orientation is inherent and cannot be intentionally altered, for example, through therapy. Marches celebrating gay pride (pride parades) are celebrated worldwide. Symbols of gay pride include the rainbow flag and pink and black triangles. Even though gay pride parades are to some degree attempts to eradicate homophobia, floats often flaunt stereotypes of gay men in exaggerated female or risqué outfits. Exaggerated images make the "evil" sexual images more familiar and funny, and consequently, less menacing. At least, that is their hope.

The 2002 San Francisco Parade astonished Guatemalan-born Claudia Ochoa when she saw men holding hands with men, rainbow flags flying high in the Castro, gay men and lesbians going out and not worrying for their safety. Ochoa, a lesbian, had fled Guatemala because her family wouldn't accept her homosexuality and they continued to harass her even after she moved away. They sometimes followed her and beat her. Had she remained in Guatemala, her persecution would have continued, so she moved to San Francisco. For Ochoa, the Gay Pride parade is a "historical act in our lives."

Through Gay Pride parades, the GLBT is enlightening the public about their community. Use of humor allows the straight community more interaction and makes the unfamiliar more familiar, and thus less intimidating. At the same time, more conservative community members find these activities offensive because they reinforce stereotypes.

Transgenders
(also known as Trannies)

One group that is growing in public recognition is that of transgenders. Although they are the "T" in GLBT, I've reserved this section for their rites of passage and holidays because the general reader requires more information about their lifestyle to clarify misconceptions.

Transgender is an umbrella term that describes a variety of people with gender differences. A transgender person might be a pre- or post-operative transsexual, cross-dresser, or other differently gendered person, such as a hermaphrodite (born with reproductive organs and many of the secondary sex characteristics of both sexes).

Transsexual is more of a medical term that describes people who want to change, or have changed, their gender to match their internal identity. Transsexuals are born into one gender but identify emotionally and psychologically with the other. This desire generally begins in early childhood. To express psychological identification with the desired gender, transsexuals may use hormones or have surgery to change the body. They often express that they were born in the wrong body.

Transgenders include drag performers who dress up and use the mannerisms of the opposite sex to entertain others and earn a living that way. Drag queens are generally gay, but female impersonators can be straight or gay. They are professional performers and not turned on by their clothes, in contrast to cross-dressers. Cross-dressers, also known as transvestites (a more clinical term), are generally heterosexual and like to dress in the clothing of the opposite sex for emotional satisfaction or erotic pleasure.

Sexual Reassignment Surgery (SRS) is the most effective form of changing gender, but it is also expensive and irreversible. In the United States, male to female (MTF) surgery is the more common form and runs between $15,000 to $30,000. While the genitalia changes are successful, sometimes their masculine musculature and body frame detract from the overall desired feminine effect. For breast enhancement some choose surgical augmentation; some take female hormones; some do both. Additional procedures can include liposuction and Adam's apple contouring.

Female to male surgery (FTM) occurs less often but costs more—sometimes up to $100,000. On the positive side, females can grow full beards and voices can change to deeper registers, but their newly-constructed penises may not always match expectations. In addition, females seeking male identities have to undergo hysterectomies and bilateral mastectomies for a complete masculine presentation.

Sexual reassignment procedures cost less in Canada with even lower prices in Phuket, Thailand, where Sanguan Kunaporn, M.D., works full-time as one of the most respected surgeons in the field. Between 1999 and 2004 he performed over 500 MTF Sexual Reassignment Surgeries for mostly American, Australian, and Japanese patients. In addition, he performed 600 cases of breast augmentation. Trained by Preecha Tiewtranon, M.D., a pioneer in transgender surgery and considered the "King" of sex change operations, Dr. Sanguan has also worked in the United States under a fellowship with Dr. Mutaz Habal in Tampa, Florida.

Dr. Sanguan is passionate about his work. He claims that it saves many men from committing suicide, freeing them from a psychological trap. He says his SRS patients feel their lives are transformed positively. He compares this surgery to the repair of cleft palates and other anomalies that help make patients look more normal. "These people are also human and deserve respect," he said. "I realize that there is more and more acceptance among the social community in the past twenty years, and I believe that it needs another one or two generations before transgenders will be widely accepted throughout the world."

Dr. Sanguan believes that surgery is the most important tool in helping transgenders, but not everyone can afford the surgery. Health limitations may prevent others from having SRS.

This doctor stands out for his compassion. In *Southern Comfort*, an award-winning documentary film by Kate Davis, a group of transgenders, mostly female-to-male, bemoan the attitude of most physicians. "They refuse to make us look real. They [the doctors] do it on purpose." Robert Eads, whose story is told in this film, was dying of ovarian cancer, yet twenty different doctors refused to treat his cancer. Eads characterized the role of transgendered males in society as being way down at the bottom of the food chain.

According to Eads, changing one's sex is a no-win situation. "Either you spend your life being miserable to make someone else happy, or you're going to spend your life somewhat happy knowing you're making someone else miserable." Although Eads was able to make a new life for himself and build positive new relationships, he accepts that he has caused his family to suffer emotionally.

Transgendered people need unique ways to celebrate their unique lives. They have adopted standard rites of passage to answer their needs for celebrating life.

REGENDER BIRTHDAY PARTIES

Transgender or regender birthday parties ritually recognize a person's change of sex. Even those who can't afford the surgery may still select one part of their transition to celebrate. Generally, the first observance takes place as soon as the person feels physically recovered, or at the six-month or one-year post-op marker.

Dr. Sanguan is noted for his sensitivity to the issue of patients becoming new persons—being reborn. To recognize a new identity, he and his staff bring flowers to the post-op patient and sing "Happy Birthday." Sanguan lauds patients' courage in undertaking this dramatic change, for he is aware of all the social negativity they experience and the many pressures that still lie ahead.

Commonly, the transgender/regender birthday party for someone celebrating sexual reassignment is an intimate event—no more than six at a quiet dinner. Naturally, if the patient or the patient's partner has children, the numbers will increase. Generally, the mood is of thankfulness for being able to continue on one's personal journey, yet this is not a somber event, either.

Often these parties occur only once, though some celebrate annually. Gianna E. Israel, a San Francisco Bay counselor for over 2400 patients and principal author of *Transgender Care*, relates that several persons she knows celebrate their passage from one gender to another annually by attending a local transition support group to talk to people who are at different stages of changing their sex. She recommends that birthday guests be supportive of the transition of the person's sex change.

Guests should use the correct gender pronoun.

Israel encourages attendees to honor the change of sex by referring to the person by their new one. If the patient has surgically become a woman, use "she." Do the same with transgender guests. If overt cues are hard to decipher, tactfully ask how the person would prefer to be identified, as a male or female.

Give gender-neutral gifts or those appropriate to the new gender.

She explains that unless you are very intimate with the celebrant, avoid giving clothing, makeup, or perfume to transgendered women. These choices are too personal, and it is hard to pick the appropriate colors.

If biological parents won't celebrate your journey, bring new people into your life who respect you and your efforts.

The transgender's journey is filled with many sorrows. But the journey need not be taken alone. According to Israel, one can create one's own new family and hold them close as they proceed with their new lives.

CROSS-DRESSER'S GRADUATION

While transgender surgery is a permanent change of sexual identification, cross-dressing is a temporary adoption of the opposite sex's identification—most commonly male to female. Because graduation from cross-dressing courses is generally closed to outsiders, I present no rules. I merely describe the event for your illumination. At Miss Vera's Finishing School for Boys Who Want to Be Girls, students first look at themselves in the mirror and see the girl of their dreams, and their fantasies become reality. These are genetically men who seek more skills in dressing and acting like women. Some of them have been lured there by exposure to Miss Vera's clever prize-winning ads, such as "Even the Simplest Evening Gown Can Be Ruined By a Penis."

Often students and staff celebrate completion of coursework by going to Lips, a nearby drag restaurant jokingly known as the extension campus or the academy halfway house. At Lips, everyone is in drag, including the waitpersons, such as All Beef Patty and Peppermint. The entertainers stop at each table and ask patrons if they are celebrating something. If it's the student's first time out in drag, he is asked to get up and walk around in a provocative manner, while others cheer.

Part of celebrating graduation is a toast to the person's re-birthday, even if a new identity might only be a temporary state and the person will return to his regular life after a weekend session at Miss Vera's. To prepare students for gender graduation, the school places appropriate gifts in students' rooms during an intensive femme weekend: bubble bath, perfume, and pink flowers.

What the general public may not understand is that most cross-dressers are heterosexuals who live in mainstream society and that approximately 60 percent are married. A great sense of humor pervades the atmosphere at Miss Vera's as she wryly reminds, ". . . for every woman who burned her bra, there is a man ready to wear one." "*Cherchez la femme*" (search for the woman) is the motto of the academy, where they believe in "sissy power." But Miss Vera's credentials are impressive: she is the author of hundreds of articles on human sexuality and a lecturer who has even testified for freedom of expression before a Senate Judiciary Committee chaired by Senator Arlen Specter in Washington, D.C. But, most important to her students, "She has a fabulous wardrobe."

FANTASY WEDDINGS

The ultimate desire for a cross-dresser is to be dressed as a bride and have a fantasy wedding. According to Miss Vera, bridal gowns are the number one favorite article of clothing of cross-dressers, also known as transvestites. And Miss Vera makes their fantasy weddings come true.

She cites the example of a grandfather from the Midwest. He attended her school for the purpose of becoming a bride as part of a complete wedding fantasy that included professional photos, a volunteer male to portray the groom, and a wedding ritual attended by a complete bridal entourage: tranny (transgender) bride, tranny maid of honor, two tranny bridesmaids, and Miss Vera, who gave the bride away. The day before the wedding, Miss Vera and her deans treated the bride-to-be to a bachelorette tea party.

The bride explained his need for this ceremony. He didn't want to reach the end of his days always wondering what it might have been like to experience a wedding as a bride. Satisfied with fulfillment of his fantasy, he returned to his other life as patriarch of his family. His story is not unique.

Miss Vera and her staff go to great lengths to fulfill fantasies. One student wanted to lie in a coffin dressed in a wedding gown. Permission granted. They covered a futon with a white satin sheet and pillow, placed the would-be corpse in her wedding finery on top of the death bed, and surrounded her with burning candles.

This concludes an overview of celebrations within our new cultural diversity. Obviously, the coverage cannot be complete due to space limitations and because there are as many kinds of celebrations as there are people who participate in them. Nonetheless, I have addressed the most popular forms and guidelines. The rest of the book focuses on "Ethnice-ities"—my word for celebrations in traditional ethnic and religious groups with behavior guidelines for guests who are unfamiliar with the events.

(PART TWO)

ETHNICE-ITIES

The Rites and Wrongs of Multicultural Celebrations

This section of *Come As You Aren't* details life cycle rituals, religious and secular. It presents a vantage point for observation and satisfies a curiosity about the behavior of those different from ourselves. It provides a peek at some unusual events that many of us may never be privy to observe. It may be that we have not yet had the opportunity to be placed on appropriate guest lists for these occasions, or outsiders are not allowed in.

"Ethnice-ities" documents and illuminates a wide spectrum of ritual behavior. Use it as a practical adviser for culturally unfamiliar situations. For example, what if you're invited to a Cambodian wedding? What do you bring? What do you wear? You want to go but don't want to insult anyone, nor do you want to just sit there observing without understanding. Ethnice-ities offers signposts to guide you through your multicultural adventures.

The more familiar rituals, such as graduations, retirements, and traditional church weddings, are not covered. If we have not attended, we have a least seen such events on television and in movies. At a wedding, for example, no matter the religious denomination, we know more or less what to expect when we get there. Therefore, we are not shocked when, in the middle of most receptions, the bride lifts up the long skirt of her formal white gown to expose her thigh and blue garter. We know why unwed women surround the bride and push and shove to catch the bouquet she tosses into the air. Without printed instructions, we understand that we must throw rice at the newlyweds.

The ubiquitous nature of such events and space limitations have dictated what is contained in this section. I have focused upon uniqueness, on eye-catching differences, on the unexpected qualities that make events memorable. I did not envision this volume as an encyclopedia, but rather as an entertaining look at the variety of ways in which we celebrate our humanity.

Not surprisingly, the longer immigrant groups have been in this country, such as the Irish, the more Americanized they have become. Consequently, there are fewer distinctions in their rites of passage, and obviously, I have included less about them.

In the pages that follow, the emphasis is on the newest arrivals because they are in transitional stages yet still maintain their homeland's ways. Nonetheless, some groups here for centuries, such as the Amish, have deliberately preserved their seventeenth-century traditions with minimal changes. I have included some of their rituals because of their uniqueness. But be aware: not all Amish observe customs in exactly the same way. Variations exist because of separate locations and branches of the religion.

Different countries of origin carry distinctions as well. For example, the customs of Muslims living in the U.S. vary because Muslims come from distinct areas, and each country has its own customs. For example, when Kuwaitis break the Ramadan fast, they eat dates and drink yogurt mixed with water, and then they pray; Iranians, on the other hand, pray first, then break the fast by eating dates and having tea, bread, and cheese.

Similarly, not everyone within a Native American tribe celebrates its rituals in exactly the same way. Most tribes have different branches, each with its own specialization. Other group variations occur because of economics and social status. Individuals, too, add their personal touches to tradition.

What if the description of a celebration practiced by your group differs from how you observe it? Unless customs are dictated by holy books, which rarely occurs, variety is the rule, even within the same culture. People can't refrain from putting their individual stamp on a tradition. This paradox of human celebrations being at once similar and unique makes this topic so complex and yet so fascinating.

If you are invited to a ritual that is not included in this book and have questions about how to behave, don't hesitate to ask someone from that culture. He or she will appreciate your interest. However, avoid yes/no questions. Ask open-ended ones such as "What do you recommend that I wear?" "What would be considered an appropriate gift?" "What is the most respectful way to greet the celebrants?" Be sure to ask what colors, numbers, or behavior should be avoided. At the event, observe and follow others carefully, but above all, savor the adventure of participating in another culture's celebration. Enjoy!

(4)

BIRTH CELEBRATIONS
"Have a cigar."

To ensure that the fragile new life survives without harm, families observe various customs and employ protective devices: Middle Easterners pin blue beads to children's clothing; Eastern Europeans affix red ribbons to the crib or baby carriage; Puerto Ricans tie a black and red charm on a baby's bracelet; Mexicans hang a "deer's eye" from a red string around the baby's neck; Orthodox Jews place a talisman near their baby's bed to keep away the preying Lilith. These practices thrive throughout the United States.

The newborn child represents unlimited potential. At the same time, fears for its future abound. Consequently, the family anxiously looks for omens, good and bad. For example, some believe that a baby born with a caul (the membrane enclosing a fetus) over its face foretells of second sight, that the child is destined to become a healer.

Which day of the week the baby arrives has meaning, too, inspiring a well-known nursery rhyme:

Monday's Child is fair of face,

Tuesday's child is full of grace,

Wednesday's child is full of woe,

Thursday's child has far to go,

Friday's child is loving and giving,

Saturday's child has to work for its living,

But a child that's born on the Sabbath day

Is fair and wise and good always.

ARMENIAN

FIRST TOOTH PARTY—AGRA HADIG [ahgrah ha-deeg]

GIFTS The first person to discover the tooth brings the baby an undershirt. Others bring small gifts.

WORDS Praise the baby, wishing it to grow up to be gentle and kind, the pride and joy of the family.

Although the Armenians are a disparate people, no matter where they live—Turkey, Lebanon, Armenia, the United States—they participate in this event. The party occurs when the baby's first tooth appears. Thus it is called *agra* (tooth) *hadig* (wheat), a traditional food served at this event.

The mother props up the infant on a table or on the floor and places up to five objects in front of the child. Whichever object the child selects first reveals the baby's future occupation. If the child picks a book or a bible, it means the child will be a scholar, teacher, or clergy person. If the baby chooses money, the child will become a banker, financier, or very rich. If he or she selects a hammer, the child will enter the building trades. A knife symbolizes a doctor or surgeon; a scissors foretells a life as a seamstress or tailor; a comb means a barber or hairdresser.

Hosts boil whole wheat and add sugar and spices, covering the mixture with pistachios, cloves, and cinnamon. When the baby is about to select an object, the mother throws some of this mixture on the baby's head, which has been covered by a towel.

Sometimes only females attend and only sweet foods are served. But among other families, all family members are invited and a lunch is served with many sweets as part of the menu. This is a gleeful event with much clapping, singing, and dancing with the baby. Although merriment prevails, underlying the gaiety lies a genuine concern for the future well-being of the child, its social status, and economic survival.

While Armenian American celebrations generally do not include negative portents, in other parts of the world, if a child picks up a scissors, they believe the child will become a murderer; dirt can signify an early death; a glass can foretell the life of a drunkard; and if the child chooses a deck of cards, a life as a gambler is assured.

CAMBODIAN

BABY WELCOMING

GIFTS Baby clothes or money in an envelope of any color.
Family and close friends give gold jewelry to boys and girls.

WORDS Any sentiment offering the mother and the father long life and happiness for the new child. In Cambodia, they observed a taboo against complimenting the baby. Although that custom is fading, use discretion when complimenting the baby in front of an older person.

CLOTHING They remove their shoes inside homes. Guests should do the same. Non-Cambodians who respect their no-shoes tradition are appreciated.

BODY LANGUAGE Use the *wai* [why] form of greeting. With hands pressed together in a prayerlike gesture, bring them up to just below the chin and nod slightly. Avoid male/female body contact.

In the United States, they have a party when the baby is one month old, but in Cambodia, an astrologer would be consulted about the most auspicious date for the event. Invitations are sent to family and friends using the name listed on the infant's American birth certificate. However, at home, the child is generally called by a Cambodian name. For example, Mary Mom Keo's granddaughter was officially named Malaya Joline, but at home, Mary calls her Srey Ping, first grandchild.

If the family is financially able, the party will be held in an Asian restaurant, Cambodian preferred, of course. More often, the celebration is held at home, generally in the afternoon, and up to 100 people may attend.

They decorate the house with real and paper flowers and balloons. Cambodians in the United States have adopted many American traditions, for example, balloons will be pink for girls and blue for boys. The monk blesses the baby and sprinkles holy water on it. Afterward, older family members bless the baby too, sprinkling water on it as well. The rest of the guests bless the baby by touching its face, feet, and hands and offering affirmations.

They will ask that the baby lives a long and healthy life, will bring luck to its parents, will be good, and will take care of its parents. Guests pray for the baby to be smart and that Buddha may protect it from suffering.

Family members prepare food for all guests who come with their gifts. In Cambodia, they have no baby showers and the one month party is equivalent to an American baby shower. However, younger Cambodians living in America are adapting more to our customs, so they no longer observe the baby shower taboo. They also no longer wait to open the gifts but do so right away.

CHINESE

RED EGG AND GINGER PARTY

GIFTS Typical baby gifts. Chinese frequently give money in small red envelopes available for purchase in Chinese gifts shops. Avoid white envelopes.

WORDS Congratulate the parents on their happiness. Surprise them by saying it in Chinese: "*Gung hay.*"

CLOTHING Whatever is appropriate for the setting, restaurant or home, but not too casual.

In China, they called it the "completion-of-one-month" party, a time to introduce the baby to the family and give the child its name. Held thirty days following the birth, this celebration dates back to the Zhou dynasty in the first millennium. However, in those times, due to the high mortality rates, they frequently delayed the event until the baby was three months old.

Chinese Americans call the festivities red egg and ginger parties, which take place any time after the baby's first month of life. Because red is a color symbolizing good luck, families send invitations written on red paper and at the parties distribute red-dyed hard-boiled eggs. The eggs symbolize fertility and wholeness. Guests eat them with thinly sliced, sweet pickled ginger, believed helpful in restoring the new mother's energy. The families may pile the red eggs high into a basket for guests to help themselves or place one red egg with a piece of ginger at each table setting.

Today as in ancient times, the celebration introduces the baby to friends and family. Since most American children receive names within the first few days of life, at this party they announce the child's Chinese name. Parents dress the baby in its best clothing, and guests compliment the baby's appearance and alertness.

Some Americanized families may announce the event on the society pages of Chinese American newspapers and will have the party in a Chinese restaurant. More traditional families do not publish announcements and more frequently have parties at home.

EGYPTIAN—Coptic

BABY WELCOMING

GIFTS Money or standard baby gifts.

WORDS Some older and more traditional Egyptian Copts prefer that the baby not be complimented. The younger or more educated tend not to practice this taboo associated with the evil eye. Observe others and use discretion.

CLOTHING Women should avoid wearing pants in church. No required ties and jackets for men, although older men generally wear them.

BODY LANGUAGE In church, men and women sit separately.

On the seventh day after the birth, the priest comes to the home to anoint the baby, and the family holds a party. The priest pours water into a basin, adds a small amount of salt and oil, and lights seven candles. After saying a prayer of thanksgiving, he offers incense, then anoints the baby. Later, when a girl is eighty days old and a boy is forty days old, the infants are eligible for baptism. By this time the mother is usually strong enough to attend a Sunday church service. Baptism, communion, and confirmation transpire on the same day as the regular service.

ETHIOPIAN—Coptic

BABY WELCOMING

GIFTS Baby gifts rather than money, which people give only in large amounts.

WORDS Compliments are appreciated.

BODY LANGUAGE Ethiopians show babies great affection. Frequently they kiss the hand of the newborn or touch the baby's cheek or forehead with their fingers that they have put to their lips in a kiss.

After the baby arrives, guests bring the new parents congratulatory cards and flowers, especially red roses. To make the new mother strong, the family feeds her *genfo* [gun-foe], a mushy, oatmeal-like grain that is easy to digest. When people come to greet the new child, the family feeds them *genfo* as well, to welcome them to the new family situation.

The baptism is not a naming ceremony. Boys are baptized at forty days and girls at eighty days. The babies are completely immersed in the baptismal font. If the child is a boy, the godfather brings the baby to the priest, who, when finished with the immersing, blessing, and anointing of the child, hands the baby to the mother. The same procedure takes place with a baby girl except that the godmother brings her to the priest.

Adults may be in national dress at the baptism. Afterwards, while still in church everyone partakes of *injera* [een-jay-rah] (unleavened bread), tea or coffee, or soft drinks. Later they adjourn to a big luncheon at the home of the newborn's parents. A priest or one of the elders says a prayer over the unleavened bread. Then they feast and party. No formal gift-giving takes place at this time.

HAWAIIAN

BABY WELCOMING

GIFTS Close family and friends contribute to a potluck meal at a luau celebrating the baby's birth and at the first birthday. Standard baby gifts or money is given. Certain family members prepare traditional handcrafted gifts. In the past, when a woman was pregnant, a quilt design for the new baby would appear in the mother's or grandmother's dream. She made the quilt during the pregnancy and presented it upon the baby's birth. Quilts are treasured heirlooms for the child, as are other labor-intensive gifts such as *lei hulu* (feather lei) or a pandanus-leaf fan or *lauhala* (pandanus) basket.

WORDS Avoid complimenting the baby, or the gods might take it away. To protect the child, admirers pick out an unfavorable physical characteristic to comment upon. "Oh, what a flat nose spread out all over its face." "Oh, what big ears," meaning just the opposite. Sometimes Hawaiians use uncomplimentary words as terms of endearment. *Pupuka* (poo-poo-kah) means what an ugly child, but when spoken in a loving manner has the opposite meaning.

CLOTHING Sandals without socks, aloha attire (floral clothing, muumuus for women, tropical-print aloha shirts for men), shorts for outdoor luaus, slacks for indoor luaus. Clothes should be comfortable because participants may be sitting on the ground or floor while eating.

The birth of a child is significant because it means the continuation of the culture. In the old days, if the firstborn was a girl, the maternal grandparents would *hanai* (adopt) the child—the child lived with the grandparents, who assumed the responsibility of teaching the Hawaiian culture and genealogy to the girl. If the firstborn was a boy, the paternal grandparents adopted the child, *punahele* (favorite child), and teaching Hawaiian culture and genealogy to the boy was their responsibility. In the old days, when Hawaiian culture was strictly an oral tradition, ensuring the transmission of the lore to the next generation was vital to the survival of the people. This is the motivation for such adoptions.

Nowadays, the structure and pressures of modern living have made adoptions less feasible. Add to this the common separation of families with some on the mainland and others living in the islands. As a result, the tradition has been modified by having the firstborn spend vacations and as much spare time as possible with the appropriate grandparents. If no grandparents are available, an elder aunt or uncle takes over.

When the baby is born and at the first birthday, the family has a luau, which must include the traditional foods of the gods: roast pig prepared in an underground oven, fish, banana, sweet potato, taro, coconut—*kinolau* [key-no-lau] (spirit forms of the gods). Hawaiians eat these foods not only for nourishment but also for spirituality. As they ingest the foods, they become godlike and strengthen their mana, insight, and wisdom.

The luau is a gathering of friends and family, a joyous event with singing, dancing, and food. Customarily, each person brings a dish, and all lend a helping hand. Each person has individual responsibilities: set up tables and chairs; decorate; prepare *emu* (roast pig); serve the food; clean up; play music; bring ukuleles, guitars; and dance the hula, all as gifts for the honored child.

HMONG [mong]

BABY WELCOMING

GIFTS Baby clothes and toys.

WORDS Most of the older generation believe that if they compliment the baby, evil spirits will take it away. While the younger generation claims not to believe in this, refrain from commenting positively about the child. They themselves make comments such as "The baby smells of poo-poo." By acknowledging the child, they are revealing their admiration, but by saying something uncomplimentary, they are protecting the baby, too. For some of the older Hmong, the prohibition against compliments extends to grown children.

BODY LANGUAGE Older Hmong avoid body contact with members of the same and opposite sex. A married woman disrespects her husband by smiling at or shaking hands with a man. In contrast, the younger generation is beginning to adopt the hugging traditions of their American school mates. To be prudent, avoid all body contact.

Neither Chinese or Lao, the Hmong are a distinct racial group who originated in China and spread to Vietnam and Laos. During the Vietnam War, the CIA recruited them to fight for us, but after the fall of Saigon, they would have been murdered had they remained there. Thus our government brought them here as refugees, mainly from Laos. Approximately 200,000 live here primarily in Wisconsin, Minnesota, and California.

During labor, Hmong women prefer not to cry and reveal their pain. Moments after birth, the baby receives a silver necklace to warn the spirits that the child belongs to the family and is not a slave. In some Hmong communities, the women sew caps covered with flower designs *paj ntaub* [pah-dow] to fool the evil spirits into thinking the baby is a flower.

If doctors are willing to give them the placenta, the Hmong bury it in the backyard, an adaptation of a custom from their home country (Laos) of burying it beneath the central pole of their homes. If the first born is a male, they dry the umbilical cord, boil it with a piece of oak, and use it for medicine. They feed it to a seriously ill person.

For one month following childbirth, the new mothers eat only boiled chicken with broth and rice three times a day. They may add special homegrown herbs. The chickens must be freshly killed each day to meet the mother's nutritional needs. Store-bought chickens are unacceptable.

Three days after birth, they have a ceremony where they announce the baby's name and call back the baby's soul, which might have been frightened away during birth. If the family is Catholic, they may delay the ceremony until the baby is one month old. For the baby's protection, they tie white strings around its wrists, which remain until they fall off or disintegrate on their own. These strings install the protective spirits within the body and prevent the soul from being abducted.

INDIAN—Brahman
(the highest caste in Hinduism)

BABY WELCOMING

GIFTS Baby clothes and other typical baby gifts.

WORDS Although it is permissible to compliment the child, it is better not to say too much. To counteract the evil eye, after someone compliments the baby, a family member rubs her palm over the baby's forehead, then cracks her knuckles, one at a time. The sound of each cracked knuckle forces away the evil eye.

CLOTHING Elegant dresses, silks only for Indian women. Avoid black. Remove shoes and socks.

BODY LANGUAGE Use the *namaste* [nah-mah-stay] for greetings. With hands pressed together in a prayerlike position, bring them up to just below the chin and nod slightly.

BABY NAMING—*NAMAKARMA* [nah-mah-car-mah]

GIFTS Typical baby gifts.

WORDS Avoid compliments.

CLOTHING Indian guests wear silks. Non-Indian guests wear good clothing as they might for a church christening. Avoid wearing black. Remove shoes and socks when entering the home and/or temple.

BODY LANGUAGE One should not look at the baby too much or too long. Indians greet each other and outsiders with the namaste [nah-mah-stay]. With hands pressed together in a prayer-like position, bring them up to just below the chin and nod slightly.

On the baby's eleventh day of life, the priest comes to the home to bless the baby, who is dressed in ordinary clothes and lying in a cradle. In fear of the evil eye, parents place a black dot on its face, often on the chin, to detract from the child's appearance. This also deters people from complimenting the child. If someone inadvertently compliments the baby, the power of the evil eye can be removed by one parent placing salt in each hand, waving it over the baby's whole body, then dissolving the salt in tap water and letting it run down the drain. After the child reaches the age of one, fear of the evil eye lessens.

After the baby's birth, parents consult with an astrologer about the baby's planetary influences. The astrologer suggests an appropriate ritualistic name, which the priest announces along with a modern name. Often the ritualistic name is the same as that of one of the gods or goddesses, so that in everyday life if there is no time to pray, just by calling the name of the child, the parents are also mentioning the name of the gods.

The priest blesses the child and so do the guests.

BABY'S FIRST BIRTHDAY

For the baby's first birthday, most Hindu's prefer to go to India, where they offer the baby's hair in temple. Girls' heads are completely shaved, and boys' heads are shaved except for a small tuft at the back of the head. In the United States, they do it symbolically by snipping a piece of hair and saving it in a plastic bag for their next journey to a temple in India.

During the ceremony, they build a fire in a two-by-two-foot brick square. Several priests pray for the well-being of the child and pour *ghee* (clarified butter) to make the flames flare higher, for fire is considered the witness that will carry the prayers for the child to heaven. If, according to the astrologers, the child is in danger because of harmful positioning of the planets on its birth date, the priests request that the gods be gentle and not harm the child too much.

JAPANESE—Buddhist

BABY WELCOMING

GIFTS After the child is born, grandparents present grandsons with a *kabuto* (warrior's helmet) and a warrior doll, which are never used for play. Families display them on Boys' Day, May 5. After World War II, during the American occupation of Japan, the United States banned Boys' Day because of the militaristic emphasis symbolized by the warrior objects. They changed the name to Children's Day. In the United States, they still call it Boys' Day. Similarly, grandparents present new granddaughters with a set of dolls representing the emperor and empress and their royal court dressed in traditional royal garb and exhibited on five tiers. Since only the wealthy can afford such expensive dolls, paper replicas may be substituted. These dolls are shown only on Girls' Day, March 3. If they remain on display on any other day, many believe that the newborn girl will never marry.

Others give any kind of gift, including money. If possible, place the cash in special envelopes decorated with baby motifs, which may be purchased in Japanese shops. If these envelopes are unavailable, use any kind. In all circumstances, bills should be clean, preferably new, and wrapped in white paper before being placed inside the envelope—never directly place money inside.

WORDS Compliments are acceptable.

FIRST TEMPLE PRESENTATION—HATSU MAIRI
[hot-sue-mah-ee-ree]

Once a year, parents present new babies to the temple. They are given *juzu*, a string of beads, white or crystal for girls and red for boys. The babies wear kimonos. In the past, they were wrapped in adult kimonos and dressed in red.

JEWISH

CIRCUMCISION—*BRIT MILAH* [BREET MEE-LAH]

GIFTS Typical baby gifts or money. If money, use units of eighteen, the numerical value of the two letters that make up the word chai (life) (yod = ten, chet = eight).

WORDS "Mazel tov!" (Congratulations! Good luck!)

Brit Milah means "covenant," commonly called either a *brit* or a *bris*. It refers to an agreement made between God and Abraham (Genesis 17:2) wherein God promises to bless Abraham and allow him to prosper in exchange for his loyalty. This covenant was symbolized by circumcision—where the foreskin of the penis is removed. Ever since then, Jewish families enter the covenant when the son of every Jewish mother is circumcised on his eighth day of life.

A ritual specialist called a *mohel* [móy-ell] performs the ceremony. The godmother brings the child into the room, and the godfather holds him during the prayers. The child is then handed over to one who has the most honored role, the *sandek* (godfather, in Greek), who is often a good friend or a grandparent. He holds the infant on his lap during the procedure, which is brief, generally taking less than ten minutes.

Jews believe that the prophet Elijah is present at each Jewish boy's circumcision. To represent his presence they set aside a special chair, known as the "chair of Elijah." Just prior to placing the baby in the *sandek's* lap, the godfather momentarily sets him on the chair as a symbol of Elijah's blessing.

During the circumcision, they ease the baby's pain by giving him a pacifier to suck on or a small sponge filled with sugar water. Often the *mohel* takes a wine-dipped cloth and places it in the infant's mouth, which not only acts as an anesthetic, but becomes the first partaking in the blessing of wine. After the procedure, the *mohel* bandages the baby and hands it back to the father. Sometimes, the father buries the removed foreskin.

In the past, the ceremony was frequently celebrated in the synagogue; nowadays, it is more commonly held at home. The wine is blessed (*kiddush*) and the baby is given his Hebrew name. The family then serves a celebration meal.

Spirits are high at this event, which is generally attended by the immediate family and close friends. Because of the delicate nature of the procedure, much joking takes place, for everyone is acutely aware of the need for precision. While on the surface, jokes on this occasion might be considered in bad taste, they serve to relieve the tension felt by both the men and women. One new mother described the apprehension in the room when the *mohel* arrived. A hush fell as non-Jewish and Jewish guests tensed. The rabbi broke the silence, "Okay, who's first?"

SEPHARDIC [say-fár-dick] VARIATIONS

Since Sephardim [say-far-déem] (descendants of Spanish, Portuguese, and Middle Eastern Jews) name their children for living relatives, it is likely that at least one of the newborn's relatives will bear the same name and be present at the circumcision ceremony. Consequently, when a child of Judeo-Spanish ancestry is given his name at this event, everyone else attending the ritual slaps the persons who bear the same name. This reminds them that the qualities they developed as a result of their name and their soul, will now be shared by the new member of the Jewish community.

REDEMPTION OF THE FIRSTBORN SON—PIDYON HABEN [pid-yon hah-bén]

GIFTS Traditional baby gifts, clothes, money, especially in units of 18 (see Birth/Jewish, *Brit Milah*, p. 140.).

WORDS "Mazel tov!" (Congratulations! Good luck!)

CLOTHING Not too casual.

If the firstborn child is a male, this ceremony occurs on his thirty-first day. It is a reenactment of a Biblical tradition that the firstborn must be consecrated to the lifelong service of the Lord. However, in biblical times a father could redeem his son through the proferring of redemption money. So, too, fathers today redeem their sons from priestly service through payment of a ransom, in the United States, in Israel, and wherever Jews may live.

Generally, the mother enters the room carrying the infant on a pillow and hands him to the father, who places the child and the pillow on the table. The rabbi asks the father if he wishes to surrender his son for priestly service or ransom him for five pieces of silver.

After the father announces his intention to keep his son, he makes a blessing and gives the rabbi five silver dollars. The rabbi accepts the money, announces that the child is redeemed, and blesses the child, the bread, and wine. The rabbi often donates the money to charity. Family members may say a few words. Sometimes the parents make speeches about aspirations for their son.

Exemptions to this ceremony occur if the child is born by C-section, if the mother's first pregnancy ended in a miscarriage, or if the child is the firstborn male child of a *Kohen* (priest) or of a Levite. If the thirty-first day falls on the Sabbath or a Jewish holy Day, the ceremony is postponed one day.

KOREAN

ONE-HUNDREDTH DAY PARTY

GIFTS Gold for girls or boys: rings, necklaces, bracelets. If unaffordable, any other baby gift.

WORDS Compliments are acceptable.

CLOTHING To the hosts, what guests wear is unimportant.

Whether Christian or Buddhist, Koreans have a celebration of life when the baby reaches its one-hundredth day. They have an abundance of food, but the hallmark of this event is the presentation of a one-layered, un-iced, round, white cake made of rice flour. It is always present at this event and has no candles.

LAO

WELL-WISHING CEREMONY—*SOU-KHOUANH* [SUE-KWANH]

GIFTS Any baby gift. Money in a white envelope. Hand it to the mother or father.

WORDS When tying on wrist strings, wish the mother and the baby good health and happiness. When the Lao were still living in Asia, they avoided complimenting the baby lest the evil spirits come and take it away. Since most Lao have now been in the United States since the 1980s, that belief is fading, especially among the younger people. If you decide to compliment the baby, use discretion if older people can hear you.

CLOTHING Remove shoes inside homes.

Sometime between the first and second months after the birth of a child, the Lao have a party. The highlight of the event is a well-wishing ceremony called *baci* [bai-see] or *sou-khoanh*. The ceremony welcomes the mother and the baby home from the hospital. Because of the violent nature of childbirth, they believe that the souls of the mother and baby may have been frightened away. Their straying souls are brought back by wrapping white strings around the wrists of the baby and the mother. The strings remain in place for three days, after which they are removed (see: Birth/Hmong, p. 135; Birth/Thai, p. 151; Marriage/Cambodian, p. 186; Marriage/Lao, p. 207; "Marriage"/Thai, p 212.).

Everyone who attends participates in tying on the strings. Monks are not required. A grandmother or grandfather may officiate. A feast follows.

NAVAJO

FIRST-LAUGH FEAST

GIFTS Small gifts for the child. Additionally, the host family may give small gifts to the guests, such as earrings or trinkets.

WORDS After guests receive salt from the baby, they may say "Thank you," for reminding them of their own first happiness.

CLOTHING Informal but modest.

Navajos adore new babies. Family and friends lovingly welcome the child, play with it, watch over it, especially encouraging the baby's first laugh, which always comes as a surprise, generally anywhere from three to eight months. This joyful sound is cause for celebration.

Whoever makes the baby laugh for the first time must prepare the first-laugh feast, which consists of corn, in mush form, on the cob, or canned; mutton or beef stew; vegetables; fried bread; and berries for a sweet life. The berries can be wild, canned, or served in a pie.

To make the baby laugh first is a great honor. It is also a lot of work. The person who inspires the first laugh must prepare food for twelve to fifty guests who participate in this significant meal. Guests include immediate and extended family, friends, and visitors. They welcome non-Navajo, too.

The guests line up with their food-filled plates to greet the baby, who sits on the lap of the person who made it laugh. The child holds rock salt tightly in one hand. In its other hand, the baby sometimes grasps a miniature Navajo wedding basket. As each guest steps up to the baby, the person holding it helps the baby release some of the salt from its fist onto the guest's plate. By so doing, the baby learns to be a giving person. Through this act, Navajo families instill the importance of generosity.

After the guests receive the salt, they shake the baby's hand, hug it, or give it a kiss. It is an uplifting occasion, and guests receive blessings by receiving the salt. The rock salt represents tears, the result of either laughing or crying, and although they might seem like opposite emotions, to the Navajo they are the same. The Navajo treasure both. The first-laugh feast signals what lies ahead for the child.

NIGERIAN

IBO [ée-bow] BABY NAMING

GIFTS Baby clothing and money. Place the bills directly in the baby's hands. If guests give money to the parents instead, the parents show it to the baby.

WORDS Advise babies that when they grow up, they should take good care of their parents.

CLOTHING Dressy

To Nigerians, the name of a person is so important, that if a child is wrongly named, they think it may become sick and die. Sometimes, parents go to a traditional healer, who after consulting with the spirits, advises what name to choose.

Generally, the baby is given its traditional name four months to one year after birth. The first son is named after his paternal grandfather and the first daughter after her paternal grandmother. When making these decisions the Ibo consult with the paternal grandparents.

Sometimes the grandparents may travel from Nigeria to perform the ceremony, officiated by the eldest male on the paternal side. The Ibo place the child on the floor, and in addition to bestowing a name, they give the child a pen, signifying their hopes for the child's education. This is one of the most prized desires for newborns, both male and female. They also put the child in touch with its roots. If the baby came from a family of farmers, parents will let it touch something related, like a hoe. If from a weaving family, the child will be handed a weaving stick to touch. If the family had been peanut traders, they will place a peanut in the baby's hand. Baby girls participate in the same ritual.

YORUBA [yóur-oo-bah]—BABY NAMING

GIFTS Money, layette sets, clothing, blankets.

WORDS Congratulate the parents.

CLOTHING Dressy

The following description applies to those Yoruba who are not *Orisha* [oh-rée-sha] followers (see Multiracial Families and Couples/Jewish American-Yoruba, p. 67.). Seven to nine days after birth, they name the baby. Otherwise, traditional Yorubas believe it will not outlive its parent of the same sex. The ceremony takes place at home beginning in the afternoon when guests arrive with gifts. Later, all gather around a table bearing ritual food and objects. After singing an opening hymn, the pastor allows the baby to taste or touch each of the foods and objects on the table. He describes the symbolism of each article, recites prayers for the child's well being and good character, then circulates the items for all to taste or touch. Afterward, the minister announces the baby's first and second names.

Next, while singing and bearing candles, the minister leads the parents, family, and baby into the baby's room to bless it and the baby's bed with prayers and hymns. Some may recite poetry created for the occasion. Afterward, everyone returns to the living room to enjoy traditional foods, such as fried plantain, goat stew with fufu (a glutinous substance made of boiled and pounded cassava), boiled yams, and fowl. Later, more guests arrive for music and dance, which may last all night.

Frequently the parents and baby wear new African clothing. If the grandmothers are still in Nigeria, they send their choice of names for the baby. When the baby visits Nigeria for the first time, grandmothers will call the baby by the names they have chosen. In Nigeria, this ceremony takes place outdoors, where they touch the baby's bare foot to the ground signifying that its first steps will lead it in the right direction.

PROTESTANT

CHRISTENING

GIFTS Typical baby gifts.

WORDS "Congratulations."

CLOTHING Guests should dress up for this occasion. Modest clothing. Avoid shorts and beachwear.

Protestant christenings are generally held during the Sunday service after the sermon. The child's godparents and parents stand at the baptismal font, and the godmother holds the baby, who is dressed in a white cap and christening gown. The godmother stands on the minister's left, and after starting the ceremony, she places the child in his left arm. The minister asks the godparents to speak on behalf of the child and make promises to God and renounce the devil. The godparents announce the child's name and the minister says, "I baptize you in the name of the Father and of the Son, and of the Holy Spirit." He then sprinkles or pours blessed water on the child's head. In some churches, baptism may be by immersion. The minister repeats the child's name and makes a cross on the baby's brow and hands it back to the godmother.

On some occasions the godfather holds a lit candle and the minister says, "I give you this sign to show that you have passed from shadow into light." He makes a final blessing and reminds the parents and godparents of their commitment to God and the baby. Afterward the family or fellowship may serve cake and coffee or perhaps a light lunch.

ROMAN CATHOLIC

CHRISTENING

GIFTS Traditional baby gifts and money. Sometimes godparents give the child a little prayer book and rosary.

WORDS Simple words of congratulations.

CLOTHING In church, respectful attire.

BODY LANGUAGE Kneeling is not required of non-Catholics or Catholics who have physical limitations. If the ceremony takes place during Mass, non-Catholic guests need not feel uncomfortable. Remain in place while others pass in front of you to proceed to the front of the church to accept the host and wine.

Since Sunday morning Mass is the busiest time, Catholics frequently hold these twenty-to-thirty-minute ceremonies separately in the afternoon in the middle of a Mass between the reading of Scripture and the priest's sermon. The Eucharist follows. Big parishes often have groups of twenty to thirty at a time.

Sometimes this ceremony is called baptism. In past times, christening took place soon after a child's birth. Urgency stemmed from the fear that an unbaptized child might die and not qualify for salvation. However, nowadays, the more common belief is that the Mercy of God will take care of the child, and parents may wait months, even years. The mother dresses the baby in a white cap and long gown, symbol of the wedding garment; some baby boys may wear a white shirt, vest, and short pants. Others have hand-me-down dresses that have gone through many generations. Most commonly, the priest or deacon pours water on the baby's forehead, but some churches have a baptismal font containing heated water so that the baby may be immersed.

After welcoming the child, the priest asks what name will be given, and one of the godparents replies with the selected name and adds one of a saint. Commonly, they bestow a saint's name to give the child a model of good behavior. Godparents are generally relatives and they are frequently asked to take a preparation class to learn their duties. In general, their role is to be attentive to the child's religious upbringing in the event that something happens to the parents. They serve as mentors and models and remind the child that they are baptized in the faith.

Standing in front of the font, the mother or godmother holds the baby. The priest or deacon asks the following questions of the parents and godparents: "Do you believe in the tenets of the faith?" "Do you resist evil?" "Do you wish _____ (name of child) to be baptized in the faith?" After receiving positive answers to these questions, the priest asks the godmother to hold the baby over the basin. He takes a cup of holy water, sometimes from a sea shell container, and says, "I baptize you in the name of the Father, Son, and the Holy Spirit." He anoints the child on the breast with holy oil and hands the parents and godparents a lighted candle, symbol of the light of faith. Then he speaks a prayer for all of them.

The priest places a white veil or cloth over the child's head for a moment and says a final prayer over the baby's ears and mouth so that the child will receive the word of the Lord and proclaim his or her faith. The priest concludes by blessing the parents. He reminds them of their religious duties and to thank God for this child's life.

SAMOAN

BABY WELCOMING—*ALAALAFAGA* [ALA-ALA-FANGA]

GIFTS Baby gifts. Do not bring liquor, considered offensive among traditional Samoans.

WORDS They welcome compliments to the baby.

CLOTHING Avoid shorts or cutoffs and beachwear.

When the mother and child arrive home from the hospital, the Samoan family has a formal thanksgiving for their healthy return. Extended family, a minister, *matais* [mah-ties] (chiefs), from both sides of the family attend, and the families exchange fine mats to celebrate the occasion. If the birth of the child has been difficult, family members may invite any medical personnel believed to have aided in the successful delivery.

Depicted as a kind of pot luck party on the mainland, on the islands it is more like a baby shower. Because they have adopted the baby shower tradition stateside, fewer baby gifts are given at the *alaalafaga*. They sing, read from the Bible, and say prayers for the child, mother, and family. After the prayers, the chief thanks the minister and they eat. Since eating heartily is an important Samoan tradition, in addition to eating at the party food is sent home with each guest. Close friends and family members bring money and food to contribute to the feast.

Alaalafaga always takes place at night after sundown in Samoa. Stateside, they have it at 7 p.m. or 8 p.m. They also observe this ceremony when a patient returns home from the hospital or when someone new comes to visit.

THAI

BABY WELCOMING

GIFTS Regardless of the sex, after the baby is blessed, friends and families give the baby gold: chains, necklaces, and bracelets. They also give money in envelopes. In the past, the envelopes were generally white. Nowadays, some people put money in pink envelopes for girls and blue envelopes for boys.

WORDS In Thailand, people do not compliment the baby for the first three months. If they were to say that the baby was pretty, the bad spirits might want it. To discourage compliments, they used to put a black smudge on the baby's face. Most Thais living in the United States do not follow this custom. Nonetheless, to avoid upsetting the older generation, use discretion when commenting on the child's appearance or demeanor.

CLOTHING Remove shoes when entering a temple. Step over the threshold, not on it, an inauspicious act.

BODY LANGUAGE People greet one another with the *wai* [why]. This is the most respectful form of greeting. With hands pressed together in a prayerlike position, bring them up to just below the chin and nod slightly. However, Thai customs in the United States are relaxing a bit. Some Thai may use the handshake when greeting non-Asians. Watch cues and follow suit.

Well-wishers tie white strings around the wrists of the Thai mother and child upon their return from the hospital. The mother wears the strings for two to three days. The baby wears them longer. The white strings must not be cut off, but can be removed by pulling them apart or untying them (see Birth/Hmong, p. 135; Birth/Lao, p. 143; Marriage/Cambodian, p. 186; Marriage/Lao, p. 207; Marriage/Thai, p. 212.).

When the baby is seven days old or one month old, parents bring the baby to the Thai Buddhist temple to be blessed by a monk. There is no special party, but friends and family may give gifts. In Thailand, they do not celebrate birthdays, but when Thai children attend school in the United States, they request parties just like their classmates. Parents usually acquiesce.

TIBETAN

CLEANSING CEREMONY—*BHANSEL* [bahn-sell]

> GIFTS Non-Tibetans bring baby clothes, blankets, and other useful items.
>
> WORDS *"Tashi delek"* (May all auspicious signs come to this environment).
> In the United States, it is permissible to compliment the baby.
>
> CLOTHING Dress up for this important occasion. Women should wear jewelry.
> Depending on the family, note whether or not they remove their shoes inside their
> homes and follow suit.
>
> BODY LANGUAGE After saying *"Tashi delek,"* Tibetans may briefly stick out their
> tongues to one another, indicating respect and affirmation. They use the *namaste*
> for greetings (see Giving Birth/Indian, p. 137), but the younger generation may also
> shake hands with non-Tibetan guests.

This is the Tibetan's baby's first official bath, which takes place at home two days after the birth of a girl and three days after the birth of a boy. Friends and family gather, and after they wash the baby, they sprinkle it with holy water. Guests offer a white filmy scarf to the baby, wrapping it around the infant while blessing the baby and wishing that it serve its parents well and have a long life and good health. As guests each place a scarf around the mother's neck, they slip her an envelope made of homemade Tibetan paper containing money.

In Tibet, flowers for offerings are not usually available for auspicious occasions because of the harsh weather. Instead, they use white rectangular rayon or silk scarves for offerings and prayers, a tradition maintained in the United States (see Marriage/Tibetan, p. 213; Death/Tibetan, p. 246.).

VIETNAMESE

BABY WELCOMING

GIFTS Gold jewelry for the baby girl or boy shows the highest respect and reflects on the donor's class and generosity. If unaffordable, give baby clothes.

WORDS Avoid complimenting the baby.

CLOTHING No restrictions.

BODY LANGUAGE The older generation avoids male/female contact. The most prudent acknowledgment is a slight nod. However, younger people may shake hands or even give hugs.

When the baby is one month old, the Vietnamese have a big party, especially if the child is male. They light incense on their home altars, thank the gods for the new baby, and pray for blessings on the child. Although some Vietnamese have parties for newborn girls, the celebrations are not as large as those for boys, and some families opt not to have a party for girls. Whether the babies are boys or girls, families send gifts of boiled pork and red- or pink-dyed eggs to their neighbors.

[5]

BIRTHDAY
ANNIVERSARIES

Like first-year celebrations, certain other birthdays have special meanings: sweet sixteen; decade markers, especially the "big five-oh." Among the Vietnamese, forty, fifty, sixty, and seventy are special. Yet among certain cultures, particular birthday numbers are taboo and thus go uncelebrated. For example, Chinese immigrants may ignore the fortieth and forty-first birthdays because of the death connotations connected to the sound of the word for four. Chinese men celebrate the twenty-first, thirty-first, fifty-first, sixty-first, seventy-first, and eighty-first birthdays, while traditional Chinese women celebrate their twentieth, thirtieth, fiftieth, sixtieth, seventieth, and eightieth birthdays. The differences between the men and women are tied to yin and yang principles. Yang, for males, stresses the odd numbers, while yin, the female principle, emphasizes even numbers.

JAPANESE

SIXTIETH BIRTHDAY—RETURN TO ORIGINS—*KANREKI* [kahn-ray-key]

GIFTS Money or typical gift items, especially red ones.

WORDS *"Omedeto"* [oh-meh-det-oh] (congratulations or good luck), a felicitation used at weddings and New Year's as well.

Originally for men only, Japanese women are now celebrating their sixtieth birthday as well. The Buddhist calendar contains twelve zodiac signs and five branches. One completes the cycle at age sixty and is considered reborn and entering a second childhood. A party, hosted by the celebrant's children, often takes place at a restaurant, and the celebrant wears either a red jacket, vest, or sweater, and a red hat (*chan chan ko*) like a baseball cap. Red is a distinctive feature of the event, tied to the old Japanese tradition of dressing newborns in red caps and vests, a custom rarely followed today in the United States (see Birth/Japanese/First Temple Presentation, p. 139.).

This party is lighthearted, like a roast. Family and friends give gifts. The family may display a thousand red paper origami cranes made by all the children and grandchildren in the family. These serve as symbols of longevity and good fortune. The party may be repeated at age eighty-eight and called *beiju* [bay-ee-ju].

KOREAN

SIXTIETH BIRTHDAY—*HWAN' GAP* [hwon-gop]

GIFTS Koreans put cash inside a double envelope and give it to a family representative, who keeps a tally of the givers and amounts so that reciprocity may be maintained for future gift-giving. Non-Koreans often give personal gifts believing it to be a birthday party rather than a rite of passage into old age. Avoid giving knives.

WORDS "Happy birthday" is acceptable even though it is not strictly a birthday party.

CLOTHING Dressy clothing with suits and ties for men. Older Koreans may wear traditional clothing. Remove shoes if the celebration takes place at home.

BODY LANGUAGE Among the older generation, bowing is the official form of greeting. Avoid body contact unless initiated by others.

In the United States, the children and wife give this party for the sixty-year-old man. Sixty signifies five times around the lunar calendar and the return to one's birth year. More than a birthday party, this celebration is a rite of passage into old age.

If the celebrant's parents are still alive, he wears brightly colored clothing. If they are not, he dresses in all-white traditional Korean drawstring pants, loose shirt, and vest. Wearing white signifies that he need not work anymore, that others have to serve him. One at a time, and starting with the eldest male, each of his children and their spouses followed by the rest of kin approach the celebrant and his spouse. In turn, they bow, pour a cup of rice wine, circle the cup in front of the celebrant, then offer it to him. Men bow twice; women bow four times.

Other fixtures of the ritual include a table that looks like an ancestor worship table (see Death/Korean, p. 233.), filled with foods presented in a formalized order going from sweet to sour, in an order of auspiciousness: plates piled high with dried fruits, fresh fruits, cookies, rice cakes, pancakes, dried meats, pan-fried foods, and salads.

The heart of the ritual occurs when an emcee recounts the life history of the celebrant, and family members and others add their testimonials. Drinking and dancing follow.

The elaborateness of the celebration depends on the economic and social class of the involved families. Some children may not give their parents a big party but instead send them on a cruise or on a trip to Korea.

(6)

COMING OF AGE
CELEBRATIONS
"Today I am a man."

When does a boy become a man? When does a girl reach womanhood? Depending on cultural background, the ages marking the crossover from childhood into adulthood vary. Some celebrations occur in the secular world: a debutante ball at eighteen, a party at sweet sixteen. Others occur in religious settings: a *bar mitzvah* at thirteen; a *quinceañera* at fifteen. We expend time and money on these occasions that announce to the world that our children have become adults and that we parents have achieved enough status to afford extravagant observances.

Ironically, the dominant event marking entry into U.S. adulthood is one devoid of ritual fanfare—obtaining a full-fledged driver's license. Across ethnic and gender borders, this act awards physical freedom to children, granting them the same mobility as their parents. While ceremonial expenses may be nil, the immediate costs of music, food, garb, and guests are replaced by long-range financial burdens—INSURANCE.

APACHE—Mescalero

MOUNTAIN SPIRIT DANCE

GIFTS If you attend as a tourist and pay for entrance, no gifts are expected or necessary. If you are visiting a particular girl's family, substantial gifts of food are welcome because the family must feed everyone three meals a day for four days. Choose four among the following choices: twenty-five pounds of flour, five pounds of lard, ten pounds of sugar, a sheet cake, fifty pounds of potatoes, four- to six-dozen eggs, watermelons, or cantaloupes. If you are visiting the owner of a set of mountain god dancers, give him a Pendleton blanket (about $150), Indian tobacco, cattail pollen, a good unset piece of turquoise, or the largest-size Swiss army knife.

WORDS There is little opportunity to convey verbal felicitations. One's presence implies congratulations. Additionally, an announcer or family member may request that an observer participate in an Apache dance. This honors the family and is a nonverbal expression of "Hurrah!" If you are a woman, and a family personally invites you to attend, demonstrate your happiness for them by saying, "I'm ready to cook." This means you are willing to help the family with food preparation or serving. Men say, "I can chop wood or carry water," to show, rather than speak, their praise.

CLOTHING For women, jeans, skirts, dresses, and slacks, but no shorts. Men cannot be shirtless. Avoid wearing sandals without socks because naked feet are displayed only to one's closest intimates.

GENERAL TABOOS They prohibit all recording devices: cameras, audiotape recorders, video cameras, notebooks, and sketch pads. If discovered, equipment will be confiscated and perhaps not returned. Credentialed journalists may be exempt from this rule, but only if they apply in advance for a camera permit to the Apache Tribe at P.O. Box 176, Mescalero, NM 88340. Permission is not always granted. Families who hire photographers to document their ceremonial may also be exempt, but only if they receive permission from tribal officials, who issue permits that must be hung from the camera.

This is only a small part of the girl's puberty ceremonial paying tribute to the achievement of womanhood, held after a girl's first menses. It sanctifies the role of woman. More than one girl may be feted, and variations exist at different Apache sites, for example, San Carlos, Cibique, and Mescalero.

The ceremony is a four-day/four-night coming-out party and at Mescalero always includes the Fourth of July. It fetes girls who have had their first menses since the previous year. Like puberty rites of other cultures, it is costly. Friends and family consume huge quantities of food over the four days, and the singers and dancers must be compensated. Although many Native American ceremonials are closed to outsiders, non-Native American guests are welcome at the Mescalero summer event. An outline of main features follows.

On the first day, tribal members construct a tepee of four main and eight subsidiary structure poles to house the young girls and their godmothers. Celebrants wear buckskin ceremonial garments painted yellow or bleached white with beaded symbols. Yellow represents sacred pollen and God's generosity. Singers apply the pollen to the girls' bodies.

The Mescalero Apaches reenact the legendary journey of White Painted Woman, the mythological figure who brought this ritual to the Apaches. The Mescalero say they invented the ceremony to honor and commemorate White Painted Woman. During the four days, physically and emotionally ailing tribe members approach the initiates, who are known to possess curative powers at this time in their life as the embodiment of White Painted Woman. The initiates treat them through touch and blessing and exchange pollen blessings. They must also behave according to strict rules. For example, they are not supposed to smile or laugh as this will cause premature wrinkling.

On each of the four nights, holy singers each sing at least sixty-four different songs and retell stories of their people. On each of the four nights, mountain spirit dancers bless the encampment and through their performance drive away evil spirits. Groups of four dancers impersonate the mountain spirits. Clowns and young boys dance with them. At the beginning of the ceremony, the dancers approach the central fire and the girls' ceremonial tepee four times.

The "owner" of a set of mountain god dancers sings and drums as the dancers perform. Additionally, initiates must participate in a minimum of two hours of strenuous dancing on each of the four nights. During the day, they run around a basket four times to symbolize the life cycle: infancy, childhood, adulthood, and old age. At the end of the fourth run, their uncles or brothers spill baskets of tobacco, candy, piñones, fruit, and money over them. This sets off giveaways by members of the girls' families. Folklorist Claire R. Farrer describes how relatives throw gifts of candy, oranges, apples, and cigarettes from the beds of pickup trucks. Others scramble to pick up these goodies because they consider the food and tobacco blessed.

When the fourth day has ended, and after the initiates have again done four ritual runs, the tribe dismantles the tepee and visitors leave. However, the family stays until the ninth day when they purify the girls in a yucca suds bath. In the old days, at this point girls were considered eligible for marriage; now they finish school before marrying.

Note the significance and appearance of the number four in this Apache ritual. The tepee has four primary wooden supports; the ritual lasts four days; there is a minimum of four dancers; they apply pollen to the girls in four places; the girls run around the basket four times; dancers approach the ceremonial tepee four times as a blessing. Emphasis on the number four as an omen of harmony and balance is common to many Native American tribes.

INDIAN—Brahman

SACRED THREAD CEREMONY—*UPANAYANAM* [oopah-náyah-nam]

GIFTS Clothing, books, items related to learning.

WORDS "Congratulations."

CLOTHING Best clothing. Avoid black. Men need not wear jackets or a tie, but wear a good shirt. Remove shoes and socks when entering the temple.

BODY LANGUAGE Use the namaste for greetings (see Birth/Indian, p. 13?.).

This major ceremony heralds a boy's initiation into learning; he is now ready to study the *Vedas* [vay-duhs] (ancient Sanskrit scriptures). The event occurs in one of the boy's odd-numbered birthdays, generally the seventh, ninth, or eleventh, sometimes as early as the fifth year. To symbolize his change of status, he wears white threads that go over the left shoulder, fall onto the chest, then loop under the right arm. Once initiates put on the white threads, they must wear them at all times and recite certain mantras twice a day.

JEWISH

BAR MITZVAH (FOR BOYS), BAS(BAT) MITZVAH (FOR GIRLS)

GIFTS Items emphasizing learning, such as books, or items related to the individual boy's interests. Money gifts in units of eighteen (see Birth/Jewish, Circumcision, p. 140).

WORDS "Mazel Tov." "Congratulations."

CLOTHING In Orthodox and Conservative temples, Jewish and non-Jewish men must wear yarmulkes (skullcaps). This may be an option in Reform synagogues. For those not owning their own, extras are usually placed at the sanctuary entrance. Orthodox and Conservative congregations require Jewish men to wear prayer shawls (tallit). Married women attending Orthodox synagogues must cover their heads with hats or kerchiefs, wear long sleeves, and have modest necklines and mid-calf hemlines, and no pant suits. If there is an evening party, everyone dresses up.

BODY LANGUAGE In Orthodox temples (also called shuls, or synagogues), men and women sit separately, often divided by a curtain.

At the age of thirteen years and one day, a Jewish male becomes a "Son of the Commandment," allowing him to become fully incorporated into Jewish life. This entitles him to participate in a *minyan* [mín-yon] (a prayer quorum) in the synagogue; he can be called to testify in a Jewish court of law, and in ancient times he could enter into various legal contracts, including marriage. Theoretically, from now on he assumes responsibilities for his own actions.

Preparation includes years of a Hebrew school education where he learns Jewish history and traditions. He learns to chant blessings over the Torah [toe-rah], recite the haftorah portion (selection from the Prophets), and sometimes chant from the Torah portion itself.

The ceremony takes place wherever the Torah is being read, but most commonly occurs in the synagogue during Sabbath services. The young man receives the honor of being called up to the pulpit to read a portion of the Torah and sometimes from the haftorah. Following the reading, he usually makes a speech about his relationship to Judaism and his ideals and goals. He then thanks his parents and teachers for guiding him to this moment of achievement.

Like their male counterparts, girls prepare for their bas mitzvah for several years by attending Hebrew school, where they learn to read

Hebrew and receive a good education in Jewish history and tradition. They learn to chant blessings over the Torah, to recite from the haftorah, when appropriate, and sometimes to chant from the Torah portion itself. During the *bas mitzvah*, held by Reform and some Conservative synagogues, everything is the same as it is for the bar mitzvah. Orthodox and some Conservative Jews oppose having *bas mitzvahs*. However, some modern Orthodox Jews and Conservative Jews allow them, but instead of reading from the Torah, the young women make speeches about it.

For both boys and girls, after the ceremony the parents provide wine, bread, and sweets for the entire congregation, called an *oneg shabbat*. Often they have a luncheon or an evening party for relatives and friends. New traditions may be initiated. Celebrations can be simple community meals following the service or lavish theme-centered events. Non-Jewish thirteen-year-olds are now emulating these celebrations (see Interfaith Families/faux *mitzvahs*, p. 36.).

Some backlash has occurred regarding reception galas for boys and girls. Alternatives to the conspicuous consumption aspects include donating percentages of the cash the children receive to charities or dedicating the event to a cause. At Roslyn Romero's *bas mitzvah*, on her own initiative to fulfill her mitzvah commitment, she cut off her hair to donate for wigs needed by cancer victims undergoing chemotherapy. She also gave part of the money she received to a local battered women's shelter where she had been a volunteer.

Some *bar mitzvahs* include "twinning," whereby the *bar* or *bas mitzvah* performs a proxy service for someone unable to do so himself or herself. Such was Ian's bar mitzvah in Connecticut. His family received the name and date for a Jewish boy born in Russia in the same month and of the same age. The Russian boy's name, Evgeny, appeared on the invitation; an extra chair draped with a talis, skullcap, and prayer book sat as a reminder on the *bimah*. When Ian read his Torah portion, he read an additional portion for Evgeny. He explained what he was doing in his speech and mentioned the portion about treating "strangers in your gates" as your own. They had an extra Kiddush cup at the *Oneg Shabbat*, and he gave part of the money he received to a charity that provided food and clothing for Soviet Jews.

Nowadays, twinning programs exist for Ethiopian Jews and other underprivileged children in Israel, for Righteous Gentiles, honoring those who helped save and rescue Jews during the Holocaust, and for remembrance of a specific child out of the one million under the age of sixteen who were murdered during the Holocaust.

Another contemporary variation is the *bar* and *bas* mitzvah ceremony for the elderly, especially women who, during their teens were denied such rituals because they were only available to boys at that time. In 2004, to celebrate the 13th anniversary of its opening, the Daniel D. Cantor Senior Center in Sunrise, Florida, offered *bar* and *bas mitzvahs* to seniors. Twenty-seven women and six men signed up. Some needed walkers and canes, three were blind, but all made it through the ceremony chanting prayers in front of 300 enthusiastic family members and friends. Later they joined together in a grand celebration.

Sara Sverin, 89, in a walker and legally blind, was shaking before her turn to recite her portion. The rabbi, attempting to console her, said Barbra Streisand was nervous before every performance, too. Snapped Sverin in response, "You're comparing me to Barbra Streisand?"

LAKOTA

FIRST MENSTRUAL FLOW

GIFTS In tribute to each girl being honored, the Lakota give gifts to visitors in something called a giveaway. They distribute gifts according to protocol. Items include towels, blankets, cigarettes, or bolts of cloth. They also give away food left over from the feast, where they expect guests to stuff themselves, then take home the leftovers in special containers to share with friends and relatives.

The ceremony is announced a year in advance so that family members can begin the preparations: gathering the traditional foods, sewing, beading, and quilting gifts, as well as purchasing blankets, towels, and dishes for the feast and giveaway. At the celebration, they apply red paint to the young woman's forehead and three marks on her chin to mark her entrance into womanhood. For the Lakota, red symbolizes dedication to truth as well as the Red Road, a euphemism for menstrual blood. Menstrual blood signifies the woman's capacity to create. In addition to the color symbolism surrounding red, they also include white (for virtue), represented by a white golden eagle feather tied to the initiate's hair.

Seated in a chair of respect covered with a star quilt, one or more girls go through the outdoor ceremony. This can take place just before or right after the young woman's first menstrual flow. Initiates are reminded that they are Lakota and should live as good Lakota people. Ceremonial leaders offer chokecherry juice and pemmican (lean dried meat pounded into a paste and mixed with melted fat and berries, pressed into cakes, and used for long journeys) to the grandfathers, the elderly, and Mother Earth. At this time, the girls may be given new spirit names to supersede childhood names. The new ones are used for all future ceremonies but are rarely spoken.

In pre-reservation days, women isolated themselves for four days every month. That no longer occurs. However, not all young women participate in a public ceremony. Nonetheless, all girls upon becoming women, receive advice from the older women about how to behave when they have their menstrual flow. This includes taboos against sitting around, cleaning house, or sewing. They should not cook or chew their nails or step over any men's clothing lying on the floor. They must wash their clothes separately. Most importantly, elder women emphasize the ideals of having a good home, of being good mothers and wives.

LATINA—FIFTEEN-YEAR CELEBRATION

QUINCEAÑERA
[KEEN-SAY-AH-NYÉRA]

GIFTS Money, clothing, jewelry, and personal items.

WORDS "Congratulations." *"Felicidades."*

CLOTHING Shirts, ties, and jackets for men. Respectful church attire for women.

Observed in the United States for over one hundred years, this all-day cultural, social, and religious event marks fifteen-year-old Latinas' entry into womanhood and the church. During this transition they move from being *niñas* [nee-nyas] (girls) to *señoritas* (young women). Through this ceremony, they enter into the Catholic community as young adults. The Mass of Thanksgiving for Life and the party held afterward are popular in Central America, Cuba, Puerto Rico, and wherever one finds Mexican populations on both sides of the Mexican American border. In cities away from the border, the *quinceañera* has been altered, and families may celebrate it one year later and call it either a "sweet sixteen" or "presentation."

Regional or personal variations may occur, but in all instances, the *quinceañera* resembles a wedding with its formal clothing, printed invitations, and many-tiered cake. It is a costly ritual, but family friends, *madrinas* [mah-drée-nahs] and *padrinos* [pah-drée-nose] (godparents or sponsors), help finance the event. Often their names are printed on the invitation with their duties, which include supplying the cake, limo, flowers, favors, rental hall, and traditional gifts, such as the rosary and missal, and birthstone ring. The *madrina de muñeca* [moo-nyay-caw], is the sponsor who presents the young woman with her last doll. This last vestige of childhood concretizes the dramatic transition the *quinceañera* is about to make. The wearing of makeup, high heels, and jewelry, her own missal and rosary, mark her new status as an adult.

To attend the ceremony, commonly held at a Saturday Mass, the girl travels with her entourage from home to church in a limo. Frequently, she wears a long white gown, but in some places the dress must be pink or another pastel shade. A headpiece ornaments her ornate hairdo. It may be a tiara with glass stones or made with silk flowers and ribbons.

The entourage includes her parents, grandparents, godparents, and court of honor. The court consists of fourteen couples; one couple for each preceding year of the honoree's life. The girls, *damas*, have identical gowns of a specially selected color, and their male escorts, the *chambelanes*, don tuxedos with bow ties and cummerbunds in colors often matching the girls' dresses. The honoree's mother wears a long formal gown, her father a tuxedo.

They enter the church in the following order: the court; a flower girl and boy carrying baskets of flower petals or party favors. The flower girl may also carry an altar pillow on which the honoree will kneel. The parents may walk with the *quinceañera* or she may follow alone. She stands at the front of the altar alongside her godparents. Her parents and her court stand in the first section of pews.

During the middle of the Mass, the priest directs his words toward the *quinceañera* and reminds her how lucky she is to have her parents sacrifice to give her such a celebration. He proclaims that she is now a woman and delivers words to inspire her to further study and achievement. She receives a religious medal on a gold chain, often the Virgin of Guadalupe imprinted with her name and the date. The girl delivers a speech giving thanks to her parents, the guests, the Church. Sometimes she reads from the Bible. She and her court receive communion, and as her last act, the *quinceañera* makes a flower offering to the Madonna and returns to the pews.

When the entourage leaves the church, she walks out accompanied by her male escort. Guests offer congratulations and often the family distributes party favors. The limo then carries the family and attendants to a special location for a photo session, most popularly a park setting or outside a local landmark.

Later, the family sponsors a reception in a hall, restaurant, hotel, or their home festively decorated with flowers, balloons, and streamers. After abundant food and drink, guests dance to music provided by a deejay or a band. The girl and her father dance the first dance, which is a waltz. The next dance includes her court. Regional differences occur. Mariachi music is traditional, but other Latino dance rhythms are played as well: salsa, cumbias, boleros. Miami *quinceañeras* reflect the Cuban connection, particularly in the dancing. They begin with the traditional nineteenth-century waltz, followed by a *danzón*, then move into the mambo and conga, sometimes finishing with Miami disco, Gloria Estefan, and hip-hop.

Regardless of geographical location, the girl cuts the cake, which is topped by a porcelain, crystal, or plastic replica of a fifteen-year-old girl. Guests bring gifts to the reception that she later opens at her home. The young woman receives objects representing her transition to adulthood: jewelry, religious medals, high heels, her own missal (religious guide) and rosary, rings, earrings, and bracelets.

To shift the focus away from the partying aspects to the more serious meaning of this event, priests now hold meetings with the *quinceañera*, her parents, and the court. The priest counsels about God, the Bible, and appropriate behavior. In addition, he reminds parents to be thankful for the fifteen years they have had their daughter, emphasizing their responsibility in preparing her for womanhood.

Some Latino families may celebrate the event across the Mexican border so that grandparents and others left behind may participate in this significant life's passage.

NEW AGE

CRONING

GIFTS Amethyst is the jewel that represents croning, so any piece of jewelry containing this stone is meaningful. Other jewelry as well as flowers, fruit, sentimental objects. A wand, a shawl, a crown, if she does not have one. Gifts should be individualized. Avoid jokey gift remedies for old age, such as references to dentures, wrinkles, and hemorrhoids, unless you know that the particular crone would find it amusing.

WORDS These should be from the heart and refer to wisdom, respect for age, the pricelessness of memories.

CLOTHING Purple preferred, since it is the crone's color. Often participants wear long dresses and happy, celebratory types of garments.

"We are the old women. We are the new women. We are the same women, wiser than before."

This chant embodies the spirit and purpose of croning ceremonies, to honor a woman's passage into old age. The Feminist Spiritual Community (FSC) of Portland, Maine, one of the leaders in croning ceremonies, defines cronehood as having two characteristics: the woman has entered menopause and has reached her fifty-sixth birthday. While the word *crone* often elicits negative witch-like images, women who have participated in croning ceremonies have chosen to stress the magical wise-woman aspects instead.

No standardized ritual exists. Individuals and groups have evolved their own variations, including parodies. For example, in one ceremony elders cross "the great divide" by crossing to the other side of the room and separating themselves from the younger crowd, chanting "Bleed No More," and "Eggs No More," while smashing *cascarones* [kos-kah-rów-nes] (eggshells filled with confetti) over each others' heads.

Despite the playfulness, the sustaining element found at all croning ceremonies is honoring rather than denying age. The ceremony celebrates the latter stage of life and prepares one for the next stage, including death. It is a time of empowerment, of dedication, of embracing all facets of life—the dark nights, bright mornings and evenings that lie ahead. It acknowledges the importance of the stories women have to share.

As with most rites of passage, the element of fire is significant, hence the burning of candles. At the FSC, other ritual objects include flowers, herbs, plants, stoles, crystals, and food. As each woman enters the room, two greeters welcome her by name and with hugs. All the women form a circle and begin chanting, "We are women giving birth to ourselves." Then in a chain, the women walk through a simulated birth canal and light three candles, one for those attending for the first time, one for those unable to attend, the third for all present.

One of the highlights of the ceremony is "The Decades." Standing in a circle, they first announce the decade from age ten to nineteen. Each woman says a few words describing something that occurred during that decade, and when finished, those over twenty step forward toward the center, leaving behind those who are not old enough. They repeat this process for each decade until they finish the fifties.

While sharing the decades, the women reveal their sorrows, pain, joys, achievements, and aspirations.

After the decade of the fifties, the crones and initiate step into an inner circle. The initiate sits in the center; the crones sit around her and everyone else forms a circle around them. The crones bestow affirmations on the new one such as "You are an honored and beloved woman." "You have a wealth of stories and ideas to share." Then the crones talk about what it is like being a crone and ask the new one questions about her feelings, fears, hopes, and plans for the future.

The new crone receives two gifts. The first is a stole made from braided ribbons symbolizing the weaving together of the strands of her life. She wears this at all subsequent ceremonies. The other gift is an amethyst crystal to help in her ongoing transformation.

Following the receipt of these presents, they receive more affirmations and gifts. Dancing, feasting, and singing take place with a benediction and opening of the circle. At the FSC, they close by chanting the following:

The circle is open but unbroken.

May the peace of the goddess go in your hearts,

Merry meet and merry part,

And merry meet again.

ROMAN CATHOLIC

FIRST HOLY COMMUNION

GIFTS Catholic religious gift and book stores can be helpful in making suggestions. Guests may give a child a missal, rosaries, a daily prayer book, stories about saints, money.

WORDS Christians may say, "Congratulations. You will be able to receive Communion when you attend Mass." "Congratulations, God is within you."
Others say, "Congratulations."

CLOTHING In church, respectful attire.

This occasion marks the first time the young Catholic Christian is officially invited to approach the altar and participate fully in the Eucharistic celebration called the Mass, commemorating the Last Supper. The Catholic understanding of communion is receiving the body and blood of Christ, symbolized by the host (wafer or unleavened bread) and wine or grape juice.

Generally, the first Communion takes place when children are seven or eight years of age and after approximately two years of Christian education or catechesis. The candidates participate together in this ritual on a special day on a weekend following Easter. The boys usually wear a white or dark suit and girls wear white dresses and veils with white shoes.

First Holy Communion ceremonies occur once a year at a Mass, although a large parish may have several first Holy Communion Masses. The pastor officiates over numerous elements including an entrance song, penitential rite, readings from the New and Old Testament, singing of a responsorial psalm, and a proclamation of the Gospel followed by a homily and Communion. Commonly, family members bring to the altar gifts of bread and wine.

Often a reception is held in the parish hall to celebrate the event with food, music, and dancing. Some families may elect to celebrate away from the church with family dinners or barbecues.

CONFIRMATION

GIFTS Books, a Bible, rosaries, tickets to a good movie or the theater, money.

WORDS "Congratulations. You have received the Holy Spirit. Now you may bear witness to the Christian faith in words accompanied by deeds." Non-Christians may just say, "Congratulations."

CLOTHING In the church, respectful attire.

Confirmation is a sacrament of maturity and commitment. It grounds young Catholics' connection to the Church and generally occurs when participants are in high school, but may occur earlier depending on the local diocese. It is a one-time event where the Holy Spirit enters the person to root them more deeply into divine affiliation. Confirmation is an initiation into the parish community and calls forth a more mature commitment to being an adult. To qualify, candidates often participate in parish community service projects. Confirmation preparation takes two years, with groups of candidates focused on study and prayer. Theirs is a journey toward a maturing faith within the faith community.

At the ceremony, the bishop comes to the parish community and anoints candidates and gives them a new name. This name, chosen by the candidate, is usually that of a saint who has special meaning to the initiate. The young persons wear their Sunday best, often adding a red stole or a red carnation to symbolize the fire of the Holy Spirit. During the ceremony, a sponsor accompanies each initiate as they approach the bishop to receive the anointing of confirmation. The sponsor is a confirmed Catholic, one who walks the faith journey—supports, inspires, and challenges the one to be confirmed. As part of the ceremony they celebrate the Eucharist (receiving the body and blood of Christ, symbolized by the host, wafer or unleavened bread, and wine). Following the religious service, the parish community hosts a reception to welcome the new members of the community.

THAI

NOVICE MONKS

GIFTS No gifts.

WORDS "Congratulations" to the boys and their parents.

CLOTHING Respectful attire. When entering the temple, shoes must be left outside.

BODY LANGUAGE When entering the temple, avoid stepping on the threshold. Step over it. As an outsider, it is not necessary to prostrate oneself as believers do. To avoid feeling conspicuous, sit at the back of the room. Chairs are usually provided for visitors and the infirm. If no chairs are available, sit on the floor. As a sign of respect and greeting, they use the wai [why] sign. With hands pressed together in a prayerlike position, bring them up to just below the chin and nod slightly. When people greet you this way, you should return the gesture. If this makes you feel uncomfortable, just nod.

As young as six and up to twenty-one years old, boys may participate in a rite of passage that teaches them how to live as Buddhists. The boys, called novices, live and study with monks at the temple for as little as two weeks and for as long as a summer. This is a commonplace ceremonial event in Thailand and is beginning to be observed in the United States where Thai Buddhists have a large enough community to support a temple and monks.

The occasion begins with family members taking turns to cut locks of the boy's hair and placing them in a golden bowl. Afterward, a monk finishes the job by shaving the boy's head. The act demonstrates how vanity must now be set aside. After the shaving, the novices put on white robes and move to the front of the temple where they join a procession of musicians, dancers, friends, and family members. They walk around the temple three times to show their respect for Buddha and then kneel before the monks. The head monk explains the ten rules of Buddha's teaching and in ritualized question-and-answer form, asks if the boys wish to proceed. After agreeing, the novices change from their white robes into saffron ones to begin their spiritual journey.

From then on, the boys steep themselves in the teachings of Buddha. They live and study at the temple, sleep on floor mats, give up play, music, and laughter, and eat only two meals a day, the last one at noon. They are then considered monks, but only until they return to their families. Temporary monks and nuns are commonplace in Asia.

[7]

MARRIAGE CELEBRATIONS
"I do. I do."

Feminists may cringe, but the intent of most traditional wedding celebrations is to incorporate the bride into the family of the groom; the ceremony marks a transfer of property. Indeed, prior to my own wedding in 1951, my about-to-be father-in-law likened me to an empty lot he was about to purchase but whose title was unclear. This motivated his desire to meet my parents.

Just as most couples are unaware of property exchange as the root of the wedding ceremony, they frequently don't know the reasons behind the myriad wedding customs most feel compelled to follow. For example, few newlyweds know that the wedding veil was meant to fool the evil eye as to the true identity of the bride, thus keeping her from harm before tying the knot. And what does "tying the knot" mean? In ancient times, knots offered protection against evil spirits, which was crucial during wedding preparations. In addition, the knot symbolizes interwoven affection. As for throwing rice at the couple, rice represents fertility, as do corn and birdseed or the old shoes tied to the back bumper of the couple's getaway car.

Wedding rituals can be big splashy events held at country clubs or as simple as that of fifty-five-year-old Pat Byrd and fifty-one-year-old Bill Hughes, whose 2004 nuptials took place in the garden center of the Boise, Idaho, Wal-Mart. The store manager served as the groomsman and a fabric department employee as the matron of honor. When the officiant asked, "Who gives this woman in marriage?" the answer was, "Her friends and family at Wal-Mart," a fitting response for this disabled couple who have averaged six hours a day there nearly every day since the store opened. They talk to people and walk around for exercise and always buy something to drink or eat.

AFGHAN

ENGAGEMENT PARTY

GIFTS Jewelry, housewares. Avoid giving money, considered disrespectful.

CLOTHING Best and latest-fashion clothing. Elaborate dresses with sparkle and sequins for women, dark suits for men.

BODY LANGUAGE Because Afghanis are Muslim, they allow no public body contact between men and women. Men dance with men. Women dance with women. These rules are relaxed between close family members.

This is a description of an engagement party that took place in the San Francisco Bay area in 1994. It is typical of traditional Afghan weddings occurring in this country.

The elegantly dressed engagement couple stepped out of a limo decorated like a wedding car with bows, streamers, and flowers. The bride-to-be wore a fancy pink wedding-like gown and carried a bridal-like bouquet. Her fiance wore a dark suit.

Once inside the reception hall, the family displayed wrapped gift packages on a table covered with a veil and decorated with pink and white balloons. The festive mood heightened as family members approached the bride-to-be and removed her old jewelry, replacing it with beautiful new rings and bracelets covering her fingers and wrists. Afterward, the groom-to-be placed an engagement ring on her third finger, left hand. Meanwhile, same-sex couples danced to the live music. When the future bride and groom stepped onto the dance floor, young women, clapping their hands, danced around the bride-to-be while the men danced around the bridegroom-to-be. Food was served buffet style, and dancing continued until past midnight.

WEDDING

GIFTS Housewares. Avoid giving money.

WORDS *"Mubarak"* [moo-ba-rock]. "Congratulations."

CLOTHING This is a more serious event than the engagement, so dress less ostentatiously.

This took place at the wedding of the couple described in the above engagement celebration.

A white limo carrying the groom picked up the bride from the beauty salon and brought the couple to the wedding hall. She wore a long, dark green dress with a green silk veil covering her head and carried no floral bouquet; wore a black suit and wore no boutonniere. Every time they walked together, an older female family member held a green fabric covered *Qur'an* (Koran, their holy book) over her head as a gesture of protection.

In the lobby of the reception hall, a male representing the bride and another representing the groom, plus witnesses, gathered with the *imam* [ee-mom] (priest), who was dressed in a suit. The groom was present; the bride was not. The men discussed the wedding contract, which made material provisions for the bride in the event the marriage dissolved. Then two witnesses from each side went to the bride to ask if she was willing to marry the groom. The first two times, she gave no answer; after the third request, she agreed.

The representatives and the imam signed the contract; the imam gave a speech, which the others applauded, and the men hugged one another in celebration. Afterward, they passed a tray filled with Jordan almonds to the men, which was later passed to all the guests waiting in the other room. The men threw flower petals over the groom's head, and in turn, he kissed their palms.

Later, in the main room, everyone rose as the bride and the groom entered the hall and stood in front of two fancy throne-like chairs on a platform. The couple posed for photographs and greeted their guests, who kissed each of them on the cheek three times. In front of them on a low table lay the *Qur'an*, two burning candles, a pitcher of juice, and two fancy goblets.

In small groups, guests came up to the seated couple to greet them. The others dined on Afghan food served buffet style, this time more formally presented than at the engagement party. Rice dishes abounded. Although music played, few people danced. Before long, the bride and the groom disappeared.

A change of mood occurred when two costumed dancers entered the room and swung baskets filled with burning incense. Then two eight-year-olds entered dressed like a miniature bride and groom. The wedding couple followed, the groom in a black suit with boutonniere, the bride in a traditional western white gown with train. She wore a veil over her face and carried a bridal bouquet. Again, an older female relative held the *Qur'an* over her head. When the couple reached their throne chairs, guests applauded and took turns taking photographs with them. The bride received more jewelry. Then someone placed spoonfuls of henna into the couple's right hands, temporarily wrapped together with cloth.

After the couple cut the wedding cake, they fed one another one bite and sipped juice from each other's glass. Then some women held an elegant scarf over the couple's heads to allow them privacy as they looked into a brand new mirror and for the first time saw themselves as a married couple. They opened the *Qur'an* at random, read a few lines from the opened pages, and removed the scarf. The train was removed from the bride's gown, and the newlyweds danced together alone on the dance floor. Some male guests dropped paper money over them, which children scrambled to retrieve. Subsequently, other guests danced with the wedding couple.

Costumed dancers wearing white tunics over white pants, decorated vests, and sashes tied around their waists performed while everyone gave them their rapt attention. Then the bridal couple came onto the dance floor and the performers danced around them.

At the evening's conclusion, the couple left the wedding in a limo to travel to the groom's home. Family members joined them as they entered with an older female relative holding the *Qur'an* over their heads as they stepped into their new life.

AFRICAN AMERICAN

Most African American weddings are no different than any other American weddings, guided by the rules and traditions of the churches where the rites occur or with regional differences. In a new trend, some couples are incorporating African traditions of their ancestors. For music, they may emphasize African drumming or perhaps vocals sung by Miriam Makeba; the bride may trim her gown with cowrie shells and wear her hair braided; the groom may wear a cummerbund in colorful Kente cloth, originally a ceremonial fabric worn by Ashanti royalty of Ghana, now worn by African Americans as a symbol of African pride.

QUEH-QUEH [KWAY-KWAY]

This pre-wedding custom from West Africa is an example of an adopted African tradition. *Queh-Queh* is a ritualized song and dance party. On the night prior to the wedding, friends and family dance and sing songs telling the future bride and groom what to expect when they get married. In song, they introduce all of the relatives and guests who circle the couple. It is a highly joyous event frequently filled with double entendre, especially in the songs. Often they serve black-eyed peas for prosperity, sometimes prepared in a dish called Cook-up Rice.

JUMPING THE BROOM

First brought to public attention by the televised miniseries based on Alex Haley's novel *Roots*, this custom was commonly used by slaves in the United States desiring to legitimize their unions when no clergy was available. Slave reports describe someone holding each end of the broom and the couple jumping over it, or the broom being held across the doorway inside the house and the couple jumping over it into the house. Other times, they simply placed the broom on the ground and the couple stepped over it. Newlyweds sometimes stepped over it together or one after the other.

Today, when African American couples jump over the broom, it may symbolize a positive recognition of their African heritage. It may also represent a bitter reminder of slavery. The custom seems to have antecedents among British Gypsies and the Welsh, as well. However, regardless of origin, the symbolism of the broom, which can represent the hearth and the sweeping away of an old life, is becoming a popular wedding tradition across ethnic borders. The Imperial Broom Company of Richmond, Virginia has been making and selling ceremonial brooms for nearly ninety years. Some customizations have been made, such as Jewish couples requesting that brooms be tied with a bag of sugar to ensure a clean, sweet marriage.

NEW ORLEANS

Two different kinds of wedding cakes distinguish an African American wedding held in New Orleans. The groom's cake is generally chocolate and shaped according to his occupation. If he is a physician, the cake may look like a doctor's satchel; a teacher's cake might resemble a book; if the groom drives an eighteen wheeler, the cake might be shaped like a big truck.

The other cake resembles a traditional wedding cake except ten ribbons extend from it. The ribbons are attached to trinkets buried within the cake. The bride invites her single girlfriends up to the cake and each girl selects a ribbon, then warily pulls on it to remove an attached symbol meant to reveal her fate. The worst trinkets to extract are the button and the thimble, both signs of spinsterhood. A penny means poverty; a clover, horse shoe, and wishbone signify good luck. An anchor symbolizes hope. A heart reveals that "love will come," and the fleur-de-lis foretells that "love will flower." The luckiest of all is the young woman who retrieves the wedding ring charm. She will become the next bride.

The reception comes to a rousing close with the second line dance, a tradition borrowed from New Orleans' funerals (see Death/African American/ New Orleans, p. 218.). Second line refers to the string of dancers behind the marching band and the family of the deceased. The band plays a second line song, such as "Little Liza Jane," and the father of the bride holds a specially decorated parasol, usually with white lace, flowers, and streamers. He, or another person chosen as leader, struts and moves around the dance floor performing the special steps of toe, whole foot, knee flex, and twist. The other guests follow, twirling and snapping their white hankies or table napkins in the air. The dance lasts as long as the guests have energy, and the band changes melodies to keep it going. The second line furnishes an exhilarating finale to the wedding reception and any New Orleans dance where it has become a commonplace ending.

AMISH

GIFTS Avoid giving anything requiring electricity. Generally, do not bring gifts to the wedding but send them ahead or give them when the couple comes to visit. The newlyweds display gifts sent beforehand on a table with a piece of paper identifying the donor. They welcome practical household items such as cookware, dishware, kitchen tools, pots and pans, canned food, and tools for the groom.

CLOTHING Subdued colors. Women wear dresses that cover the arms with hemlines below the knees, and modest necklines. Men wear jackets and ties.

Amish weddings exemplify the no-frills Amish life. There are no rings, no flowers, and no vocal solos. The bride makes her own wedding dress and after the wedding continues to use it as her Sunday-best church outfit. She may be dressed in it for the last time at her burial. The dress is in shades of blue or purple, unadorned and of plain design, mid-calf in length, and without a train. She wears black, high-topped shoes and a black head covering instead of a veil. She and her attendants wear white capes and aprons over their dresses.

The groom and his attendants are attired in black suits, white shirts with bow ties, black stockings, and shoes. As with other non-work-related attire, coats and vests fasten with hooks and eyes. The groom wears high-topped shoes and a black hat with a three-and-a-half-inch brim.

Weddings take place at home in November and the early part of December after the harvest season. The short wedding season causes some Amish to attend several on the same day, accomplished by staggering arrival times, for example, during the morning part or for the noon or evening meals. They hold weddings during the week, most frequently on Tuesdays and Thursdays, and not on weekends. From two hundred to four hundred celebrate the occasion with helpers arriving as early as 6:30 a.m.

The three-hour service begins at 8:30 a.m. with congregational hymn singing while the bride and groom receive instruction from the minister in another room. Later, in front of the congregation, the minister has the couple step forward to ask them questions akin to marriage vows. He blesses them, after which ordained men and fathers of the couple give testimony about marriage. The ceremony closes with a final prayer.

Immediately afterward, women prepare dinner while men set up tables in a U-shape in the living room. A special corner, the "eck," is an honored place set aside for the bride and groom, where the bride sits on the groom's left. Single women sit on the same side as the bride, and the single men assemble on the groom's side. Because of the large numbers of guests, they may have two sittings for the meal, which frequently consists of stuffed roast chicken, mashed potatoes, gravy, creamed celery, coleslaw, applesauce, cherry pie, doughnuts, fruit salad, tapioca pudding, bread, butter, and jelly. The prepared chickens come from several dozen freshly killed by the groom the day prior.

Following an afternoon of visiting, games, and matchmaking, the guests gather for the evening meal, which begins at 5 p.m. and may consist of macaroni and cheese, fried sweet potatoes, stewed chicken, cold cuts, pumpkin and lemon-sponge pies, and cookies. The wedding day ends at 10:30 p.m.

There is no honeymoon. Instead, newlyweds visit family members on prearranged times on weekends, generally spending one night or one meal with each host family. They collect wedding gifts on these visits.

The above description applies to typical nuptials taking place in Lancaster County, Pennsylvania. As with all groups, variations occur in other locations and among the many other branches of the Amish and related groups of Plain People, including the Old Order Mennonites.

It is considered a great honor when the Amish invite non-Amish (called English) to their weddings. Very few are included. If you are fortunate enough to be invited, be respectful in your demeanor.

ARMENIAN

GIFTS Money or housewares brought to the reception.

WORDS Any kind of felicitation.

CLOTHING Black is popular and considered elegant. These are formal affairs that call for fancy clothing including sequins and sparkle. Men wear dark suits and ties.

Weddings are their most significant rite of passage. When children are born, a common expression of congratulations to their parents is, "I hope that you will see your son or your daughter on their wedding day." They repeat this sentiment at birthdays, graduations, and all other major life events.

The bride's family pays for an elaborate betrothal ritual; the groom's side pays for the wedding. At the engagement party, a silver tray holds sweets that include Jordan almonds, the rings, flowers, perfume, and cognac representing the sweet things of life. The priest blesses the rings at this time and places the ring on the bride's right hand. At the wedding it is changed to the left hand. The future groom's family presents the future bride with jewelry.

On the wedding day, the family dresses the bride and brings her to church. The groom comes with his father and best man. Armenians from Iran have an additional custom. Prior to the wedding ceremony, a traditional Armenian band accompanies the groom and his family to the bride's home. Each member bears a gift: candy, decorated candles, bouquets of flowers. The groom brings the bride's gown, shoes, and veil which he has purchased. He dances with the gown; men drink vodka, and then the bride dons the dress, but the groom's brother puts on her shoes. The groom's family bedecks her with new expensive rings, bracelets, watches, and necklaces. The best man brings the car to take them to church, but when the couple attempts to leave the house, the brothers block the door until the groom gives them money to let the couple pass.

For the ceremony, the wedding couple selects godparents, generally relatives. The godparents are very important to the couple and stay involved as counselors throughout the newlyweds' lives. To demonstrate their role, they stand closest to the couple during the ceremony, the godmother next to the bride. The godfather, holding a cross, stands next to the groom. During the ritual, the couple wears crowns of gold or silver that are exchanged during the ceremony. At this time, they touch their foreheads together and hold right hands. The godfather touches the heads of the couple with the cross, after which the couple and the godparents drink wine.

Surreptitiously, while still at the altar, the bride or the groom may step on the other one's foot, signifying that he or she will be the boss of the family. Generally, the groom is the aggressor. Upon return from the honeymoon, the couple places a plate outside the door of their new home, and the groom has to step on the plate and break it to demonstrate once more that he will be the boss.

In Southern California, with the largest Armenian population, newlyweds often hire a horse-drawn carriage to take them from the church to the reception. The newlyweds enter last at the reception, and they enter dancing. After the first dance, family and friends present gold jewelry, which they put on the bride. Since most gifts are not sent ahead, the guests present them to the couple during the reception. Russian Armenians, in particular, bring jewelry and gifts of money.

Musicians play drum and horn music and sing special songs about the bride and groom. Guests dance to Armenian circle and line dances as well as Western music. While dancing, the groom's father throws dollar bills over the bride's head, and the bride's father throws money over the groom's head. Others throw money as well, all of which is collected and given as a tip to the band.

At the reception, they serve traditional foods: shish kebab, stuffed grape leaves, rice pilaf. Frequently, the groom's family makes flowery toasts about the bride. "She is ours now." "This is a flower in a garden which we came to pick." Other kinds of toasts are, "I hope you will have a long happy life together, as many children as you want, a warm family, and that you grow old together on one pillow."

CAJUN

WEDDING

GIFTS Household gifts brought to the reception, but many gifts are given ahead of time at bridal showers. Prepare to pin money to the bride's veil or the groom's suit.

WORDS "Congratulations."

CLOTHING Avoid black, associated with mourning. Men wear coats and ties; women wear nice dresses.

At the reception, the bride and groom walk around the dance floor to a traditional Cajun tune *"Marche de Mariés"* [marsh day mah-reese] (march of the newlyweds). Behind them in twos march their parents, grandparents, godparents, brothers and sisters, aunts and uncles. After the newlyweds dance a waltz, they invite the entourage to join them, which becomes the official wedding dance, *le bal de noce* [lay bol day noss] (the wedding dance).

Later, guests take turns dancing with the bride or kissing her in exchange for pinning money on her veil, which soon becomes a mass of green bills. A recent embellishment extends to the groom, who dances with guests in exchange for pinning money to his suit jacket.

An unusual feature is the mop or broom dance. An older, unmarried brother or sister of the bride or groom dances alone with a mop or broom on the dance floor. This is a form of teasing for being passed in the marrying line of succession by a younger sibling. The dancer is usually barefoot, and if the dancer is a man, he must dance with his pants legs rolled up a few inches. Bare feet and too-short pants symbolize the poverty of life without a mate. Underlying is the warning against becoming a spinster or bachelor. The single's dance encourages the dancer to find a life partner and avoid repeating the embarrassment.

A variation of this custom has an older unmarried sibling dancing barefoot, often in a tub, to remind him of the poverty of old age if he does not begin a family of his own. This dance may take place simultaneously with the wedding dance.

CHARIVARI (ALSO CALLED SHIVAREE OR CHIVAREE)

Charivari is a French word referring to a noisy serenade for newlyweds made by beating on metal objects: kettles, pans, tea trays. After the wedding couple goes home, the *charivari* band disrupts them until they offer the noisemakers money or invite them into the house for food and drink. A popular practice of eighteenth-century France, it was brought to the New World and popularized in Canada as well as in the United States. Other European immigrants brought variations of this custom, too.

In Cajun territory, any wedding merits a *charivari*. During the couple's wedding night, friends and relatives congregate outside the couple's bedroom window. They bang pots and pans and make loud irritating noises and do not leave until the bride and groom invite them inside to serve them food: cake and coffee or a full meal. Additionally, this practice is observed for widows and widowers who remarry and estranged couples that reunite.

CAMBODIAN

GIFTS Hand a money-filled envelope of any color to your table representative. Write your name on the envelope.

WORDS Praise or bless the couple.

CLOTHING Avoid black, associated with death. A wedding party is joyful; colors should be joyful, too.

BODY LANGUAGE Use the *wai* [why] form of greeting which is like the Indian *namaste*. With hands pressed together in a prayer-like position, bring them up to just below the chin and nod slightly. Avoid male/female body contact.

To set the wedding date, parents of the engaged couple consult a fortune-teller to discover if the union will be fortuitous and request the best date for the ceremony. Fortune tellers make their prognostications based upon the ages and birth dates of the couple and correlate the calculations with lunar calendar symbols such as Year of the Rat, Year of the Ram, Year of the Monkey. The fortune-teller draws upon special knowledge gleaned from many years of studying the relationships of the sun, moon, and the stars.

The wedding ceremony begins at the girl's home about 8 a.m. and lasts until early afternoon. The groom and his family arrive in a procession with offerings of fruit presented in pairs: pineapple, orange, apples. The groom's party also presents a Cambodian cake and jewelry to the bride: rings, bracelets, necklaces, sometimes a sword to chase away evil spirits. They place offerings of incense, candles, flowers, and a small plate of fruit on an altar in front of a statue or picture of Buddha. The bride is attired in an ornate brocade wraparound skirt with many bracelets, anklets, necklaces. The groom may wear baggy pantaloons and jacket or a Western-style suit. During the course of the ceremony and reception, they may change their outfits three to four times.

A Buddhist monk cuts a lock of hair from both the bride and groom and combines the locks in a bowl to symbolize the sharing of their lives. As a blessing, elders may tie knots in a white string bracelet for each of them (see Birth/Cambodian, p. 129; Birth/Hmong, p. 135; Birth/Lao, p. 143; Birth/Thai, p. 151; Marriage/Lao, p.207; Marriage/Thai, p. 212.).

If the families have access to a Cambodian restaurant, they hold their receptions there. If not, they go to a Chinese restaurant. At the reception, the bride and groom frequently change into a traditional Western, white wedding dress and tuxedo or dark suit. At the end of the meal, the couple visits each table. As they approach, all guests at that particular table rise, and a representative of the table, usually the oldest or most respected, hands the envelopes of money he has collected from his table mates to the bride and groom. He blesses the couple at this time.

Sometimes if younger people are at the table, they will tease the couple, coaxing them to kiss each other or playfully encourage them to eat from the same banana. Although they serve Cambodian food, they always have an American-style wedding cake—in appearance only. Although it looks the same, it tastes less sweet and has a coconut flavoring. Festivities continue with dancing to Cambodian and Western music.

CHINESE

GIFTS Avoid giving clocks, a death omen, or scissors, a symbol of separation. During the reception, when the bride comes to each table to serve tea, leave a red envelope containing money on the tea tray. These envelopes can be purchased in Chinese gift shops. If you do not have access to these envelopes, avoid leaving money in a white envelope, associated with death.

WORDS Avoid talking about illness, death, or sadness of any kind. Focus conversations on happiness.

CLOTHING Females avoid wearing black or white, associated with death. For men, suits other than black are preferred.

Red invitations with gold lettering are sent in red envelopes. The Chinese wrap gifts in red, as well. If the couple is Christian, the ceremony follows the rules of the particular church. If they are Buddhists, the ceremony may take place in a temple or in the bride's home. Regardless of religion, they hold reception banquets in Chinese restaurants where the bride changes from a Western-style white gown into a red *cheongsan* [chong-san] ceremonial gown. Sometimes she will have more than one change of costume.

Family and close friends frequently give gold or jade jewelry, and the bride wears all of it even if it means many rings on every finger and bracelets up to her elbows. This demonstrates how affluent and generous the new family is. The new mother-in-law provides a red comforter for the bridal bed.

An ornamental centerpiece, perhaps a silk flower with a poem, embellishes each table. The family and close friends make many speeches; then they serve the banquet food. Desserts may consist of dates and fruit, connoting fertility, and lotus petals, representing harmony for the new couple.

Before dinner, the bride's first duty is to kowtow to her in-laws. She serves them tea and in return receives jewelry and red envelopes filled with money. She later visits the guests' tables to serve them tea.

EGYPTIAN—Coptic

ENGAGEMENT

GIFTS Only close friends present gifts. The future husband is the only one to give jewelry to his future bride.

Since parents prohibit their daughters from dating, the only acceptable form of courting follows an official engagement ceremony officiated by a priest and performed either in church or at the bride's home. Girls may be as young as sixteen years old, but more often are between the ages of eighteen to twenty-two. After the engagement ceremony, which is financed by the girl's family, the girls may go out with their intended husbands.

At the ceremony, the bride wears a colorful dress, never white. She also does not wear any headdress. If the couple holds the ceremony in church, the choir sings and prayers are said. Whether in church or at home, the priest places wedding rings on the ring fingers of the couples' right hands. At the party held afterward, the intended groom presents his future bride with more jewelry. In the event that he later breaks the engagement, she keeps the jewelry and all gifts. If she breaks it, she must return everything.

WEDDING

GIFTS At the reception, place household gifts on a designated table. They welcome money, too.

WORDS In English, "Congratulations." In Egyptian, *"Mabarouk"* [mah-bah-rock] (blessings).

CLOTHING Dressy clothes for both men and women. Women avoid wearing pants.

BODY LANGUAGE Men and women sit separately in church.

The bride wears a traditional, Western-style gown and veil at the church ceremony. The groom has on a regal gold robe over his suit or tuxedo and a red sash (*zinnar*), which represents his covenant with God. The couple walks in procession from the door of the church up to the altar.

During the forty-five to sixty-minute ceremony, the choir sings, and the only musical accompaniment comes from cymbals and a triangle. The priest offers prayers and anoints the couple with oil, and the bride and groom exchange vows. During the latter part of the ceremony, the priest places gilded crowns decorated with jewels on the couples' heads. From their right hands, the couple removes the rings they have been wearing since their engagement ceremony and gives them to the priest, who ties three knots around them. Later, the priest unties the rings and toward the conclusion of the ceremony places the bride's ring half way down on her ring finger, left hand. The groom then pushes the ring into place. In turn, the priest places the other ring halfway on the groom's ring finger, left hand, which the bride pushes into place. There is no drinking of wine and there is no bridal kiss.

The groom's family holds the reception in a hall where they have a wedding feast, which includes lamb, grape leaves stuffed with rice and meat, turkey, chicken, and Egyptian pastries. They dance to both Western and Egyptian style music.

ETHIOPIAN—Coptic

GIFTS Household gifts brought to the reception. Giving money is not an Ethiopian custom.

WORDS All forms of congratulatory expressions. Wish them the best.

CLOTHING Dressy. Too casual clothing is considered disrespectful.

BODY LANGUAGE Inside the church, men sit separately from the women, but if space is limited, they disregard this rule.

Wedding festivities consist of three separate events. First, the religious ceremony takes place in a Coptic Church. Right after the ceremony is an intimate reception in a park. A large evening reception in a hall or hotel follows.

A distinguishing characteristic of the wedding ceremony is the *caba* (mantle), an ornate, often gold-trimmed robe worn by the bride and groom over their wedding clothes whether traditional or Western style. His robe is gold and hers is white. If they choose to wear traditional Ethiopian attire, their head coverings are close-fitted, gold-colored, and jewel-trimmed hats. Frequently, they display the Ethiopian flag in the back of the church behind the priest. The ceremony consists of vows, songs, prayers, blessings, and an exchange of rings. During the ceremony, the couple kisses their holy book, but they do not kiss each other inside the church.

Only close friends and family attend the park reception amid many flowers. They serve special drinks, *teje* [tedj], a mead, made of honey and hops, and *tela* [tell-lah], a kind of beer made from fermented barley, corn, and hops. Ethiopian music enlivens the scene. After a few hours guests leave and change into more formal clothes to wear at the elaborate, large open reception held in either a hall or hotel, depending upon the financial resources of the groom. The bride and groom greet each guest upon entry, and they always serve Ethiopian food, even in hotels that cater only American food. In such situations, the Ethiopian community members bring in the food.

FILIPINO

GIFTS For the reception, be sure to have dollar bills, $1 to $100, ready to pin on the bride. Men line up for a two-minute dance with the bride, and women do the same for a dance with the groom. Pin the money anywhere. This money is expected in addition to wedding gifts, which may be brought to the reception.

WORDS Any words of congratulations.

CLOTHING Avoid black, associated with funerals. Women should avoid wearing white, which is thought to compete with the bride.

Listed on the formal wedding invitation may be the headings of *ninong* [nee-nong] and *ninang* [nee-nang] or nino [nee-no] and *nina* [nee-na]. This refers to sponsors, usually affluent family friends who provide gifts, generally money to cover the costs of the wedding, honeymoon, or setting up housekeeping. These sponsors guide and encourage the couple throughout their married lives. The invitation also lists the names of the entourage as well as the parents.

Generally held in a Roman Catholic Church during a full Mass, the ceremony lasts about one hour. Two candle sponsors each light and place one small candle on opposite sides of a unity candle located near the priest. Together, the bride and the groom proceed to the unity candle. Each takes a light from the smaller candles, and jointly they light the unity candle.

Later, a white veil physically links the couple and symbolically unites their families. One end is pinned to the shoulder of the groom that is furthest from the bride, and the other end is draped over the bride's head. The veil encloses the two of them together as one of the steps toward union. Afterward, the priest links the couple once more by placing a *yugal* (a white braided cotton cord shaped like the number eight) over them. This cord represents a lifetime union.

GREEK ORTHODOX

GIFTS Household items. Money in envelopes.

WORDS "Congratulations."

CLOTHING Dressy clothing for women. Suits and ties for men.

This service lasts approximately one hour during which time the following acts take place.

THE BETROTHAL

The Priest begins the service by offering petitions and prayers on behalf of the couple. The Priest petitions God for His blessings of the rings and three times blesses the couple with the rings. The blessing alternates between bride and groom, symbolically entwining their lives.

THE RINGS

The rings are placed on the third finger of the right hand of the couple, according to biblical tradition. The koumbaro (best man) exchanges the rings three times, taking the bride's ring and placing it on the groom's finger and vice versa. The rings are the symbol of bethrothal, and the exchange signifies that in married life the weakness of one partner will be compensated by the strengths of the other; the imperfections of one by the strengths of the other. This exchange of rings denotes that by themselves, the newly-betrothed are incomplete; together they are complete.

THE CANDLES

The couple is handed candles which they hold throughout the service. The candles are likened to the lamps of the five wise maidens of the Bible, who because they had enough oil in them were able to receive the bridegroom. The candles symbolize the spiritual willingness of the couple to receive Christ, who will bless them through this sacrament.

PETITIONS AND PRAYERS AND THE JOINING OF THE RIGHT HANDS

The bride and groom join right hands as the priest reads the prayer that beseeches God to "extend Thy hand from Thy holy dwelling place and join these Thy servants. Unite them in one mind and flesh." The couple continues to keep their hands joined throughout the remainder of the service to symbolize their oneness as a couple.

THE CROWNING

The crowning is the climax of the wedding ceremony. The maid of honor and the best man hold crowns tied with a common ribbon above the bride's and bridegroom's heads. This symbolizes unity. During the ceremony, the best man picks up the crowns and crisscrosses them three times over the couple's heads. The couple is crowned as the king and queen of their own little kingdom, their home, which they will rule with wisdom, justice, and integrity.

THE COMMON CUP

Referring to a Gospel reading where Christ converted water into wine and offered it to newlyweds, the "common cup" of wine is given to the couple. This denotes the mutual sharing of joy and sorrow. From this moment on the couple will share everything in life—joys as well as sorrows—and they are to bear one another's burdens. Their joys will be doubled and their sorrows halved because they will be shared.

CEREMONIAL WALK

The priest leads the couple in a circle around the table on which are placed the Gospel and the Cross. This is the first time the couple walks together as a married couple. During the walk a hymn is sung to the Holy Martyrs to remind the couple of the sacrificial love they are to have for each other in marriage.

FINAL BLESSING

The Priest blesses the bride and groom, and at the conclusion separates their joined hands, reminding them that God and only God may break the marriage between them.

HAWAIIAN

GIFTS Nowadays, young Hawaiians register at department stores and have bridal showers. If you have nothing material to give, the finest tribute would be to pick flowers from your own backyard and string them into a lei to adorn the couple. This advice applies to all other Hawaiian occasions, as well.

CLOTHING Aloha attire, colorful floral prints for muumuus and shirts, which can be worn in church and temple. Shorts are unacceptable at formal events.

BODY LANGUAGE At all occasions, acknowledge elders with a kiss. Hawaiians kiss on one cheek. Kiss the couple, the parents, and the grandparents. Avoid handshakes, considered offensive. In ancient times, Hawaiians greeted one another by going up close and pressing nose to nose and inhaling each other's essence. When the first Caucasians landed, the Hawaiians called them *haole* [hah-oh-lay], which means "not of the same breath." Caucasians smelled different. Kissing has replaced the inhalation form of greeting.

Hawaiians may be of varied faiths, and religious ceremonies follow the dictates of either the church or temple. In either situation, they incorporate Hawaiian elements. For example, before the ceremony, a chanter dressed with a coverlet, *kilui* [kee-loo-ee], which is like a sheet tied over one shoulder with a traditional Hawaiian design on it, welcomes the guests and calls on *ke akua* (God), for His blessings. The groom wears a formal aloha white shirt with *lei maile* [mah-ee-lay] intertwined with white jasmine and *pikake* [pee-caw-kay] blooms. The bride has on a white gown or white *huloku*, a more fitted long dress with a train. Her bouquet may include floral leis worn during the reception. Over their tuxedos, the groom and his ushers may have *pikake* garlands, stole-like leis of maile, a fragrant leafy vine intertwined with jasmine or stephanotis, worn only on special occasions. Instead of a traditional veil, the bride may wear a *lei haku* (a crown of braided leaves and flowers).

At the reception they serve foods for the gods, which when eaten bring the spirits to the people. The menu varies with the ethnicity of the wedding couple. Frequently they serve Chinese, Japanese, and Korean dishes along with roast pig. They serve *poi* (taro paste), roast pig, *lomi* (salted salmon), sweet potato, chicken long rice with green onions (a kind of chicken noodle soup), and coconut pudding.

Wedding reception locations depend on the affluence of the families. They may take place in posh hotels, recreation centers, or in backyards. Regardless of location, entertainment is a highlight. The family brings their instruments to play and accompany singing. Then to honor the wedding couple, each person gets up and does a hula. All hulas are individualized, and over time people develop their own signature dance. One hula dance teacher explained that Hawaiians express all that is within them when they dance the hula. She calls it "aloha in motion," and explained that when one dances as a gift, one's love and emotions for the family pours forth. "All of it comes up and enhances your dance."

HMONG [mong]

GIFTS Money in an envelope. Avoid giving anything red, such as red towels or blankets, or wrapping anything in red paper. Red is a taboo color symbolizing blood and foretelling danger. If someone dreams of red before leaving on a trip, the person cancels the trip.

WORDS "Congratulations."

CLOTHING No restrictions.

BODY LANGUAGE Although it is appropriate for Hmong males to shake hands with non-Hmong females, Hmong married women may not shake hands with any men. They must also avoid smiling at other men, considered an insult to their husbands. Unlike other Southeast Asians, the Hmong use no physical greeting gesture. They do not sit on the floor, and they use spoons instead of chopsticks.

The Hmong have several acceptable forms of marriage, and in all forms, the girl lives with and becomes a part of the boy's family. The first called *zij poj niam* [jhee-paw-niah], means bride capture, where a young man of nineteen or twenty takes a girl as young as thirteen to his home and consummates the marriage. Before entering his home with the girl, the boy kneels before his parents, asks for their help in proving his decency. The parents bring a rooster and circle it over the couple's heads to bless their union. Afterward the young man sends two male representatives to the girl's family home. They present $100 to the father and $100 to the mother, give each one a cigarette and kneel twice in front of each parent.

If the girl's family is unhappy with the union, they will try to get her back, but if the girl doesn't want to go home, she will stay in spite of her parents' opposition. Sometimes the boy's family gives the girl's family extra money to appease them, and sometimes the girl's parents complain about the young man merely as a form of bargaining. For the first three days at her new home, the girl does nothing. If she is shy, she stays in her room and people come to visit her there. After three days, her husband's family expects her to participate in household chores. The bride capture custom is waning because many young women now wish to pursue their educations and careers rather than being tied down to raising families at such a young age.

Elopement is another form of marriage. Parents may also arrange marriages when their sons are between the ages of fifteen and eighteen and daughters are thirteen to fifteen. Both sides agree on the bride price, which symbolizes that the wife will be highly valued and treated well when she moves in with her husband's family.

They also practice a form of mutual consent marriage where neither the bride nor her parents know in advance that a marriage proposal is going to occur. The young man consults with his family about the most propitious time for marriage to the young woman of his choice. Family members choose a date that falls on an even number and is close to the new moon. Hmong avoid marrying on rainy days.

In the late afternoon or evening, the groom-to-be meets with two wedding specialists and a third man, who serves as their porter. They bring the equivalent of bamboo backpacks to carry to the girl's home. One is filled with blankets, the other with food. They also bring along a bridesmaid and a large black umbrella.

The girl's parents are completely surprised, as may be the future bride, when outside the front door one of the weddings specialists sings a song to announce their presence. They ask the parents to open the door. Once the entourage enters, the specialist sings another song and hangs the closed umbrella on the wall. The umbrella signifies that the boy's family will protect the bride.

The boy's representative makes a monetary offer for the girl. Generally, there is a $500 variance in negotiation, and families of brides today generally receive about $6,000 to allow their daughters to marry. The groom's side gives cash only, which is immediately counted and carefully examined. If the girl's family agrees to make a wedding party, which often takes place the next day, the boy's side gives an extra $500 to $600. In addition, the boy's side must set aside extra money for the girl's special relatives, such as uncles.

Once the financial arrangements are settled, the bride leaves her home with the groom and his representatives and travels to her husband's home. On her way, she must not look back at her former home. To welcome the couple at the groom's home, his family sets out a plate with offerings of two freshly killed chickens, a boiled egg, lit candle, and cooked rice.

The wedding party takes place at the bride's house. She wears a traditional Hmong dress and headdress, one typifying her homeland region. Family members give her jewelry, costumes, money in envelopes, pillows, blankets, and other household items. At the party, someone collects the money and keeps a list of donors. During the party, they have a long table filled with food for the men, who drink beer and make ritual toasts. Following this, wedding specialists from the bride's side sing songs. Afterward, her family gives blessings and presents gifts of money, jewelry, and costumes.

One year later, if the bride is caught in an affair or if she is lazy or does not fulfill her household chores, or the in-laws dislike her, the boy's family will send her back to her family with $300. They call this "washing the parents' door." In contrast, if the girl runs away or she doesn't want her husband any more, she must return to her family who must repay the money. The Hmong have a very low divorce rate.

INDIAN—Brahman

PRENUPTIAL CEREMONY—*MEHNDI* [mendee]

This custom involves drawing henna designs on the hands and feet of the bride-to-be. It is found with variations throughout South Asia, the Middle East, and parts of North Africa and practiced by Hindus, Muslims, and Sephardic Jews. It takes place at a pre-wedding ceremony where female relatives gather to anoint and beautify the bride.

They make a thick, smooth mixture of ground henna leaves mixed with water, lime juice, and oil, which becomes a paste after being left to sit overnight. Applying it like paint, they create designs on the skin and leave it to set. When washed off, the henna leaves a stain that varies from pale orange to a rich brown. The longer the paste is left on, the deeper the color and the longer it will last.

Specialists paint patterns on brides' palms, fingers, backs of hands, and sometimes the bottoms of their feet extending up to the ankles. Designs can be lotus flowers, intricate lacy or bold geometric designs. Frequently, they draw fertility symbols or configurations to ward off the evil eye.

During arranged marriages of the past, the bride and groom never saw each other until their hands were symbolically joined over the ceremonial wedding fire. The bride's face was veiled, and the only glimpse of her was her ornamented hands. Although in the United States brides and grooms are generally not strangers to one another, the *mehndi* tradition persists and is spreading outside of traditional ceremonies to become a fashion statement.

WEDDING

GIFTS General household gifts or merchandise gift certificates brought to the reception.

WORDS Any felicitations.

CLOTHING Best clothing, but avoid black. Females also avoid white, a mourning color.

BODY LANGUAGE People greet one another with the namaste [nah-mah-stay], a sign of respect. With hands pressed together in a prayerlike position, bring them up to just below the chin and nod slightly (see Marriage/Lao, p. 207.).

Brides from South India wear red except those from Andhra Pradesh, who wear white and gold. The bride's sari is made of nine yards of silk, three more yards than that used for standard saris. For the wedding, it must be tied in a particular way, and after the wedding the bride may wear it only for ceremonies in front of a ritual fire, for example at her child's first birthday celebration. The groom is bare-chested and wears a *dhoti* [doe-tee], a single length of cloth wrapped to form pants with a pleat in front. Neither wears shoes or socks.

The wedding couple sits together before a burning fire, considered the witness. They pour *ghee* (clarified butter) on the fire to keep it burning strongly. This means the fire god is listening to them. Those in charge make certain that the fire remains burning until the ceremony is over. Meanwhile, the priest recites the mantras. In Sanskrit, the groom promises to protect his wife and children and provide for their material needs. Often, these promises are translated afterward into English. Similarly, the bride must promise to care for their home and children.

After the couple walks around the fire three times, the bride sits in her father's lap as her husband winds a yellow thread smeared with turmeric paste around her neck and ties it with three knots. This is the moment when they are officially united, when he literally "ties the knots." Later, the string is often replaced by a gold chain, and the bride wears it throughout her life to safeguard her husband. She discards it only when she becomes a widow.

Guests throw flower petals at the couple after the knot-tying, and the petals must come from fragrant flowers, never non-fragrant ones. They frequently use carnations, roses, and jasmine. A reception follows, but not necessarily on the same day.

IRANIAN

GIFTS The Iranian community has now adopted American ways, and they have bridal showers and register at department store wedding-gift departments. Generally, the groom's family pays all wedding expenses, and the bride's family provides most of the household items.

WORDS *"Tabrik arz mikonam"* [tah-bréek-arz-meé-ko-nam] ("I congratulate you).

CLOTHING Dressy apparel for women; black is acceptable. Suits and ties for men.

As a part of the Iranian wedding ceremony, the person officiating, a mullah or civil official, asks the bride if she will agree to all the provisions in the marriage commitment. According to tradition, she is not supposed to say "yes" the first time. She keeps quiet and smiles. After the third time, she agrees.

The event takes place in the largest room in the bride's home or in a reception hall. If the latter, the wedding couple sits on a bench, preferably on a platform area. In front of them on the floor are pieces of a handwoven Persian multicolored cloth (*termeh*). A stand-up mirror sits upright on it, one large enough for the wedding couple to see themselves. On either side is a candelabrum. On a colorfully painted wooden tray rests rue (*esfand*) [es-von], an herb used to keep away the evil eye. Another tray holds a long, thin flatbread alongside feta cheese, and a plate filled with washed mint, chives, tarragon, and basil.

While a ceremonial speech takes place, two young women hold a piece of cloth over the heads of the bride and groom. Then a happily married young person takes two large cones of sugar (approximately one to one-and-a-half feet) from the cloth on the floor. The cones are decorated with ribbons or flowers. The woman comes up behind the bride and the groom and rubs the flat ends of the sugar cones together so that the granules fall onto the cloth above the couple's head. While doing this, she blesses the couple.

After all married women have taken turns grinding sugar over the newlywed's heads, the remainder of the cones is returned to the floor, and the couple holding the sugar-filled cloth shakes it so that the granules fall on the bridal couple, who attempt to get away without a sugar shower. The ground sugar symbolizes wishes for a sweet future.

ITALIAN

GIFTS Money. One wedding coordinator at an Italian Catholic church advises that at her church, close friends of the bride and groom never give anything under $100. That would be looked upon unfavorably. They are expected to give $300 to $400 per couple, family members even more. Other guests can figure out proportionate amounts depending on their relationship to the couple.

WORDS Old timers say, *"Tanti auguri"* ("Best wishes"). They may also express wishes for a male child, *"E figli maschi"* [eh fée-lee moss-key].

CLOTHING Dressy.

BODY LANGUAGE Lots of hugging and kissing.

Incorporating ethnic roots into contemporary wedding receptions, Italian Americans dance the tarantella and hire musicians to play Neapolitan love songs strummed on mandolins at their weddings. *Confetti*, white sugar-coated almonds, are a hallmark of the reception. Formerly, guests threw them at the bride and groom as a wish for fertility, but that became a dangerous practice. Now, instead, the candy-covered nuts are wrapped in little net bundles and presented at each place setting at the reception meal. The candy comes from Sulmona, *confetti* capital of Italy.

The newlyweds give *bomboniere*, small party favors, to their guests as a thank you for attending, and more extravagant gifts to each member of the wedding party—for example, silver or crystal dishes, often running $25 to $30 each. Add to this the cost of dinners which may be $120 per person, and Italian parents spend a lot on weddings. However, the tradition of *la busta* [boo-stah] (the envelope) helps defray those expenses. After leaving the reception line, guests place money-filled envelopes into a decorated container: a box, mailbox, or birdcage placed on a special table.

Some wedding couples have eliminated the receiving line. Instead, the bride and groom visit each table to greet their guests. This becomes an opportune time to accept money-filled envelopes as is commonly done at Chinese and Vietnamese weddings. However, some Italian couples have now adapted *la busta* to match the famous opening wedding scene in the movie *The Godfather*.

In that film, wearing a silk money purse hung from her shoulder, Connie, Don Vito Corleone's daughter, moved table to table collecting envelopes from those in debt to her father. To emulate this, some brides are ordering large (ten-by-ten-inch) silk shoulder purses to stash the cash-filled envelopes when greeting their seated guests. Designers at Saks Fifth Avenue in Manhattan make *le buste* in fabric matching the wedding gowns.

Other Italian Americans look askance at this. "Too gauche." Old timers comment, "Why, we used to do that during the Depression." In those times of financial hardship, while going through the receiving line, guests commonly handed the bride and groom an envelope with money for living expenses. What makes *la buste* new is having the bride collect with a specially made purse, à la Connie Corleone.

JAPANESE—Buddhist

GIFTS Money, given in special envelopes with appropriate designs and characters and marked for the occasion by *mizuhiki* [mee-zoo-hee-key] (colored ties), (see Birth/Japanese, p. 139; Death/Japanese, p. 230.). These ties may be attached to the envelope or merely printed on the envelope. For weddings, the ties are gold. At the reception, someone receives these envelopes and logs in the amounts of money with the names of the donors. If you do not wish to give money, standard wedding gifts are also appreciated. Avoid giving a matched set to the couple. When giving a husband/wife gift, there should be a slight difference between his and hers, either in color, size, or design. Avoid giving an even number of objects. Traditional Japanese believe that one should not give something that can be divided. That explains why Japanese sets of dishes come in odd numbers and why gifts for the wedding guests are odd-numbered.

WORDS During the reception, the best man makes a toast by saying, "*Banzai!*" (one thousand wishes). However, because of the word's negative connotations associated with World War II, they may substitute "*Kampai!*" (good luck). The best man says the word three times, then takes a drink. Well-wishers join in.

During the ceremony, the priest pours *sake* [sah-kay] (rice wine) into two small sake cups, and the bride and groom sip from each other's sake cup in three sets of three sips totaling nine. Note that the number of times they drink the wine is an odd number. Even numbers indicate that a set is complete, that it is over. That is why they often use even numbers at funerals.

At the reception both Christians and Buddhists display one thousand *origami* [oh-ree-gah-mee] (folded paper) cranes which bridesmaids have helped to make. These are strung together and often hung from a tree. They are good luck symbols, generally gold in color, and sometimes marked with a Chinese character that bodes well for the couple's future.

An older person often reads poetry. The bride's parents give a token gift to guests like souvenir matches or origami cranes.

JEWISH—Orthodox

GIFTS Household items and money placed in an envelope or greeting card are welcome.

WORDS During the ceremony, after the groom successfully breaks the glass, people shout, "*Mazel tov!*" (congratulations or good luck).

CLOTHING Suits for men, women in below-the-knee dresses with modest sleeves and necklines. Men should wear yarmulkes, and a boxfull is usually available for those who do not own one. Non-Orthodox married women cover their heads with hats or scarves.

BODY LANGUAGE Depending on the level of observance, some Orthodox may not separate men from the women, but more commonly males and females sit separately from one another during the ceremony and at the reception. As a form of modesty, separation rules apply to the dance floor as well.

Shortly before her wedding day, the bride visits a *mikvah* [mick-vah] (ritual bath) and undergoes ritual immersion. This represents a spiritual cleansing in preparation for the approaching marriage. Many bridegrooms also observe a ritual immersion in a *mikvah* but are not required to do so. On the day of the wedding, the couple fasts from morning until after the ceremony.

The bride wears a traditional white wedding gown and the groom wears a long white *kittel* (smock) over his regular clothing. Men wear the kittel at their weddings, on *Yom Kippur* (Day of Atonement), and at their funerals. Just prior to the ceremony, the bridegroom and other males gather in a separate room for the signing of the marriage contract, called the *ketubah* [keh-too-bah]. This is a legal contract in accordance with Jewish civil law where the husband guarantees to support his wife. Written in calligraphy in Aramaic, the document is dated according to the Hebrew Calendar. *Ketubot* [keh-two-boat] range from simple pieces of paper to highly decorated parchments designed with flowers, vines, and lions.

The *ketubah* must be signed by two witnesses who are not related to either side. The groom formally accepts its terms by taking hold of a handkerchief handed to him by the Rabbi on behalf of the bride. When finished, the men escort the groom in a singing procession toward the bride who has been waiting in another room. Seated upon a throne-like chair, she blesses and greets family and friends who come to share in her joy, offer her blessings, and sample delicacies arrayed at the laden bride's table.

When the groom meets the bride on her throne, he partakes of a ceremony known as *badeken* (veiling). By placing the veil over her face he confirms that he is marrying the right person and avoids the possibility for deception that caused Jacob to marry Leah instead of Rachel as described in Genesis. The marriage ceremony follows and takes place under a *chupah* [khu-pah, rhymes with book-a] (bridal canopy) which is supported by four poles. It is often made of velvet with embroidery and fringe, other times of flowers, or may be a *tallit* [tall-eét] (prayer shawl), a gift from the bride to the groom. *Chupah* means covering or protection and symbolizes the wedding couple's new home together.

The bride's parents accompany her down the aisle. When she arrives at the *chupah*, she walks around her bridegroom seven times. During the service, the couple shares a goblet of wine and receives seven blessings. Then the groom places a plain gold band, on the bride's right index finger, considered the finger of intelligence because it is the one that points at the words when reading the Torah. Next, the rabbi reads the wedding contract aloud and formally presents it to the bride.

At the conclusion of the ceremony, the groom breaks a glass with his foot. There are many different interpretations of this act, but traditionally it has meant to keep the ceremony from being totally joyous by reminding that no joy can be complete since the destruction of the Temple in Jerusalem two thousand years ago, or it may serve as a reminder that at such a joyous time, one must still be aware of sadness and pain existing in the world.

The newlyweds leave the *chupah* amidst singing and dancing and adjourn to a private room. Originally, this is where they consummated the marriage. Today, it is a time alone together to share a few private moments and break their fast. Soon afterward, they rejoin their guests who have already begun the wedding feast.

Dancing occurs, but men and women dance in separate circles and a fabric screen may separate the dance floor for this purpose. One of the highlights is the chair dance where the bride and groom, seated in chairs, are hoisted into the air and danced around. This is a highly joyous moment. Because dancing with the opposite sex in public is considered immodest, the bride and groom hold opposite ends of a scarf or handkerchief.

To entertain and evoke laughter at the reception, some people may don costumes and women may wear silly hats or rainbow wigs.

SEPHARDIC CEREMONIES

In addition to many of the Orthodox customs, a few days prior to the wedding, the women may have a henna party where they paint symbolic designs on the hands of the bride (see Marriage/Indian, Mehndi, p. 196.). These symbols offer protection from the evil eye. Depending on whether the bride's background is Moroccan, Syrian, or Judeo-Spanish, the bride alone will have her palms and feet decorated for joy and happiness, or she may have just the palms done, or just the right hand. In some situations, all females in attendance will have their hands beautified by henna designs, as well. They may present the bride with a *hamsa* [khóm-zah] (a hand-shaped pendant) for further protection from the evil eye from which brides are most vulnerable.

REFORM AND CONSERVATIVE CEREMONIES

Compared to Orthodox rituals, Reform and Conservative ceremonies are less complex. There is no separation of males and females. They emphasize gender equality rather than differences. For example, instead of the groom presenting the *ketubah* to his bride, the rabbi may hand it to the newly wedded couple, each holding a part of the usually framed document. Their mutual carrying of it symbolizes that each partner must uphold his/her part of the contract.

Often the bride and groom express their love for each other by reciting poetry or personal variations of the wedding vows during the ceremony. At the reception, during the chair dance, brides and grooms may touch one another. Interpretations of the breaking of the glass may include a statement about the symbolic grinding out of violence, hatred, and evil.

KOREAN

ENGAGEMENT—*YAK KON SIK* [yock-cone-sheik]

This very formal occasion is often the first time the groom's family meets the bride's family. An emcee introduces each side of the family giving biographies and histories of each member of the family. Alone and together, the couple sings traditional songs without musical accompaniment.

An important feature is giving gifts to the future bride and groom. If wealthy, the family of the future groom presents the future bride with three sets of jewelry, each set containing a necklace, earrings and bracelet, and each set comprised of a different semi-precious stone, such as sapphires or rubies. They are presented in a *ham* [hom], traditional wooden box. The bride's side presents the future son-in-law with a suit and an expensive watch. In Korea, the bride's family provides the groom with an apartment. Traditionally, the bride's family gives the future mother-in-law an expensive gift. In the United States it may be a fur coat. To not present expensive gifts on this occasion brings about a certain humiliation.

WEDDING

GIFTS Money in any color envelope with your name written on it. Frequently they set up two tables at the reception to collect monetary gifts, one for the bride's guests, the other for the groom's guests. A close and trusted relative guards the collection and tallies the amounts. Housewares are acceptable, but if you give knives, you must receive $1 from the couple to preserve rather than sever the relationship.

WORDS Any form of congratulations.

CLOTHING Dressy clothes show respect. Avoid wearing white, associated with funerals. Females avoid wearing white hair ribbons, also a mourning sign. If the couple has a traditional Korean ceremony, remove shoes before entering the room.

BODY LANGUAGE Nowadays, in most situations, it is acceptable to kiss the bride. Avoid hugging family members. The most respectful form of greeting and salutation is the bow. If you feel uncomfortable with this gesture, nod your head.

Frequently, Koreans hold wedding ceremonies at commercial wedding halls, often located in the Korean business district where they can have both a Western-style and Korean-style wedding, one immediately following the other. At the Western-style wedding, the bride and groom wear traditional Western garb, but afterward they often have a brief ceremony where bride and groom change into traditional clothing. The bride wears a blouse with wide rainbow-striped sleeves, flared skirt of lively colors and vivid embroidery, and a beaded hat, sometimes adorned with jewels. She wears two red dots, like stickers, on her cheeks, reminiscent of the painted rosy cheeks of the past. The groom wears an embroidered blue robe and a *samo* (stiff, black, high crown hat with "wings" on the sides).

During this part of the ceremony, the bride and groom stand in front of the groom's family, who are seated all around them. The bride and groom bow to each other, share *sake* [sah-kay] (rice wine), offer fruit and wine, and bow to each member of the groom's family. Then they sit down and receive blessings from the groom's family. As a means of protecting the couple from evil influences, the groom's family throws nuts to the bride. How many she catches foretells how many children she will have.

Another prognosticator of future children is tied to the behavior of the bride and groom. Since a wedding is a serious occasion, the wedding couple is not supposed to smile. If the bride smiles, it means that her first child will be a girl.

SIXTIETH WEDDING ANNIVERSARY

GIFTS Hand money in envelopes to someone in charge who collects, records, and tallies amounts.

WORDS "Congratulations."

CLOTHING Good clothing.

For this anniversary, the entire traditional Korean wedding ceremony is reenacted in a restaurant, nightclub, or hall. The anniversary couple enters through the main entrance of the room in full Korean wedding regalia, including the bride's rosy-cheek stickers. From afar, the couple may look just as they had sixty years earlier. However, age and arthritis betray them as they attempt to bow, sit down, and rise. It is both humorous and touching to witness.

All the events of the wedding are repeated; an emcee details their individual and couple histories; they display a formalized food table; each relative offers them rice wine; guests sing and dance.

LAO

GIFTS Household items, but avoid giving knives or anything sharp. Money may be enclosed in any color envelope. Write your name and address on the outside and deposit it in a slotted, decorated box sitting on a special table at the reception. If a box is not visible, present the envelope to the person who appears to be in charge.

WORDS All felicitations.

CLOTHING Guests should dress up. Lao women have certain skirts and scarves they wear only when going to temple or attending weddings. The skirts contain many gold threads. In the past, guests would not wear black to a wedding, and in some families this taboo persists. Women wear skirts rather than pants, but no miniskirts. At the home ceremony, remove shoes. If the reception is in a hall and people sit on mats on the floor, remove shoes.

BODY LANGUAGE Avoid kissing the bride. The groom won't kiss her either. There is no kissing at all. Avoid hugging or kissing family members. The respectful greeting for elders or other honored persons is the wai, which is like the Indian namaste (see Marriage/Indian, p. 196.) They will return the gesture.

Prior to the wedding, the families consult in temple with the priest as to the best date for the wedding based on astrological implications. The day before the wedding ceremony, close friends and relatives come to the bride's home for a pre-party where they assist in preparations. During this time, they eat and drink with gusto. The major task, however, is to prepare food for the wedding and to build two identical towers of a flower and leaf arrangement used only at weddings, *pha kouane* [pah kwan]. These towers sit on the floor on a silver or aluminum tray. From these trays, they build a tower about two and a half feet tall constructed of flowers of all colors and kinds except those that have thorns. In Laos, they use banana leaves in the construction, but away from Laos they substitute green, folded paper to which they attach the flowers. Depending on whether the family is from northern or southern Laos, they place different kinds of food offerings at the base of the flowers. These may be rice, whole chickens, eggs, candles, fruits, and sweets. These offerings feed the ancestor spirits.

Generally, the morning ceremony lasts two to three hours and most frequently takes place in the bride's home, where she awaits the groom, his family and other guests. A shaman performs the ceremony. The bride wears a traditional Lao gown with a silk, gold patterned skirt, while the groom wears a dark-colored sarong, often topped by a long-sleeved shirt or military-type jacket.

A striking feature of the Lao wedding is the bride's hairstyle, *kao phom* [cow-pomm], a particular fashion created by a hair specialist who spends up to three hours fixing it. The hairdresser pulls the hair up away from the face and ties it into a bun at a straight angle without one single strand of loose hair. Then the bun is decorated with gold chains and gold jewelry topped by a gold umbrella-type object resembling a flower that sits at the very top of the bun, called *pak pin kao* [pock-pin-cow]. Sometimes these objects have been kept in families for generations. If a bride's family does not own one, they may borrow one from a friend.

During the ceremony, the shaman ties white strings around the wrists of the wedding couple and temporarily connects them to the two towers of flowers and himself. After receiving blessings from the shaman, the bridal couple presents nicely wrapped gifts to their parents, such as a skirt for the mothers or some fabric for a shirt or blouse. Then the couple asks their parents for blessings or forgiveness for any wrong doing in their pasts. In turn, the parents wish them good luck and bless the marriage. Afterward, all the guests tie white strings around the wrists of the wedding couple and offer their blessings in a *baci* [bai-see] or *sou-khoanh* [sue-kwanh] ceremony (see Birth/Cambodian, p. 129; Birth/Hmong, p. 135; Birth/Lao, p. 143; Marriage/Cambodian, p. 186; Marriage/Thai, p. 212.).

They hold the reception in the evening either at home, in a restaurant, or in a hall. While guests are dining, the wedding couple visits each table with a bottle of liquor and a shot glass. The couple thanks the guests for being there, serves the elderly first, then friends of the parents, then the rest of the guests, who all drink from the same glass. The bride and groom drink, too.

Live music and dancing take place. The bride and groom dance first, traditional Lao style in a circle (*lam vong*), but they do not touch one another. Then the parents dance, after which everyone is invited to join in. The men dance inside an inner circle; the women dance outside. Only family members and close friends may dance with the bride, no one else.

When a man wishes to dance with a woman he invites her by performing the *wai* [why] gesture by pressing his hands together in a prayer-like position and bringing them up to just below his chin and nodding slightly.

When the dance is finished the couple makes the *wai* sign to one another as a thank you and form of respect.

MEXICAN

ROMAN CATHOLIC

GIFTS Household items, money in wedding congratulations cards or plain envelopes. Gifts may be sent ahead or brought to the reception.

WORDS *"Felicidades."* [fay-lee-cee-dá-dess] "Congratulations." "May you have a long happy life together."

CLOTHING Suits and ties for men. Nice dresses for women. Dressy pants suits.

BODY LANGUAGE Men may greet each other with an *abrazo*, a hug and simultaneous pats on the back.

The priest performs the marriage in the middle of a Mass. After the exchange of vows and the rings, one of the *Padrinos de Arras* [pah-dreé-nose deh ár-rahs] (sponsors in charge of the money and rings), hands thirteen dime-like coins encased in a heart-shaped or pillbox-sized chest to the priest, who hands it to the groom, who in turn, gives it to the bride. Symbolically he is saying, "I will always take care of your material needs." Her acceptance means that she will use the money to take care of their household.

In the nineteenth century, this custom meant that the groom would give the bride his future earnings, which would be plentiful. After the bride accepted the coins, which in those times were real and often of gold, she spilled them. They then became the property of the officiating priest, to be used for furnishing the church or distributing to the poor.

In modern services, after the vows, a lasso of silk and flowers or two cords or ribbons are placed over the couple as they kneel. This signifies that they will be together always.

NIGERIAN
Ibo [ée-bow]

GIFTS Since the bride's family provides most of the gift items, money is preferred.

WORDS "Long life." "Good Health." Give marital advice: "Don't go to bed mad." "Marriage is for better or for worse." "You must have good communication."

CLOTHING Dressy.

Following a typical Roman Catholic or Protestant church ceremony, the wedding party and friends move to a large hall for a reception that lasts about five hours. The breaking of kola nuts by a male elder is the most important part of the ritual. The elder takes the nut and begins a prayer consisting of a series of affirmations such as: "May the marriage last," "May they live in peace," "May they have children both male and female," "May they not bring shame to the family." After each statement, everyone responds with *Ibo* words, "*Ise*" [ee-say] or "*Ofor*," [oh-for] both meaning "Amen." At the end of the prayer, the kola nut is broken and everyone claps. Other guests make toasts, and everyone samples the bitter-tasting nut.

As an adaptation of the African dowry tradition, in the United States, the bride's family participates in the custom called "sending her home." The bride's family buys most of the items to help their daughter start a new household in her husband's home. Items may include furniture, cooking utensils, clothing, perhaps a car. The family displays the gifts outside the new home, but they do not bring them indoors until after the wedding ceremony. These items demonstrate the family's support for their daughter and publicly announce, "Thank you for being a good daughter."

Because as many as five thousand people may attend, a Committee of Friends organizes fund-raising to assist. If other Nigerians cannot afford to give money, they volunteer to bring food: baked chicken, pans of rice. Friends provide at least eighty percent of the food.

SAMOAN

GIFTS Bring paper money to put on the bride during her dollar dance. Place gifts on a table set aside to receive them. Give housewares or money tucked inside congratulatory cards or plain envelopes.

WORDS *"Talofa fa'amálo"* [tah-lów-fa-fa-ah-máh-low] "Congratulations."

CLOTHING Respectful church attire.

Samoans are Christians, most belonging to Congregational churches. Therefore, wedding ceremonies take place in church and follow the customs of the particular denomination. Inside the church, the wedding couple looks like any other with the bride in a traditional white gown, groom in a tuxedo, and their attendants in coordinated outfits. Full-fledged Samoan traditions surface at the reception.

All Samoan rites of passage are noted for their joyousness and generosity, and wedding receptions are prime examples with the emphasis on singing, dancing, feasting, and having a good time. Immediately after the church ceremony, the bride and groom change into traditional outfits. Often the bride's dress is of natural colored woven fabric trimmed with brilliant red and yellow feathers around the neckline, waist, and mid-calf hemline. She also wears a head ornament of red and white feathers.

The groom wears a *lavalava* (wrap-around skirt) with a white long shirt over it and a white floral lei. If they hold the reception outdoors, he will be shirtless. Some of the female guests wear muumuus (loose brightly colored dresses) and the men may wear *lavalavas*.

Reception activities include presenting the bridal couple with fine mats, traditional singing, and dancing by performers in native costumes accompanied by a Samoan band. In one of the highlights, the bride dances alone in the middle of the dance floor and guests attach dollar bills to her clothes or stick them to her body, which is easy to do because she has oiled herself with coconut oil. This not only makes the money adhere but makes her body shine as well. The bride alone receives the money while she dances, but her husband dances close by as a sign of support.

Whole roasted pigs lying on wooden pallets and placed on the floor in front of the head table are another specialty. Roasted pigs presented in such a fashion are hallmarks of Samoan feasts. The pigs are prepared in underground rock-lined ovens in backyards or at commercial bakeries that have sufficient-sized ovens to accommodate them. The higher the social status of the couple, the more roasted pigs are displayed.

A tradition apt to surprise first-time guests is the appearance of cardboard boxes, the size that holds two dozen canned drinks. These sit at individual place settings and may contain a whole fish, a whole chicken, cooked yam, large slabs of corned beef, pork ribs with potato salad, cold noodle salad, fruit salad, and a canned soft drink. Guests are expected to sample the food but take most of it home to their families in the cardboard containers. This tradition reflects the strong Samoan emphasis on community sharing.

THAI

GIFTS Bring them to the reception. The bride receives jewelry from her husband's family. Give envelopes with money, and write your name on the outside and hand it to the person who seems to be in charge. If you give a household gift, avoid knives or anything sharp. Avoid giving handkerchiefs, representing future tears. Avoid giving matches, a symbol of danger.

WORDS Wish them a successful, long life together.

CLOTHING Dressy clothes. Avoid black.

BODY LANGUAGE Traditional people use the wai gesture as a sign of respect (see Marriage/Lao, p. 207.). Younger, more Americanized Thai may be open to shaking hands, hugging, or kissing. Observe others before you act.

Thai customs vary according to region. In the northeast they resemble those of neighboring Laos. Outside, customs seem to mix. Prior to the temple ceremony, people tie white strings around one wrist of the wedding couple. Each guest takes a piece of precut string and ties a knot in the middle and then ties it to one wrist of the couple's hands. This is a form of blessing. The act is repeated at the wedding ceremony and later at the reception (see Birth/ Hmong, p. 135; Birth/Lao, p. 143; Birth/ Thai, p. 151; Marriage/Cambodian, p. 186.).

The ceremony takes place at home or at the temple. In a one-hour ceremony, the monk blesses the couple, who are dressed in traditional Thai costumes. The monk talks about Buddha's teachings and gives five rules for married life, that include being honest with one another and advising the husband to provide for his wife according to his economic status.

A respected elder, one who only has been married once and has remained with his partner his whole life, blesses the couple. The couple kneels in front of him and he links them together by placing a loop of white thread on their heads. Then over their hands, he pours sacred water into bowls of flowers. Guests follow suit as a means of anointing the bride and groom. Before leaving the temple, the newlyweds offer food and money donations for the monks. Later, they celebrate at an evening wedding reception, generally held in a Thai restaurant where, as a part of the festivities, they dance Western style.

TIBETAN

GIFTS White scarves, money in envelopes, offerings of tea and rice wine. Anything but shoes, which symbolize parting company.

WORDS "Have a long, good life together."

CLOTHING Dressy.

BODY LANGUAGE Avoid kissing the bride. Use the namaste for greetings (see Marriage/Indian, p. 196). The urbanized younger generation may shake hands.

A young Tibetan man who wishes to marry sends two friends to the home of the young woman he has selected. They bring her parents tea and champagne or a rice wine called *chang* [rhymes with song]. The emissaries ask for the young woman's hand, but the parents never make a commitment. They say they must consult with their daughter.

Two to four weeks later, the friends return bringing more tea and chang. If the girl or her parents do not like the young man, her parents will say their daughter is not ready at this time. If the girl and her family are interested, parents make no commitment. However, lack of rejection signifies agreement.

The third visit is akin to an engagement ceremony. The groom sends four or five people with many gifts for the bride and her family. They present tea, expensive fabric, and white scarves to everyone (see Birth/Tibetan, p. 152; Death/Tibetan, p. 246.). They give the bride's mother one or more trays holding small white fabric bags filled with paper money rolled up in vertical cylinders.

Each bag is tied with a white scarf and looks like a flower. These bags are called *nureen* (payment for milk) and show gratitude to the mother for nurturing the bride-to-be.

The families set the wedding date according to astrological calculations, and the day before the nuptials, the bride's family hosts a party. Everyone dons colorful Tibetan clothing, hats, and shoes. The bride wears a *patu*, a black wig with two cone-like rolls of hair standing upright on each side of her head. A Y-shaped woven fabric strip, adorned with turquoise and coral, attaches to each cone, its tail reaching midway down the bride's back. The bride also wears elaborate and large turquoise earrings and a turquoise necklace that looks more like a breastplate.

During the evening, the groom takes five arrows that have been bound together with braided strips of silk in the five sacred colors of blue, green, red, yellow, and white, and inserts them vertically down the back of the bride's dress. The upper half is visible. She removes them before sleep.

On the wedding day, at about 10 a.m., the groom's emissaries drive in cars decorated with colored ribbons to pick up the bride to take her to the groom's family's home. One of the escorts carries a painting of a deity. Another escort replaces the arrows into the back of the bride's dress. Meanwhile, at the groom's home, the bride's emissaries hang scarves in the sacred five colors on his front door and one scarf on the inside door leading to the home altar.

Before the bride enters her future home, a boy offers her *chima* [chi-máh], a mixture of roasted barley and wheat seed, which she flicks into the air three times. She then dips her ring finger into the *chang* (rice wine) three times and flicks it, too. Once inside, the bride joins her groom who waits for her seated in front of the altar. Guests offer white scarves to the wedding party accompanied by envelopes filled with money. They make additional offerings of tea, rice wine, and the *chima*. At the late-night conclusion of the ceremony, as guests leave, they form a circle, sing, burn incense, and offer the chima to the gods three times. Upon leaving, each guest receives a white scarf.

VIETNAMESE

GIFTS Red money envelopes often hold $50 from a single person and $100 from a couple. In addition to money, other gifts may be given, but avoid giving handkerchiefs, which presage tears; clocks, which are omens of death; and scissors or knives, which symbolize the severing of a relationship. Avoid giving anything white, such as towels, pillowcases, or candles because white is associated with funeral rituals. Give pink linens because pink and red are associated with good luck.

WORDS Congratulations.

CLOTHING Good clothing.

If they are Christians, the wedding ceremony takes place in church and the bride wears a traditional Western white wedding gown. If they are Buddhists, the ceremony takes place at the temple or at home in front of an altar. In both situations, they hold dinner receptions at a restaurant. The bride changes into a Mandarin-style red gown embroidered on the front with an entwined dragon and phoenix and worn over baggy pants.

The bride may change into different colored outfits at different stages during the event—during the ceremony, when greeting guests, when cutting the cake. Nowadays, she wears a white, Western-style bridal gown at the end of the reception. Bridesmaids, too, change outfits. All the men and women in the bridal party wear headpieces called *khan dong*. The men wear them lower on the forehead and the women wear them more like a crown.

In Buddhist families, the groom's family arrives in procession at the home of the bride with offerings of roast pig, red-dyed sticky rice, tea, red wine, brandy, and cakes covered with red cloths with gold fringe, and a black lacquer box holding the two wedding rings. Servings are double, everything in twos. They place the gifts on the altar inside the bride's home. The altar, decorated with gold-trimmed red covers, holds additional offerings of incense, flowers, fruit, and red candles.

The couple kneels and bows before the shrine to pay their respects to the bride's ancestors. After the bride thanks her parents and they advise that she live up to their expectations, they place the rings on their fingers and the groom's mother and sisters present the bride with gold jewelry. The couple eats some of the food, and then the groom and his family, taking some of the food they have brought to the bride's home, leave and repeat the ritual at the home of the groom.

When guests arrive at the reception, generally held in a Vietnamese or Chinese restaurant, they sign their names on a piece of red fabric. Later, one person from each of the round banquet tables for ten collects red envelopes containing money from each single guest or each couple (see Marriage/Chinese, p. 187; Marriage/Italian, p. 199.). This money defrays the cost of the banquet. When the bride and groom visit the table, a self-appointed envelope-gatherer hands the envelopes to the bride, who in turn gives them to one of her bridesmaids for safekeeping. In exchange, the bride gives a small wedding token to each guest, for example, a miniature wedding shoe or flower or tiny wine cup.

The newlyweds live with the groom's family. They strongly believe that the bride and groom must be the first ones to sit on their wedding bed. Sometimes the mother-in-law prepares the wedding bed and locks the bedroom door so that no one accidentally breaks this taboo. If a pregnant woman were to sit on the bed, it would foretell of arguments between the bride and groom.

[8]

DEATH CELEBRATIONS
"Ashes to ashes, dust to dust"

We have control over most rites of passage. Even with birth, we have a pretty good idea when it will occur, so we have time to prepare. With death, we never know. Unless the deceased has left explicit instructions, planning for the ritual is hurried. Even if someone has been lingering near death, the final moment shocks us and that frequently prevents us from efficient organizing.

Because of its mystery, many customs shroud death. If mourners do not strictly conform to funeral rites and mourning customs, the deceased might be negatively affected in the afterlife. Even worse, spirits of the dead might linger on earth too long and interfere with the living.

Most immigrants from the early twentieth century and before now observe mainstream death rituals. These practices have become homogenized through time, traditional religions, and the standardizing influence of the mortuary industry. However, the heavy influx of late-twentieth century immigrants has changed that. Funeral practices have become more complex, designed to meet the needs of these newest grieving families, who tend to cling to the traditions of their homelands, especially in times of sorrow. Some of these changes include larger-sized family participation, more personal involvement in the preparation of the body, more days and nights of final farewells.

AFRICAN AMERICAN

NEW ORLEANS OR JAZZ FUNERAL

Spirited funerals with traditions rooted in West Africa and the West Indies are a tourist attraction of New Orleans. Famous jazz musicians, such as Louis Armstrong, Jelly Roll Morton, Bunk Johnson, and Kid Ory developed their licks playing at these joyful processions. Until the 1960s, only jazz musicians received these heavenly send-offs. Since then, any New Orleans resident qualifies for this colorful burying ceremony.

In the past, slow-stepping, white-gloved pallbearers carried the casket from the mortuary onto the hearse, and a marching brass band played hymns in a dirge-like tempo: "Just a Closer Walk with Thee" or the "Old Rugged Cross." Somberly they placed the casket into one of New Orleans' above ground graves, but as mourners marched away from the cemetery, melancholia transformed into jubilation when spectators joined in the parade and began their feverish "second line." (Second line refers to the group that marched behind the musicians.) The second line set up its own syncopation as a counter rhythm to the beat of the brass band (see Marriage/ African American/New Orleans, p. 179.).

Nowadays, second line dancers may dance from the church into the cemetery. Carrying an umbrella decorated with sequins, feathers, flowers, or fringe, the leader of the second line struts along the funeral route. Those who follow imitate his exaggerated motions until the line becomes a sinuous snake dance—bobbing, zigzagging, and gyrating through the streets. Sometimes a group of dancers circles a single dancer or duos who perform their own routines. The soloists dance free-form with myriad dance styles: cakewalking, stamping, jumping, crossing of feet and legs; but the second liners maintain their special steps: toe, whole foot, knee flex, and twist.

Although not costumed, sometimes second liners roll up their trousers or add handkerchiefs around their necks or wear them as headbands. Some wear white aprons; others in addition to the leader carry decorated umbrellas, too. A dancer without an umbrella grasps an unfolded white handkerchief between thumbs and index finger. As the second liners dance, they unfurl and snap the handkerchiefs overhead in time to the music.

Frequently, as the second line weaves around the city and excitement swells, they stop at a tavern to have a quick one or perhaps a free one at places that once served as watering holes for the now deceased.

No longer exclusively African American, the second line is open to anyone to participate and sometimes grows to hundreds of dancers. Anyone can join in the fun and wait with both anticipation and sadness for what is often the closing signature tune, "When the Saints Go Marching In."

AMISH

GIFTS Prepared food for the family. A condolence card or note. Avoid giving flowers.

WORDS "My condolences to you and your family."

CLOTHING For women, dresses with arms covered, modest necklines, and hemlines below the knees. Avoid open-toed shoes and jewelry. Wear minimal or no makeup. For men, jackets, ties, and white shirts.

Like Amish weddings, funerals take place at home, and customs vary according to particular branches of their religion. Most Amish communities now embalm the dead to give time for relatives to travel to the funeral. In Lancaster County, Pennsylvania, family members wash the body before the undertaker embalms it. The mortuary returns the body to the family home dressed in long underwear. Family members dress the men in a white shirt, white vest, and white pants, and women are dressed in their wedding day white capes and aprons, sometimes the same dresses.

Generally, Amish woodworking shops produce the coffins, shaped wider at the shoulders than at the head and feet, with a simple white lining. They place the coffins inside the house and observe a wake or night watch for two days. The funeral takes place on the third day. Sometimes so many people attend, that they hold two simultaneous services, one in the house, and another in a barn for the overflow. After the closing prayer and benediction, the minister delivers a brief obituary.

Graveside, the congregation may sing a hymn followed by silently saying the Lord's Prayer. Frequently the men remove their hats when the minister speaks. Often four pallbearers bear the coffin, usually neighbors and friends, but sometimes male kin. After the ceremony, they serve a simple funeral meal at home. One must be invited to attend an Amish funeral and those few non-Amish who were close friends with the deceased will be included.

ARMENIAN

GIFTS No gifts.

WORDS "I'm sorry" and other simple words of comfort.

CLOTHING Black.

After the person dies, the family visits the home of the deceased to drink bitter coffee. They drink bitter coffee again after the funeral. Emotions are openly expressed; some may wail during the services. At the burial site, Russian Armenians drink vodka and toast the departed and help shovel the dirt onto the lowered casket. When mourners return home, they immediately enter the bathroom to wash their hands.

The family holds a dinner immediately after the funeral, then again at forty days, and at the one year anniversary of the death. Sometimes hundreds attend the dinner immediately following the funeral, served in either the church hall or a restaurant. They prepare shish kebab, rice, and chicken. On the seventh day after the funeral, they hold a service at the cemetery and serve food afterward, especially Russian Armenians. On the fortieth day, the priest comes to the cemetery for Mass, and afterward the family rents a place to serve lunch or dinner. At the one year anniversary of the death, they publish a notice in the Armenian newspapers inviting anyone who desires to attend a dinner for the soul of the deceased.

BUDDHIST

The U.S. mortuary industry has made numerous adaptations to serve the needs of the growing Buddhist population. Some bury; others cremate. Often the funeral homes work in concurrence with religious astrologers, who determine which dates are the most auspicious for services. Some funeral homes allow twenty-four-hour tape-recorded chanting of Buddhist monks. They install ceiling fans and fire-resistant tile floors to allow for indoor incense burning. They supply tables for constructing temporary shrines, and some companies have installed kitchens for the preparation of ritual food. At the grave, family and friends often leave food, ranging from full plates to a solitary orange.

Additionally, outdoor incinerators may be provided so mourners can burn paper money, paper replicas of homes as large as six feet, and cars—often Mercedes-Benz, clothing, and other items believed necessary for the journey to the next world and an easy life thereafter.

One funeral home in Orange County, California, built a separate chapel according to Vietnamese ritual needs, which included a large viewing room to allow the relatives and friends, sometimes numbering up to seventy, to watch the body entering the furnace.

Services may be held at the funeral home, and laypersons, with or without monks, chant appropriate prayers. They have a large photograph of the deceased on a stand or table near the casket, and at the temple they offer flowers and fruit and burn incense. As a sign of mourning, family members may wear white headbands and arm bands.

They remember the dead each year in August on Buddhist All Souls' Day, when they hold special temple services. Memorial services are important observances.

CAMBODIAN

GIFTS Money, enclosed in an envelope of any color. If the deceased was a husband, give it to the widow. If the deceased was a widowed mother, give the envelope to the eldest or most responsible child.

WORDS Express your sadness. Praise the deceased. Tell the family that you share in their loss. Tell them you are sorry that they have lost such a fine person.

CLOTHING Mourners wear white or black. Guests wear black or dark colors.

BODY LANGUAGE Use the *wai* [why] as a respectful greeting. Press hands together in a prayerlike position and bring them up to just below the chin and nod slightly. Avoid male/female body contact.

When a person dies, the family prepares a basket filled with the objects the deceased will need in the next life, such as new clothes, rice, medications, cooking, and eating utensils. If the person lies dying at home or in the hospital, to give him or her confidence the family shows the patient the basket full of objects; this lets them know that their material needs for the next life will be met.

At the internment ceremony, the monk prays over the body before the coffin is lowered into the grave. Seven days after the death, the family has a ceremony at home and dedicates the objects in the basket to the spirit of the dead. A monk officiates to assist in steering the spirit toward a good place so he can be reborn again at a higher level.

CHINESE

BUDDHIST

GIFTS At the ceremony, survivors of the deceased hand out red envelopes containing money to thank people who helped during the ceremony, such as the minister or priest, drivers, pallbearers, eulogizers, soloists or musicians. In addition, as guests leave the service, they receive red envelopes containing a coin and a piece of candy. Flowers may be sent to the mortuary, not to the home. They should be white or yellow, never red. The family avoids bringing flowers home from the cemetery. When making condolence calls, bring prepared food, pastries, and depending on financial need, a white envelope containing cash.

WORDS General expressions of condolence.

CLOTHING Nothing flowery or flashy.

Sometimes a New Orleans-style jazz band parades through Chinatown. The procession usually passes by the deceased's home and place of business. Next comes an open car displaying a large photo of the deceased decorated with white flowers and sometimes carrying the sons or grandsons of the deceased. The hearse follows, trailed by other cars carrying family members. If the family is Buddhist or Taoist, the first son may walk in front of the hearse carrying an incense burner. The procession follows a zigzag course ensuring that the hearse not cross over its own path. To do so brings bad luck. At the funeral home, sometimes Christians will also burn incense as part of their Chinese heritage. The family may hire professional mourners to wail and shriek during the ceremony.

In front of the tombstone or stele, they burn three sticks of incense and place offerings on a red cloth sometimes holding a rice wine bottle with two wine cups, and perhaps a bowl of uncooked rice or fresh fruit. Nowadays, after the ceremony, family and friends go to a Chinese restaurant for a special meal. In the late nineteenth century, in California as well as in some places in China today, they place a whole barbecued pig, a whole parboiled chicken, a plate of *dim sum*, a bowl of rice, and sometimes fresh fruit in front of the tombstone. These are offerings to the spirit of the newly departed and the ancestors. In addition, they offer fake money called hell notes, symbolically used to help the deceased buy their way out of hell. This money is burned in an adjacent incinerator along with other paper replicas, clothing, houses, TVs, Mercedes-Benz, items thought to provide luxury in the afterlife.

In the past, when they did not go to a restaurant after the ceremony, those attending ate the graveside food offerings instead of burning them. Food offerings occur at the one year memorial and subsequent annual feeding of the souls. The spring holiday *ching ming* is equivalent to a community memorial day with a general cleaning of the cemetery and graves followed by food and flower offerings.

Today at the restaurant following the service, they avoid having an even number of tables, for this might repeat the pattern of death. In addition, those paying for the funeral home services generally do not write checks because ultimately the checks return to the signers, and the death symbol would also return. Instead they prefer to pay in cash.

Some mourners refrain from visiting other people's homes until thirty days have passed.

EGYPTIAN—Coptic

GIFTS Flowers, food for the family, or money placed inside a condolence card.

WORDS "May you not see sorrow again." "May the Lord console you." When a young person dies, they frequently say, "May the remainder of his expected years be added to your life."

CLOTHING Black. Men wear dark or black suits with black ties. Women wear black dresses, no pants. Women mourners and guests wear no makeup. Red is taboo.

BODY LANGUAGE Men and women sit on separate sides of the church.

Prior to the funeral, family members and close friends go to the home of the deceased to drink black coffee. The funeral generally takes place three days after death. Inside the church, they place the closed casket facing east. This is in accordance with the layout of the church which is always built on an east/west axis. The congregation looks eastward; the priest looks westward. The coffin is placed parallel to the people, facing east, because they believe that the Lord will come from the east.

Although they no longer use professional mourners, the family cries and wails during the ceremony. Mourners wear black, and women in the immediate family may wear chapel veils. The graveside ceremony is brief, just a prayer or two. Family members do not shovel dirt over the casket.

ETHIOPIAN

GIFTS Money or food brought to the mourners' home. Those who bring food are expected to eat with the mourners.

WORDS Expressions of encouragement such as "Be strong." "It is a matter of time." "Your pain is my pain." "If you need help, call on me."

CLOTHING Black for women and men, who must also wear black ties.

Most Ethiopians prefer to be buried in Ethiopia, and if possible, the community raises money to ship the body home. If not, they hold the ceremony approximately two to three days after death. During the religious service they pray and have eulogies and much crying takes place. They display a lot of emotionality, including wailing. Commonly, friends weep openly.

Following the burial, they have a funeral meal, and everyone brings food to the home of the deceased for three days, during which time the family stays at home in respect for the dead.

Forty days after the death, the family goes to church to pray for the deceased, and close friends and relatives return home with the mourners. At this time, if the main mourner is a widow, she will be encouraged to discard her mourning clothes and return to a normal life. In spite of well-intentioned urging by friends and family, widows and widowers usually ignore the advice until one year has passed.

HAWAIIAN

GIFTS Money in white envelopes. Guests also place leis over the casket as a sign of respect.

CLOTHING Subdued colors in Western or aloha wear.

BODY LANGUAGE As a message of condolence, guests must approach the elders of the family and give them a hug and a kiss on one cheek. Kisses and hugs for the rest of the mourners are signs of respect.

The deceased wears traditional aloha clothing, a muumuu for a woman, preferably white or one of her favorite colors, and an aloha shirt for a man. The deceased may also wear traditional jewelry of gold, koa wood, or kukui nut. Sometimes they place a Bible or a Hawaiian hymnal in the casket. They may also use a Hawaiian flag casket coverlet draped over the casket instead of an American flag. The immediate family may be dressed in white.

At the service, whether or not the deceased is Christian or Buddhist, an elder gives a blessing in Hawaiian which may also be translated into English. This elder, *kahu*, may be either male or female. If the deceased was of royalty or very high status, they will post pairs of *kahili*, poles topped by colored feathers. Sometimes during the vigil, two women or men will maintain a twenty-four-hour watch, one at the head of the casket and the other at the foot.

In the old days, family members or professional mourners would wail. That tradition has been modified, and family members may still wail or some wailing may precede the eulogy or reading from the Twenty-third Psalm. In addition to prayers and readings from the Bible, they also chant. Often they have Hawaiian music—guitar, stand-up bass, and ukulele— playing favorite songs of the deceased.

During the church or temple service, attendees bring leis to place on the casket. They place a *hala* fruit lei at this time because it signifies separation, the end of one era and the start of another. They also wear the *hala* fruit lei at New Year's and retirement celebrations. The *hala* fruit is a pod that is combined with either a ti leaf or a fern. If you give one of these leis to someone at New Year's or at a retirement celebration, you never place it over their head or else you might sever the relationship. Instead, you hand the lei to the other person, and the recipient places this special lei around his or her own neck.

A memorial feast follows at a luau-like celebration. It is not a somber event because they believe the deceased has joined his ancestors. When possible, prior to death, they may hold a celebration of life with the dying person present to hear the tributes that will be paid him or her after they die.

HMONG [mong]

GIFTS Money enclosed in a white envelope and handed to the family representative in charge. If you are not sure who this is, ask. At the funeral, they publicly declare amounts given, and if the amount is generous, two or three family members may approach the donor and show respect for the generosity of the guest by bowing to that person. They do not send written acknowledgments.

CLOTHING Red is taboo. In Hmong culture, red represents blood and therefore is dangerous. This prohibition is so powerful that during the Vietnam War, if family members of a soldier dreamed of something red, they would ask their leader for permission for the soldier not to go to the front line. If they send a nasty note to someone and enclose a red tissue, it means, "We will be enemies forever."

BODY LANGUAGE Older community members avoid body contact. They do not use any physical greeting gesture. If a married Hmong woman shakes a man's hand or smiles at another man, she disrespects her husband. Some of the younger generation may shake hands with non-Hmong.

Hmong dread autopsies. They believe that an autopsy in this life causes the person to be mutilated in the next life. An autopsy also drives the soul to return and brings illness to family members and their descendants. Moreover, they believe that embalming may cause future misfortune.

Many of the complex Hmong traditional practices have been altered or eliminated by the Hmong living here. One major reason is that most deaths occur in the hospital where family members have no access to the body. For example, they cannot wash and dress the deceased immediately following death. Later, however, they place *paj ntaub* [paw-dow] (hand-stitched fabric) inside the coffin to insure the spirit's wealth and dress their dead in special shoes believed needed for the journey to the afterlife. Made of woven hemp, the shoes turn up at the toes allowing the souls to safely walk on dangerous paths, step over valleys of snakes, and cross the big river on their way to the spirit world.

Another conflict arises because of the authority of mortuaries and their inflexibility of scheduling; Hmong prefer to bury in the afternoons because they believe the souls of the dead leave the body at sunset. If buried in the morning, the souls might return. Other problems arise with animal sacrifice, an important aspect of funeral rituals in Laos that conflicts with laws here. However, funeral directors allow Hmong mourners to bring in a live chicken which must be immediately removed. The sustained loud playing of the *queej* [cane] (six reed pipes inserted into a wooden wind chamber) and funeral drums during visitation in the mortuary cause other grieving families to complain, especially since the pipes and drums must play for at least three days. If there is no *queej* player at the funeral, the soul of the deceased won't be guided on its journey and will not be reborn. Not only that, it might make relatives sick. Some funeral homes request that the music not be played during concurrent services of non-Hmong.

They must have wooden caskets that are pegged and glued; they permit no metal or plastic. To allow the spirit to escape, the grave liner has no bottom. Sometimes they confer with a geomancer (a specialist who divines the best physical site) about the most propitious site for the grave; the best places are those with a view of the mountains. They decorate the graves by placing stones in patterns over the grave. If the family has become Christian, they adorn it with a cross. At the burial, they engage in ceremonial wailing and ritual drumming, and following burial, they return to their homes for a ceremonial meal.

Thirteen days after burial they conduct a soul-releasing ceremony to ascertain whether the deceased's soul has agreed to return to the spirit world. While difficult to carry this out in this country, some still are able to do so. They create the replica of an upper body dressed in traditional Hmong clothing. To distinguish between male and female, they put a hat on the head for a man and a turban to represent a woman. Afterward, they place the mannequin on a large woven bamboo plate and an elder invites the soul of the deceased to return home to take residence inside the mannequin. In the late afternoon, they carry the mannequin to a small hill or slope in the road, remove the mannequin and allow the plate to roll down the hill. It must roll down three times and fall face down or the action must be repeated. When the plate falls face down after three complete rolls, it signifies that the soul has agreed to leave for the spirit world. Seeing the plate fall face downward is the major method of ensuring that the soul is departing for the spirit world. It qualms anxieties of those left on earth. This marks the official end of the funeral.

INDIAN—Brahman

GIFTS Bring food to the mourners' home during the twelve days after the death. During the twelve days, friends may also send flowers to their home. Avoid offering money.

WORDS "I'm sorry."

CLOTHING Solemn colors, black preferred.

Brahman households possess sealed copper containers containing Ganges water. Therefore, if anyone is on his deathbed, they unseal the container and pour the holy water into the dying person's mouth which is the equivalent of anointing them with Ganges holy water. Then they allow the person to die.

Hindus believe that life deeds influence whether or not they will be reborn, but the words they speak prior to the moment of death have significance, too. If the dying person chants the names of the gods at their last breath, they will go directly to heaven. Thus they will not have to be reborn, which is their greatest desire.

The priest invokes prayers within a few days of death. Often there is a delay to allow family members to gather. In this country, both men and women witness the cremation ceremony, and the eldest son pushes the button to set off the crematorium. After witnesses leave, they pour water on their heads. When they return to their own homes, they take a bath, wash their hair, and wash their clothes. Through this purification act, they symbolically divest themselves of death.

They believe that the soul is still present for twelve days after death. During this time, they demonstrate their grief by crying. In India, they hire professional mourners to wail, but they do not observe this in the United States. During the twelve days of mourning, the family refrains from cooking in their home, so others bring food to them. On the thirteenth day, which is the day they believe the soul departs, crying ceases so as to release the soul. Mourners are not allowed to go to temple until this date, and if they miss this particular time, they can't enter the temple until after the first year.

On a weekend soon after the funeral, they hold a memorial service. In addition to chanting and singing, the priest gives a talk, or a friend may give a sermon. This is not a sad occasion because they believe that the soul has gone on to better things.

JAPANESE—Buddhist

GIFTS Koden [coe-den] is a monetary offering to the family of the deceased, originally used for incense, now used to cover other funeral expenses. If economic assistance is not needed, the family donates the money to charity. If you are not closely connected to the family, $20 would be an appropriate amount. Enclose the money in special envelopes marked by black and silver ties (see Birth/Japanese, p. 139; Marriage/Japanese, p. 201). Give the envelope to a family representative or receptionist. If you do not have access to these envelopes, a plain white envelope will do. The money should be clean, preferably new bills, and wrapped in white paper before being placed inside the envelope. The representative collects the *koden* and marks down the amount given and the name of the donor. This information is given to the widow (if the deceased was a married man), who then logs the information into a *koden* book. She uses this book as reference for giving an equal amount when someone in the donor's family dies. In acknowledgment of the donation, the family may send a card or token gift in return, frequently a book of stamps because it is practical and easy to mail. However, in urban centers, this custom is beginning to fade. As an alternative, the family may send notification that a donation has been made to some charity.

WORDS "Sabishiku narimashita desho" [sah-bee-she-coo-nah-ree-mah-she-tah deh-show] (You must be terribly lonely). Avoid saying, "He or she has gone to a better place."

CLOTHING Somber colors, not necessarily white or black.

Many Japanese Buddhist funeral traditions have been eliminated. Mourners no longer wear white clothing, nor do they use professional mourners. In addition, they do not burn paper houses or cars or money as funeral offerings.

The tolling of the bells signals the beginning of the temple service. The bells are struck in a particular funeral sequence: twice, followed by a crescendo and decrescendo, then five times followed by another crescendo and decrescendo, then a final three times. During this time, the guests rise and the pall-bearers bring in the casket. The casket is usually open during the service.

The ceremony proceeds with chanting; incense offerings by family, relatives, pallbearers, and congregation; prayers; eulogies; and a sermon. The funeral ends with a family representative giving words of appreciation to those attending the funeral and those involved in conducting it. Then they close the casket.

After the funeral, the family sometimes gives rice crackers to those who attended. Generally, in urban centers where large numbers of people attend the service, there is no large gathering to eat following the funeral. Cremation or burial usually takes place the morning after the funeral. Memorial services take place on the seventh, thirtieth, and one hundredth day. During this time, mourners offer incense, plain white rice cakes, and white flowers. At the thirty-day and one-year ceremonies, the family shares a meal together following the service.

A special memorial service occurs at the *obon* [oh-bone] festival each summer at a *hatsubon* [hot-sue-bone], a ceremony to honor the return of the departed the first year after their death. Mourners go to the temple, burn incense, and send floating lanterns into the ocean. The lights guide the souls as they journey back to the spirit world.

JEWISH—Orthodox

GIFTS Avoid sending flowers, either to the cemetery or to the home. Food may be brought to the house. For the Orthodox, anything cooked must be kosher and sealed. Fresh fruit is always appropriate. They sometimes request donations to charity in the deceased's name.

WORDS Avoid references to the afterlife. "I'm sorry" is acceptable. Since the departed can no longer speak, one should observe silence in their presence. If speech (other than prayer and eulogy) is unavoidable, it should be in undertones.

CLOTHING For women, long-sleeved clothes in somber colors with hemlines mid-calf or longer. Necklines must be modest. Suits and ties for men. They must wear a yarmulke (skullcap) during the service and graveside. Extras are available for those not owning any. Married women cover their heads with either a scarf or hat.

BODY LANGUAGE During the service, men and women sit separate from one another.

At the funeral chapel Orthodox Jews employ a *shomer* [show-mare], someone who guards the dead until burial and prays over the body as a sign of respect. These *shomrim* [shom-reem] are observant Jews, often students or semi-retired people. Shifts last twelve to twenty-four hours and the *shomer* is supposed to remain awake the entire time, continuously reciting psalms and other religious texts to uplift the deceased's soul. Some *shomrim* receive pay for their work, while others perform this service on a volunteer basis.

The body must be buried as soon as possible without embalming. They place it in a wooden casket, which remains closed. Caskets must be kosher, which means that rabbis supervise construction: they are not built on the Sabbath and they use only vegetable glue, wooden dowels, and no metal, including screws. Kosher caskets have holes on the bottom to promote the quick decomposition and swift return to earth.

At services they read from the psalms, and one to three persons may give brief eulogies. Men and women sit separately.

After the body has been lowered into the grave, everyone helps shovel dirt over the body. They do not leave until it is almost completely covered to ensure that the body has been properly buried. Regardless of which branch of Judaism, before leaving the cemetery, the rabbi tears a black ribbon affixed to the lapels of the immediate family. This simulates the rending of clothing, an ancient symbol of mourning.

Following interment, people wash their hands as they leave the cemetery or before entering the home of the mourners. At the home, they eat a religious, formal meal consisting of boiled eggs, representing life, and bagels, which, through their roundness, symbolize the life cycle.

The family of the deceased observes a seven-day mourning period called *shiva*. They sit on low stools to signify that their station in life has been lowered. Likewise, they cover mirrors to demonstrate their lack of concern with their appearance. An older explanation for covering mirrors was that whoever looked into the mirror and saw oneself may become the next to die.

Visitors come during the *shiva* to bring comfort to the mourners. They may bring food to the house but not take food away from it. A *minyan* (ten male Jews who have been *bar mitzvah*) gather during the morning and night to say the appropriate prayers.

Mourners burn a memorial candle for seven days following the funeral. On the one year anniversary of the death, as reckoned by the Hebrew calendar, family members light a twenty-four-hour memorial candle. At the one year death anniversary or earlier, they have a brief ceremony to unveil a grave marker. All branches of Judaism observe this custom. On subsequent cemetery calls, mourners may leave a pebble on the gravestone as a token of their visit.

SEPHARDIC FUNERALS

Children and pregnant women should not come to the cemetery. In the old days, no women came to the cemetery. They call the first post-funeral meal the *huevo* [oo-éh-vo] (egg) when each person eats a hard-boiled egg to symbolize the circle of life. The meal takes place in the synagogue or at the mourners' home and includes kashkaval cheese, Greek olives, and bread. They conclude with a blessing after which they eat raisins for sweetness to compensate for the bitterness of the loss and as a hopeful sign for the future.

KOREAN

GIFTS Flowers may be sent during the three-day preburial rites. Give money in envelopes only at this time. Names of donors should be written on the outside of the envelope. Families receiving guests at home appreciate food.

WORDS "I'm sorry for your loss," and any other sincere expressions of sympathy.

CLOTHING Black or somber colors, nothing floral. If the three-day period is held at home, remove shoes before entering. At the forty-ninth day ceremony, men wear suits and ties. Women wear clothing comfortable for sitting cross-legged on the floor. Pants suits are acceptable.

BODY LANGUAGE When entering the temple, step over, not on, the threshold.

Three days before the funeral, guests visit and pay their respects to the deceased. This may take place at the family's home, a rented hall, or at a mortuary. At the entry, someone seated at a table receives donations placed in white envelopes and offers a guest book to sign. They display a black and white, framed photograph of the deceased, a floral arrangement, and incense on a table. Female family members of the deceased may wear white traditional Korean dresses. Male family members may wear black suits with white handkerchiefs around their arms.

Guests approach the table, and if the family and visitors are Buddhists, they light an incense stick, kneel, then bow to the photograph. If they are Christian, there will be no incense or bowing. Instead, guests approach and acknowledge the photograph or say a silent prayer to the deceased. They serve food and drink during this preburial mourning period.

Most Christians prefer burial. Each family member throws dirt on the coffin, beginning with the closest family member and on to the furthest. At Buddhist funerals they burn imitation money for the deceased to take into the afterlife. Often they place a complete meal in front of the casket to offer nourishment to the departed soul. Funerals take place on odd-numbered days because even numbers are unlucky. They loudly express their grief and prefer to pay in cash rather than by check so that death won't return with the canceled check.

Buddhists prefer cremation. Ashes may be sprinkled at a lake or ocean. Korean Buddhist temples have a special room with photos of the deceased, many burning candles, burning incense, and a Buddha image in the center of the room. They make food offerings there, as well.

As a sign of mourning, some wives and daughters of the deceased wear white, flat ribbons attached to barrettes for approximately two weeks to one month.

Both Christian and Buddhist families hold memorial services on the forty-ninth day after death, and at one and two years. At Buddhist temples, they place vegetarian food and many kinds of fruit on the altar. During the ceremony, the monks chant and a Zen master gives a sermon. Someone approaches the altar and takes a small piece of each kind of fruit, places it on a plate, and takes it outdoors to feed the hungry ghosts. After the ceremony, they burn an article of the deceased's clothing outdoors to symbolize that the deceased is truly dead. At the conclusion of the ceremony, the family and close friends go to a restaurant, frequently a Chinese restaurant, for a special meal.

At the one year memorial, *jesa* [jay-sah], mourners gather at the cemetery for an ancestral-worship ceremony. They create an ancestor-worship table that includes piles of apples, Korean rice cakes, oranges, and other fruits. This small low table holds a framed picture of the deceased. Family members bow to their ancestors: males twice, females twice, but sometimes four times. Afterward, at nearby picnic tables, they eat the food they have placed on the table.

LAO

GIFTS If invited to the home ceremony, bring fresh fruit offerings or prepare some special food the family enjoys. Prior to the funeral, enclose money in an envelope and place it on the family's home altar.

WORDS Any expression of condolence.

CLOTHING Black or somber colors. Avoid brightly colored clothing or floral prints.

BODY LANGUAGE Avoid hugging, kissing, or shaking hands with the mourners. Instead, they will appreciate it if you perform the *wai* [why]. With hands pressed together in a prayerlike position, bring them up to just below the chin and nod slightly. They will return the gesture.

From the day of death until the funeral ceremony, the monks visit the house of the bereaved every day to pray for the dead and give comfort to the family. On the morning of the funeral and prior to the mortuary service, the monks come to the house to participate in a custom called *het boun* [het boon] (make offerings) for the deceased. Family and friends bring fresh fruit, cookies, and other sweets. The family provides food for the monks and the guests. The monks eat what they want first, then give the rest to those who wish to take home the leftovers. This food is considered blessed. The family presents new yellow robes to the monks. In addition, sons of the deceased don yellow robes and shave their heads to become Buddhist monks for the day (see Death/Thai, p. 245.). When the ceremony is over, the sons remove their robes and become lay persons once again. Close female friends dress in all white as part of this ceremony. Afterward, the Lao go to the mortuary, where the monks chant and burn incense for the dead. The funeral service ends at the mortuary.

Most Lao cremate their dead. Those who can afford it prefer to take the ashes back to Laos, where they place them inside family tombs—memorial towers made of brick and cement that sit alongside the walls of temple grounds.

MEXICAN

Customs vary according to church denomination. Generally, Mexicans have an open casket, and cremation is uncommon. Viewing of the body is important and it must be dressed in the best or new clothing. The family usually requests all-night visitations, and the funeral service itself is generally quiet and solemn. Large numbers of family members attend the service. They commonly have a week-long recitation of rosaries and observe anniversary rosaries. Large numbers of family members attend.

DAY OF THE DEAD—*DÍA DE LOS MUERTOS*
[dée-ah day los moo-áir toes]

In addition to rituals dictated by the varieties of religions to which Mexicans belong, some may observe the folk custom of Day of the Dead, memorializing deceased family members. This occurs during the two-day period of November 1, All Saint's Day and November 2, All Soul's Day. On All Saint's Day, families go to the cemetery and clean and beautify the graves of the deceased. For All Soul's Day they prepare an *ofrenda* [oh-frén-dah] (altar) at home, displaying a photo of the deceased with memorabilia and favorite foods of that person as well as seasonal treats such as Day of the Dead bread, shaped like corpses or round with cross-bones on them, and spun sugar candy skulls. They believe the dead do not go directly to their final resting place but once a year come home for a brief visit. The altar welcomes them. These rituals are more common in U.S./Mexican border states.

Sister Karen Boccalero, of the Sisters of St. Francis, founder and driving force behind Self-Help Graphics, a community-based art gallery located in East Los Angeles, was instrumental in reintroducing the Aztec-based Day of the Dead back into the U.S. Latino community. In the 1970s, Self-Help Graphics became a showplace for the spectacular altars they created. Fittingly, when Sister Karen suddenly died on June 24, 1997, in gratitude and love, the Latino community constructed a huge altar to honor her.

Friends and artists adorned it with bunches of marigolds, the traditional Day of the Dead flower. A large photo of Sister Karen framed by bramble branches became the centerpiece. The altar was packed with artwork from her protégés, fruit offerings, incense, her signature items of a box of Marlboro cigarettes with a box of matches next to her favorite brown ceramic Mexican ashtray. Other items included plants from her magnificent gardens in which she took pride, Aztec figurines, statues of Catholic praying women, pieces of tapestry woven in Mexico, etchings, and words that were reproduced on her rosary card from Mahatma Gandhi's Seven Sins in the World: wealth without work; pleasure without conscience; knowledge without character; commerce without morality; science without humanity; worship without sacrifice; politics without principal. Sister Karen spent her life fighting these evils.

On the Day of the Dead following her death, friends and artists created another altar for her. Franciscan nuns led prayers at her grave, then led a procession of forty on a one and one-quarter mile trek from the cemetery to Self-Help Graphics. They gathered at Sister Karen's altar, still covered with mementos to lure her spirit's return.

MUSLIM

GIFTS Avoid giving material gifts. Respect for the deceased and the survivors is the greatest gift. Depending on ethnicity, flowers are welcomed.

WORDS "My condolences." "May God give you patience." "I hope that this will be your last sorrow."

CLOTHING Men in dark suits with black ties, women in black. Avoid wearing light colors. Avoid wearing red. Avoid open displays of jewelry containing non-Muslim religious symbols, such as Stars of David, crosses, and signs of the zodiac.

Surprising as it may seem, some American Muslims living in cities where they do not have their own mortuaries use Jewish funeral homes because many customs are the same. For example, they oppose embalming, forbid cremation, and must bury the dead within twenty-four hours after death. In a small Muslim community outside of Minneapolis, they have imported special waters to bathe the deceased and a special cotton used for wrapping the corpse in order to comply with Saudi Arabian burial traditions.

Frequently, family members prepare the body with oils and fragrances. Husbands may prepare their wives, wives prepare husbands, and children are prepared by either. For the unmarried, widowed, or divorced, only women prepare women, and men prepare men. Before the burial, they wash and shroud the body. The funeral service generally takes place in a mosque, but may also be held in a funeral chapel or at the cemetery away from the grave. They generally request closed caskets.

The leader at the funeral is an *imam* [ee-mam] (priest) who leads a prayer and asks God for forgiveness. The body is laid on the ground or table. The *imam* stands in front and faces Mecca, while others stand behind him in rows. No bowing or prostrating occurs during the service.

Before lowering the body into the grave, they turn it slightly so that it rests on its right side. In the final resting position, the body faces Mecca. If Mecca is to the north, they dig the grave in an east-west direction and place the head side of the body on the east. They say prayers as they lower the casket. Crying is acceptable but wailing is not.

Among Iranian Muslims, the funeral home prepares the body which is interred in a cemetery among other Muslims. The deceased wears a white shroud and is placed in the simplest wooden coffin. The ceremony primarily takes place graveside, where they serve dates and *halvah*, a special sweet, to those assembled. Good friends recite from the *Qur'an* and they say a special prayer for the dead called *namazeh mayet* [nah-mah-zéh mah-yét]. Once the body is in the ground, mourners and guests may throw in three handfuls of dirt to help fill the grave. With the first handful they say, "From the earth did we create you." With the second they say, "And into it shall we return you." With the third, they say, "And from it shall we bring you out once again."

After the ceremony, Muslims gather at a home or in a hall where they serve tea, coffee, and *halvah*. For the first week of mourning, some people have memorial ceremonies at home or in the mosque where they recite from the *Qur'an*. On the fortieth day in the evening, they hold a ceremony with a big dinner, almost like a wedding dinner. They recite from the *Qur'an* and talk about the deceased. This event is repeated at the one year anniversary with an even bigger meal.

For some Muslims, for forty days after the funeral, female relatives visit the grave every Friday, their Sabbath. They place a palm branch on the grave and distribute cakes to the poor. Sometimes widows wear black for an entire year.

NATIVE AMERICAN

GIFTS Water, because they consider it sacred, and it is especially appropriate when burial ceremonies last over a day. Food and money.

WORDS They prefer silence. Avoid words of condolence. Avoid offering them your prayers.

CLOTHING Respectful attire, nothing colorful. If you are a non-Native American, avoid wearing anything that might be construed as Native American clothing or jewelry. This is highly offensive.

TABOOS Do not record the event on video or audio recorders, with cameras of any kind. Their songs and dances must stay within the family and are not to be shared with outsiders.

As with most groups in this book, there are many variations, but generally, outsiders have to be invited to a funeral, which ordinarily takes place on the burial ground on a reservation or allotted land, shortly after death. Depending on the status of the person, the ceremony may last from one day up to two weeks. Most people are buried horizontally, but medicine men may be buried in a sitting position with many artifacts. Sometimes, those considered "bad people" are placed face down. Singing and dancing take place at nighttime only. Mourning lasts for one year. During this time family members refrain from singing or going to celebrations, powwows, or sweat lodges. A common sign of mourning is for immediate and extended family to cut their hair.

HOPI
They cover the face of the deceased with a cotton mask, which symbolizes the rain cloud. Mourners silently lower the body into a grave located in an obscure place and surround it with prayer sticks. After they cover the grave, they leave a bowl of food to feed the soul on its journey to the spirit world. Four days later, women mourners return to the grave and place another bowl of food there. After that, they believe the soul has safely returned to the spirit world and normal activities resume.

REDEDICATING DISTURBED BURIAL SITES
When Native American burial sites have been disturbed, steps must be taken to ask for forgiveness from the affected spirits. Tribal representatives

must have a ceremony to ease the disturbance of the dead. Medicine people and spiritual leaders pray over the physical remains and make offerings. Commonly, they leave handmade tribal gifts such as baskets as well as clothing, tobacco, food, and sage, which they place on top of the grave. If bones have been disturbed, they must rebury them. Usually, the ceremony is attended by spiritual leaders and descendents of the particular tribal group. Ceremonial details vary according to tribe.

On May 10, 1997, tribal leaders of the Miwok and Pomo tribes and hundreds of other Native Americans and local residents gathered before sunset at the Mission San Francisco Solano in Sonoma, California, for a memorial service to bless the 900 tribal members buried under First Street.

They blessed the ground and those prohibited from burial in the nearby cemetery designated for Christians only. "We don't want them to think they're forgotten," explained one tribal member. The Native Americans didn't want angry spirits to return. They could counteract this possibility through the rededication ceremony, demonstrating that they protected their dead.

After the blessing and prayers, tribal leaders burned sweet grass, and afterward, traditional Pomo dancers performed. In addition to blessing the site, they raised money for a future monument that will be erected containing the Christian names of those buried. To cover its costs, the local tribes prepared and sold dinners to the locals who enthusiastically supported the cause.

REBURIAL—CHIEF LONG WOLF

In 1992, when Elizabeth Knight, of Worcestershire, England, first read a lament on the tragic life of Chief Long Wolf, she became captivated by his plight. An Oglala Sioux warrior, he had lain forgotten in a London Cemetery since 1892, stranded from his native people in South Dakota. Knight vowed to return him to his ancestral burial grounds at Wounded Knee, and after five years of personal detective work and diligence, she fulfilled her promise.

Chief Long Wolf had been wounded at the brutal Battle of the Little Bighorn, and joined Buffalo Bill Cody's Wild West Show rather than stay in South Dakota and live as a member of a vanquished people. He spent the rest of his life performing in Cody's troupe touring the U.S. and Europe. In 1892, at age fifty-nine, Chief Long Wolf died of respiratory complications in London. Cody purchased a grave for him at Bromptom Cemetery, later shared with Star, the seventeen-month-old daughter of another Sioux troupe member, Ghost Dog. The child had died after falling from a horse.

Elizabeth Knight's pledge became a reality when, on September 26, 1997, the Chief's coffin was removed from the cemetery, 105 years after its original burial. A horse-drawn black carriage slowly carried the buffalo-hide-wrapped remains of the chief and Star. To the accompaniment of Indian drums, relatives in native dress marched behind.

The reburial service commenced in London's St. Luke's Parish Church combining Native American and British church traditions: Indian drums and organ music; Sioux prayers and biblical verse; Native American headdress and Anglican robes; Indian medicine men and English clergy.

A descendent of the author whose story had impassioned Knight read from the Bible. An English quartet sang a Lakota memorial song, and two of the Chief's descendants intoned hymns in Lakota and English. A tribal spiritual chief prayed over the coffin and after a final hymn, the bodies were carried from the church by four men in morning coats. A hearse transported the chief's flag-draped coffin to an airplane for the final lap of its journey.

Wilmer Mesteth, an Oglala Sioux tribal spiritual leader in attendance proclaimed, "It [return of the body] means he's set free. He'll be among his own people. His bones will remain with us. The spirit remains with the bones and the bones will finally be at rest among his own."

Two days later, the ceremony resumed at Wolf Creek, South Dakota. At first, the coffin remained inside a tepee surrounded by flowers. Then nine pallbearers bore it up a steep hill to a grave at Wolf Creek Church Cemetery. Seven of the nine were powwow dancers in traditional dance regalia; the other two were chiefs in feather bonnets. Mourners followed, and en route to the cemetery the entourage stopped four times to honor the four directions. At the burial site, traditional Lakota songs and prayers preceded the internment. Rather than feeling sad at this reburial ceremony, Chief Long Wolf's people rejoiced. He was finally home.

ROM—Gypsy

GIFTS Only family and other Rom give gifts. For an outsider to give a gift would seem presumptuous.

WORDS Anything sincere is appreciated, or positive words including remembrances of what made the person unique: "He sure did love those cigars."

CLOTHING For the three-day or six-week tables, guests wear dressy, dark, formal clothing. Avoid pastel colors or white. Avoid wearing casual clothing, short pants, or casual dresses. The Rom view the lower half of the body as sacred and dangerous, so it must be covered. However, they also understand that outsiders don't know their customs. They expect that outsiders have their own rules to obey and watch closely to see if they observe them or not. If not, they ask, "Why would you give up your traditions?" or "Does he think he's a Gypsy?"

Ordinarily the Rom prefer to die outdoors, but if they die in the hospital, all traces of blood must be removed from the room. Family members place the corpse next to an open window with a lit candle under the bed. This provides a lighted way for the spirit to travel to heaven.

At the funeral home, they hold a boisterous three-day feast. Large groups gather, and feasting takes place the night before and the morning of the burial. They bring huge amounts of food and drink to the mortuary and sometimes set up barbecues outside the building. During the night, mourners bring food to the deceased and place familiar items into the casket such as telephones, toothbrushes, lipstick, cigarettes, whiskey, and cash. An elder presides at the funeral service.

During the six weeks after the death, the family gathers the deceased's belongings and clothing, everything but the jewelry, and tosses them into a body of moving water for the deceased to wear in the spirit world. The most honored man in the group says a prayer over the objects and clothing.

A unique custom called the *pomana* [poe-máh-nah] (black feast or table) takes place at three days, six weeks and one year after death. For the six-week feast, the family rents a hall or banquet room in a hotel to accommodate hundreds of guests for an elaborate ceremony. At one end of the banquet table they provide a place setting for the deceased so ornate that it may consist of gold dishes, gold utensils, and the finest linens.

Next, they place personalized objects at the place setting. For example, if the deceased was a male smoker, they may leave the finest cigars. If the deceased was a female who loved Entenmann's cookies, they stack boxes of Entenmann's cookies for her pleasure. An elder stands near the place setting, says prayers in Romany, burns incense over it and the gifts displayed in a different corner of the room. Here family and friends exhibit extravagant items for the deceased to use in the next world: fine luggage, a certificate for a vacation, jewelry, envelopes containing money. Offering these gifts sends a message that the spirit of the deceased is still among them and receiving these luxurious presents. Later they distribute the gifts to the family of the deceased.

The gifts are for people to enjoy here as a symbol of what the deceased's spirit could or would enjoy if it were still embodied. The people eat the cakes and say, "I'm eating this for you."

"Wearing the Suit" is another significant custom of the *pomana*. Rom believe that the spirit of the deceased is on earth until the one year feast. At the six-week *pomana*, they outfit a surrogate for the deceased in an expensive suit of clothing, including hat, undergarments, and shoes. If the deceased was a female, her outfit includes underclothing, even makeup. It is an honor to be chosen for this role, but before giving the outfit to the chosen person, the elders may burn incense over it for purification. The person who wears the suit is symbolically saying, "I'm wearing it here; she [the deceased] is wearing it there [in the spirit world]."

At the *pomana*, some Rom may go up to the person wearing the suit and speak to him/her just as they might interact if the deceased were truly among the living. They may even apologize for past wrongdoings. This custom has variations because other Romany families believe that to talk to the dead person you have to go to the cemetery. Through the ritual of the wearing of the suit, the deceased is given a little more time on earth to enjoy life and be remembered. All of these acts demonstrate the Rom's strong belief that the spirit of the dead person stays among the living for a year before moving on to the next state of being. The Romany goal is for the deceased to be happy and not wander the earth.

After the six-week feast, the person who wears the suit and accoutrement is supposed to wear it to parties and special occasions until the year is over. This is a great honor, and everyone who sees the person in the outfit then remembers the deceased and talks favorably about him or her. At the one-year celebration, the person wears the suit again but afterward sends it to an unknown destination. The suit-wearer may hang the suit on a tree or shrub where someone unknown can take it, or throw it into a body of moving water, or bring it to the dry cleaners and never pick it up.

One must be invited to attend any Rom event, including a funeral. Usually this occurs because the person is a good or helpful connection, such as an attorney.

SAMOAN

GIFTS Money enclosed in a card. In return, Samoans have a custom called *sua*, which is a thank you for the gift. After some days have passed, members of the deceased's family may come to call bearing gifts of a can of soda, five yards of fabric, and turkey. These gifts substitute for the traditional island gifts of coconut, tapa, and pig. They also bring a tray holding chicken, crackers, and a fine mat.

CLOTHING Dress for church. In the past, everyone wore black, then later all white. Sometimes families request all white. Above all, respectful and comfortable clothing.

Typically there is a lag of one week to ten days between the time of death and the Samoan burial. They need that amount of time to gather the family, many of whom fly in from the islands.

The women dress the bodies, frequently in white. Women may be buried in white wedding dresses; men may be buried in white suits, sometimes black. They cover the body with a veil, just as they might do to keep insects off the body if the service were being conducted in Samoa, but in the United States, they frequently substitute lace for veiling. They cover the coffin with lace, as well.

Customs vary with the status of the deceased. Sometimes they have an open coffin for a grandmother. If her children know she loves flowers, they give her lots of flowers. "You want to do your best for the grandmother," explained one Samoan, "but it's always according to status." If the deceased is a chief, he has to have a fine mat unwrapped and on top. Women mostly have lace.

A small choir sings and the Samoans drape the casket and surround it with fine mats of handwoven grass or leaves. These mats circulate among families and appear at all rites of passage. They place dollar bills on the body and include highly valued family possessions inside the casket as well, such as a watch or other jewelry.

Before closing the casket, the spouse or oldest child pours perfume over the body. The family gets together, sometimes while the person is still alive, and decides who will perform this act, called the last bath. It is a great honor to be chosen for this final loving task. During the interment, they sing and throw flowers, especially rose petals. The mood is not somber; a warm, lively atmosphere prevails.

THAI

GIFTS At home visitations, give money in envelopes and write your name on the outside. Someone is usually in charge of collecting them.

WORDS "I'm sorry." At the same time, you may hold the hands of the family, but only if you see others doing the same. No joking. Do not talk too loud or laugh. Silence honors the dead.

CLOTHING Black or white clothing.

BODY LANGUAGE Avoid smiling. At the temple, guests should sit and refrain from talking. Temple members sit on the floor. If you are uncomfortable in this position, look for some chairs at the back of the room. The *wai* [why] is the most respectful form of greeting (see Death/Lao, p. 235.). When entering the temple, step over the threshold, not on it.

In Thailand, rites take place at home from three to seven days before the funeral. People come to pay their respects at this time and hosts serve them food. This custom is beginning to change and in the United States, the body may be taken directly to the temple. The most important day is the last day at the temple before the body is cremated. In front of the body they place a photo of the deceased, offerings of incense, oranges, and flowers. Generally, the family wears black, although those from Northeast Thailand wear white.

Whether at home or at the temple, services occur only in the evening. At the ceremony, an even number of monks, preferably four, chant. Sons of the deceased become monks for the day; they shave their heads and don orange robes and participate in a monk's temple ceremony (see Death/Lao," p. 235.). By doing this, the sons ensure that their parent will more easily reach heaven. After the funeral, the body is most commonly cremated. Ashes may be kept at home, thrown into a river or ocean, or returned to Thailand. The Thai Buddhist Temple contains a special room where people keep ashes in a pagoda-style container with a displayed photo of the deceased. They regularly place offerings there. Families observe one hundred days of mourning.

TIBETAN

GIFTS The first few days, guests come to the mourners' home for lunch and offer white scarves and envelopes with money. This recurs at the fourth- and seventh-week death anniversaries.

WORDS The Tibetans offer words of condolence while offering scarves placed around the mourner's neck. "Don't worry." If the deceased was elderly, they say, "She lived well. She led a long, good life."

CLOTHING Subdued colors.

BODY LANGUAGE *Namaste* [nah-mah-stay] is the most respectful form of greeting (see Marriage/Indian, p. 196.).

Prior to death, friends offer the dying person sips of holy water. A monk or lama comes to the hospital or home to say prayers and pour grains of colored sand from a sacred sand mandala over the crown of the dying person. This allows the person's spirit to exit from the top of the head.

The funeral takes place three to seven days after death and is determined by astrological calculations, but services do not take place on weekends, considered inauspicious times. During the ceremony and prior to cremation, monks chant, burn incense, and guests lay white scarves over the casket (see Birth/Tibetan, p. 152; Marriage/Tibetan, p. 213.). For seven days afterward, family members and friends make offerings to monks at monasteries. For forty-nine days following the death, the family prepares a dough of barley mixed with honey, milk, butter, sugar, and dried fruits. A small part of this mixture is offered into a flame three times daily to feed the spirit of the deceased. This ends on the forty-ninth day when they believe the deceased finds a way of reincarnating as a human or another life-form, or goes directly to heaven.

LOOKING FOR MORE INFORMATION?

Print and Online

Acain, Angeline. 2004. "The Chen-Hayes Family of New Jersey and Their Child from the Heavens." *Gay Parent.* March-April, 12-14.

Ancelet, Barry Jean, Jay Edwards, and Glen Pitre. 1991. *Cajun Country.* Jackson: University Press of Mississippi.

Andersen, Ruth E. 1999. *The Color of the Sun.* An unpublished manuscript.

Anderson, Terje. 1986. "Halloween, Queen for a Day. *Out in the Mountains.*" 11 November. http://www.mountainpridemedia.org/oitm/issues/1986/11nov1986/queen.htm

"A NigerianYoruba Naming Ceremony in the Washington, D.C. Area." 2005. http:/www.folklife.si.edu/Africa/photo2.htm

Ayers, Tess, and Paul Brown. 1999. *The Essential Guide to Lesbian and Gay Weddings.* Los Angeles/New York: Alyson Books.

Bahti, Tom. 1982. *Southwestern Indian Ceremonials.* Las Vegas, NV: KC Publications.

Baron, Marta, Liza Steinberg, and Beth Hall. 1998. "Building Racial Identity: Hair Is an Adoption Issue." Pact, An Adoption Alliance. http://pact.best.vwh.net/press/articles/identity-hair.html

Bartholomew, Dana. 2004. "Bar None: 'Faux Mitzvahs' a Rising Trend With Non-Jews." *Daily News* (San Fernando Valley, CA), 1, 26.

Berkowitz, Bill. 2004. "Christian Right Plans Holy Havoc for Halloween." 18 June. http://www.alternet.org/module/printversion/9937

Bernstein, Elizabeth. 2004. "More Non-Jews Celebrating Faux Bar Mitzvahs." *The Wall Street Journal.* 14 January. http://sfgate.com/cgi-bin/article.cgi?file=/news/archive/2004/01/14/financial1013EST0066.DTL

Berry, Jason. 1995. *Spirit of Black Hawk.* Jackson: University Press of Mississippi.

Beyer, Debra. 2004. "Be Our Guest: Weddings Put Couples' Hosting Skills to the Test." 17 February. *Los Angeles Times,* 1,3, Wedding Supplement. www.latimes.com/extras/weddings

Bliatour, Bruce Thowpaou. 1993. "Hmong Death Customs: Traditional and Acculturated." In *Ethnic Variations in Dying, Death, and Grief: Diversity in Universality,* edited by Donald P. Irish, Kathleen F. Lundquist, and Vivian Jenkins Nelsen. Washington, D.C.: Taylor & Francis, 79-100.

Blumenfeld, Amy. 2003-2004. "Mixed Families, Jewish Choices." My JewishLearning.com. http://www.myjewishlearning.com/index.htm

Booe, Martin. 2001. "Viva Hanukkah: Potato Latkes Are Delicious with a Little Salsa." *Los Angeles Times Magazine,* 11 November, 8.

Brunvand, Jan Harold, ed. 1996. *American Folklore: An Encyclopedia.* New York: Garland Publishing.

Bumstead, Alden. 2002. "Blaxicans and Hinjews—A Language for the Lives We Lead." 19 November. *Poynteronline.* www.poynter.org

Cantú, Norma E. 2002. "Chicana Life-Cycle Rituals." In *Chicana Traditions: Continuity and Change,* edited by Norma E. Cantú and Olga Nájera-Ramirez. Chicago: University of Illinois Press, 15-34.

Caplan, Jeremy. 2004. "Om-Shalomers Come of Age: Children of Jewish and Hindu Parents Are Emerging as a New Cultural Subset." *Forward.* 16 January, 16.

Chavez, Annette. 1996. "Queen for a Day." *Los Angeles Times,* Westside Weekly, 8 December, 1,7.

Chin, Soo-Young. 1991. "Korean Birthday Rituals." *Journal of Cross-Cultural Gerontology* 6: 145-52.

———. 1989. The Role of Ritual for Korean American Elderly. *Frontiers of Asian American Studies.* Pullman: Washington State University Press, 127-39.

Clines, Francis X. 1994. "73,000 Times in 22 Tongues, Vow: 'I Do'"; *New York Times,* 30 October, 41.

Coffin, Margaret. 1976. *Death in Early America: The History and Folklore of Customs and Superstitions of Early Medicine, Funerals, Burials, and Mourning.* Nashville, TN: Nelson Publishing Co.

Cohn, Meryl. 1995. *"Do What I Say:" Ms. Behavior's Guide to Gay & Lesbian Etiquette.* Boston/NewYork: Houghton Mifflin Company.

Colton, Michael. 1995. "A Lasting Union: Eight Days of Lavish Parties and Ancient Rituals Forge a Marriage of Families." *Los Angeles Times,* 26 July, E1, 4.

Crohn, Joel. 1995. *Mixed Matches: How to Create Successful Interracial, Interethnic and Interfaith Relationships.* New York: Fawcett Columbine.

Daniels, Susan. 1989. "Funeral Customs of the New Americans." *The Director*, July, 10-16.

Diamant, Anita. 1993. *The New Jewish Baby Book*. Woodstock, VT: Jewish Lights Publishing.

Dobrinsky, Herbert C. 1986. *Sephardic Laws and Customs*. Hoboken, NJ: KTAV Publishing House.

Doi, Mary L. 1991. "A Transformation of Ritual: The Nisei 60th Birthday." *Journal of Cross-Cultural Gerontology* 6: 153-63.

Dongre, Archana. 2004. "Cross-Culture Parenting: American Parents Who Adopt Indian Kids." http://library.adoption.com

Donohue, William, Rabbi Adam Mintz, and Rabbi Joseph Potasnik. 2004. "'Chrismukkah' Holiday Shamefully Plagiarizes." *Forward*, 10 December, 8.

Dresser, Norine. 1994. *I Felt Like I Was from Another Planet*. Menlo Park, CA: Addison-Wesley.

———. 1991. "Marriage Customs in Early California." *The Californians*, November/December, 46-49.

———, 2005. *Multicultural Manners: Essential Rules of Etiquette for the 21st Century*. Hoboken, NJ: John Wiley & Sons.

———. 1996. "Remaining Safe from the Remains." *Los Angeles Times*, 20 April, B7.

Dumas, Firoozeh. 2004. *Funny in Farsi*. New York: Random House.

Dundes, Alan. 1996. "'Jumping the Broom: On the Origin and Meaning of an African American Wedding Custom.'" *Journal of American Folklore* 109: 433, 324-29.

Dunnette, Paul. 2001. "A Call for Cultural Understanding." *Connection*. December, 1, 5.

"The First American *Bat Mitzvah*." 1997. From *Chapters in American Jewish History*, reprinted in *Forward*, 7 November, 7.

Garfinkel, Renée. 2004. "Homogenization Trap: Kaddish for Grandpa in Jesus' Name Amen." *B'Nai B'rith*, Winter, 15.

Gilanshah, Farah. 1993. "Islamic Customs Regarding Death." In *Ethnic Variations in Dying Death and Grief: Diversity in Universality*, edited by Donald P. Irish, Kathleen F. Lundquist, and Vivian Jenkins Nelson. Washington, D.C.: Taylor and Francis, 137-45.

Glaser, Gabrielle. 1997. *Strangers to the Tribe: Portraits of Interfaith Marriage*. Boston/New York: Houghton Mifflin.

Goldberg, Christine. 1994. "Choosing Their Futures, a Custom for Babies." *Western Folklore* 53 (April): 2, 178-89.

Goodheart, Adam. 2004. "Change of Heart." *AARP Magazine.* May & June. 37-41, 75.

"Grief and Loss: Funerals, Memorial Services and Rituals." 2003. http://www.planet-therapy.com/

Groves, Martha. 2004. "Journey to Fill in the Blanks." *Los Angeles Times,* 17 December, A1, 36, 37.

Guidelines for Display Committees. 1994. San Francisco, CA: NAMES Project Foundation.

Hansen, Barbara. 1995. "Quinceañera: Cinderella for a Night." *Los Angeles Times,* 9 February, H10.

Harris, Scott. 2004. "Judaism Is Hot, Hot, Hot." *B'nai B'rith.* Winter, 8.

"Hatred and Cowardice: Evil's Twin Pillars." 1999. *The Canadian Jewish News.* 19 August. http://www.cjnews.com/pastissues/99/aug19-99/editorial/editorial.htm

Harlow, Ilana. 1997. *Beyond the Grave: Cultures of Queens Cemeteries.* Woodhaven, NY: Queens Council on the Arts.

Hartman, Susan. 1997. "For Bar Mitzvahs, a Revival of Spirit." *New York Times,* 13 March, C1, 10.

Hawxhurst, Joan C. 1998. *The Interfaith Family Guidebook.* Kalamazoo, MI: Dovetail Publishing.

Hayasaki, Erika, and Joel Rubin. 2004. "School Yuletide Observances Shift Into Neutral." *Los Angeles Times,* 22 December, A1, 34.

Hazen-Hammond, Susan. 1995. "Kinaaldá: Coming of Age in the Navajo Nation." *Arizona Highways,* March, 14-19.

Herman, Valli. 2004. "Happiness on a String: For $25.99 It's Yours." *Los Angeles Times,* 5 August, E2, 3.

Holmes, Kristin. 1996. "Today's Funeral Directors Live Up to Diverse Customs." *Philadelphia Inquirer,* 2 January, B1-2.

"Hopi: Following the Path of Peace from Native American Wisdom." 1994. San Francisco: Chronicle Books.

Hostetler, John. 1972. "The Amish in American Culture." *Historic Pennsylvania Leaflet,* no. 12.

Howe, James. 2004. *Kaddish for Grandpa in Jesus' Name Amen.* New York: Atheneum Books for Young Readers.

Hur, Sonja Vegdahl, and Ben Seunghwa Hur. 1997. *Culture Shock!*: Korea. Portland, OR: Graphic Arts Center Publishing Company.

Hurwitz, Allison. 2003. *Information Packet: The Adoption of Chinese Girls by American Families.* May. New York: National Resource Center for Foster Care & Permanency Planning at the Hunter College School of Social Work.

Israel, Gianna E., and Donald E. Tarver II, M.D. 1997. *Transgender Care.* Philadelphia: Temple University Press.

Jerris, Rabbi Miriam. 2004. "Finding One's Role as a Grandparent in an Interfaith Family." *Jewish News Weekly.* 20 July, 6b (seniors supplement).

Jones, Carolyn, Nanette Asimov, and Jose Vargas. 2003. "No-Booze Halloween a Drag on Castro St." 1 November. *SFGate.com.* http://www.sfgate.com

Jones, Leslie. 1995. *Happy Is the Bride the Sun Shines On.* Chicago: Contemporary Books.

Jones, Rose Apodaca. 1997. "Vows for the Heart and for Vietnam." *Los Angeles Times*, 27i August, S4.

Kabaker, Harvey. 1971. "Moni at Six Months: The Ogunfiditimis Name a Daughter." *The Evening Star* (Washington, D.C.), 17 May. http://www.folklife.si.edu/africa/evestar.htm

Katz, Jesse. 1997. "New Orleans Parade Tradition Advances Black Men's Image." *Los Angeles Times*, 4 September, A5.

Kay, Julie. 2004. "Eighty-nine-year-old Bat Mitzvah Girls." *Forward*, 17 December, 13.

Kendall, Laurel. 1996. *Getting Married in Korea: Of Gender, Morality, and Modernity.* Berkeley: University of California Press.

———. 1985. *Shamans, Housewives, and Other Restless Spirits: Women in Korean Ritual Life.* Honolulu: University of Hawaii Press.

Keys, Lisa. 2001. "For Many, the 'December Dilemma' Loses Its Sting." *Forward.* 21 December. 1, 14.

Kim, Diana. 1993. "Love, Armenian Style." *Los Angeles Times*, 19 August, J1, 5.

Klein, Sybil. 1995. "The Celebration of Life in New Orleans Jazz Funerals." In *Feasts and Celebrations in North American Ethnic Communities*, edited by Ramón Gutiérrez and Geneviève Fabre. Albuquerque: University of New Mexico Press, 101-8.

Kluckhohn, Clyde, and Dorothea Leighton. 1962. *The Navaho.* New York: Anchor Books.

Kraybill, Donald B. 1989. *The Riddle of Amish Culture.* Baltimore: Johns Hopkins University Press.

Kress, Marlyn. 2003. "Raising a Jewish-Chinese Daughter in North America." My Jewish Learning.com. http://www.myjewishlearning.com .

Lakota: Seeking the Great Spirit from Native American Wisdom. 1994. San Francisco: Chronicle Books.

La Ferla, Ruth. 2003. "Generation E.A.: Ethnically Ambiguous." *The New York Times*. 28 December. www.nytimes.com

Leonard, Jack. 1997. "Nun's Contributions to Chicano Heritage Recalled at Festival." *Los Angeles Times*, 2 November, B2.

Leonelli, Laura. 1993. "Adaptive Variations: Examples from the Hmong and Mien Communities of Sacramento." Unpublished paper delivered at the Southwestern Anthropology Association meeting, San Diego, CA, April.

Levin, Sunie. 2003. *Mingled Roots: A Guide for Grandparents of Interfaith Children*. New York: UAHC Press.

Liptak, Karen. 1992. *North American Indian Ceremonies*. New York: Franklin Watts.

"Longtime Customers Wed at Wal-Mart." 2004. Associated Press. 23 August. www.cnn.com

Lowery, Steve. 2004. "Just Another Wedding Expo: Gay and Lesbian Event Trudges On, Politics Be Damned." *OC Weekly* (Orange County, CA), 23 July. 10.

Macomb, Susanna Stefanachi. 2004. "Celebrating Diversity in the U.S." InterfaithNews.net. July. www.interfaithnews.net

Magenta, Gary. 2000. "Leave a Plate of Matzoh for Santa." Dovetail Institute for Interfaith Family Resources. Reprinted online: http://www.beliefnet.com/story/58/story_5858.html

Magida, Arthur J., ed. 1996. *How to Be a Perfect Stranger*. Woodstock, VT: Jewish Lights Publishing.

Matlins, Stuart M., and Arthur J. Magida, eds. 1997. *How to Be a Perfect Stranger*. Vol. 2. Woodstock, VT: Jewish Lights Publishing.

Mahany, Barbara. 2004. "Mitzvah Envy." *Chicago Tribune-Online edition*. 29 August. www.chicagotribune.com

Marech, Rona. 2004. "San Francisco Bay Area's Gays Cheer Banner Year." *SFGate.com*. 22 June. www.sfgate.com

Maxwell, Evelyn. 1993. "When Your Grandchild Celebrates a Different Faith." *Dovetail: A Newsletter By and For Jewish-Christian Families*. April/May, 2–3.

McLane, Daisann. 1995. "The Cuban-American Princess." *New York Times Magazine*, 26 February, 42.

"Merry C-Word." 2004. *Los Angeles Times*, 21 December, B12.

Meyer, Nan. 2004. "My Granddaughter's Baptism." *InterfaithFamily.com* Network. www.interfaithfamily.com

Moore-Howard, Patricia. 1982. *The Hmong—Yesterday and Today*. Lansing, MI: Collection of MSU Museum.

Mulford, Kim. 2004. "Workshops Address Special Needs of Interfaith Families at the Holidays." *CourierPostOnline.* 17 June. http://www.courierpostonline.com/columnists/cxmu121303a.htm

National Association of Colleges of Mortuary Science, Inc. 1994. *Funeral Services and Ceremonies.* Dallas, TX: Professional Training Schools, Inc.

Navajo: *Walking in Beauty.* 1994. From *Native American Wisdom.* San Francisco: Chronicle Books.

"New CD *Marry Me* Supports the ACLU's Efforts to Win Marriage for Same-Sex Couples." 2004. *Queery.com*, 9 December. http://www.queery.com/sybfusion. cgi?templ=q-item2.tpl&category=Q-i

"Newlyweds Show Gay Pride." 2004. *The Miami Herald.* 28 June. http://www.miami.com/mld/miamiherald/news/9028403.htm?template

Ngo, Qui. 1994. "Buddhist Funeral Rites." Unpublished article, Cypress College of Mortuary Science Department, Cypress, California.

Oppel, Shelby. 2001. "A Chance to Break Bread—and Barriers." *The Oregonian*, 26 November, A1, 6.

———. 2002. "Muslims, Others Share Meal in Quest for Understanding." *The Oregonian*, 11 November, C1, 4.

Osbey, Brenda Marie. 1996. "One More Last Chance: Ritual and the Jazz Funeral." *Georgia Review* 50 (Spring): 1, 97-107.

Paddock, Richard C. 1996. "165 Gay Couples Exchange Vows in S.F. Ceremony." *Los Angeles Times*, 26 March, A1, 18.

Padilla, Steve. 1990. "Death's New Face." *Los Angeles Times*, 5 March, B1, 8.

Paulson, Amanda. 2003. "The Changing Face of Love." *The Christian Science Monitor.* http://www.csmonitor.com/2003/0115/p11s02-lifp.htm

Perman, Stacy. 2005. "High Profile Kabbala." *Hadassah Magazine*, January, 25–29.

Pollard-Terry, Gayle. 2004. "A Shout Rings Out." *Los Angeles Times.* 16 October, E1, E19.

Powers, William K. 1977. *Ogalala Religion.* Lincoln: University of Nebraska Press.

Prager, Dennis. 2004. "Born-Again President—White House Hanukkah." *Los Angeles Times*, 19 December, M1.

Przybys, John. 2004. "All Are Welcome: With Open Arms." *Review Journal* (Las Vegas). 12 August. www.reviewjournal.com

Rich, Tracey R. 2001. "Judaism 101. What Do Jews Do on Christmas?" http://www.jewfaq.org/xmas.htm

Rivenburg, Roy. 1992. "An Ancient Vigil." *Los Angeles Times*, 14 September, E1,2.

Rochlin, Margy. 2004. "To Tree or Not to Tree." *Los Angeles Times*, 21 December, B13.

Rosenbaum, Mary Heléne, and Stanley Ned Rosenbaum. 1995. *Dovetail: A newsletter by and for Jewish-Christian Families.* February/March, 3-4.

———. 1999. *Celebrating Our Differences: Living Two Faiths in One Marriage.* Shippensburg, PA:Ragged Edge Press.

Rosenberg, Shelley Kapnek. 1998. "A Jewish Rainbow: Transcultural and Transracial Adoption." *Adoption and the Jewish Family: Contemporary Perspectives.* Philadelphia, PA: Jewish Publication Society. www.interfaithfamily.com

Rourke, Mary. 1997. "In the Spirit." *Los Angeles Times*, 21 December, E1.

Salcedo, Michele. 1997. *Quinceañera!* New York: Henry Holt and Company, Inc.

Sanders, Gabriel. 2004. "Meppy Chrismukkah!" *Forward*, 3 December, 13.

Schulweis, Harold M. 2003. "Beyond Interfaith Marriage." Rabbi Harold *Schulweis Archives.* Rosh Hashona. http://www.vbs.org/rabbi/hshulw/interfa_bot.htm

Scott, Stephen. 1988. *The Amish Wedding.* Intercourse, PA: Good Books.

Shanley, Jason. 2004. "It's Gay Pride Time." *Pride*, May-June, 40-42.

Sherman, Spencer. 1988. "The Hmong in America." *National Geographic*, October, 586-610.

Smiley, Lauren. 2004. "Ms. Behavior Has the Do's, Don'ts of Gay Marriage." *Boston Globe.* 14 June, B7.

Smith, Lynn. 1997. "Ashes to Ashes, to Ashes, to Ashes." *Los Angeles Times,* 10 April, E1, 5.

Story, Paula. 1997. "Same-Sex Couples Use Festival Ceremony to Affirm Their Bonds." *Daily News (Southern California)*, 22 June, 12.

Sturgis, Ingrid. 1997. *The Nubian Wedding Book.* New York: Crown Publishers.

Sullivan, Meg. 1996. "Marriage, American Style." *University of Southern California Chronicle*, 22 April, 15:29, 1, 6.

Sutherland, Anne. 1975. *Gypsies: The Hidden Americans.* New York: Free Press.

Sway, Marlene. 1998. *Familiar Strangers: Gypsy Life in America.* Urbana and Chicago: University of Illinois Press.

Tempko, Florence. 1991. *Jewish Origami.* Torrance, CA: Heian International, Inc.

Tilsner, Julie. 2004. "Celebrating the Holidays in an Interfaith Family." *The Baby Center.* http://www.babycenter.com/refcap/baby/babyritual/9838.html

Tobin, Jonathan. 2004. "Joining the Party." *Jewish World Review.* 3 February. http://www.jewishworldreview.com/0204/tobin_2004_02_02.php3?prin

Trippett, Frank. 1981. "In Louisiana: Jazzman's Last Ride." *Time.* 20 April, 10-11.

Tugend, Tom. 2001. "Furrow Sentenced." *The Jewish Journal of Greater Los Angeles.* 30 March. http://www.jewishjournal.com/home/preview.php?id=6673

Vera, Veronica. 2002. *Miss Vera's Cross-Dress for Success.* New York: Villard.

Vera, Veronica. 1997. *Miss Vera's Finishing School for Boys Who Want to Be Girls.* New York: Doubleday.

Vilanch, Bruce. 2004. "Boo! We're Gay!" *The Advocate.* 9 November. www.advocate.com

Ward, Edna M. 1992. *Celebrating Ourselves: A Crone Ritual Book.* Portland, ME: Astarte Shell Press.

Wardle, Francis. 1999/2000. "Children of Mixed Race—No Longer Invisible." *Educational Leadership.* Volume 57/Number 4. Understanding Youth Culture. Pages 68-72. http://www.ascd.org/ed_topics/el199912_wardle.html

Weiner, Stacy. 1996. "Thank Heaven for Little Girls." *Jewish Monthly,* June-July, 26-31.

Weiss, Vikki, and Jennifer A. Block. 2000. *What to Do When You're Dating a Jew: Everything You Need to Know from Matzah Balls to Marriage.* New York: Three Rivers Press.

Williams, Darice. 2004. "Non-Jewish 13-Year-Olds Celebrate Faux Bar Mitzvahs." *Tribune Review.* 3 December. http://www.pittsburghlive.com/x/

Winton, Louise A., ed. 1985 "Ontario, Canada:Commemorative Services of Ontario.

Wittenburg, Mary, and Amanda Paulson. 2003. "All in the (mixed-race) family: a US Trend." *The Christian Science Monitor.* http://www.csmonitor.com/2003/0828/p03s01-ussc.htm

Wolcott, James. 2005. "The Gay Divide." *Vanity Fair.* February, 82-84.

Wolk, Martin. 1999. "Aryan Leader Says L.A. Shootings Part of Race War." *Reuters.* 20 August. http://www.rickross.com/reference/furrow/furrow12.html

Wolff, Jana. 2000. *Secret Thoughts of an Adoptive Mother.* Honolulu: Vista Communications, Second Edition, Revised.

Wride, Nancy. 2004. "More Than One Claus in His Contract." *Los Angeles Times,* 22 December, B1, 7.

Yurchenko, Marine, and Sam Abell. 1991. "Birth and Childhood." *Life,* October, 10-21.

Other Resources

ADOPTIONS

Bal Jagat Adoptions

> 9311 Farralone Ave.
> Chatsworth, CA 91311
> 818-709-4737
> www.baljagat.org

Families with Children from China—www.FCC.org

> www.adoption.com
>
> www.adoptachild.US
>
> www.adoptivefamilies.com
>
> www.pactadopt.org
>
> www.rainbowkids.com

GAY/LESBIAN/BISEXUAL/TRANSGENDER

Gay Parent magazine
P.O. Box 750852
Forest Hills, New York 11375-0852
www.gayparentmag.com

Growing Generations, a full-service surrogacy and egg donation agency dedicated to assisting members of the gay and lesbian community in the creation of their families.

> www.growinggenerations.com

Parents and Friends of Gays and Lesbians—www.pflag.com

> www.twobrides.com
>
> www.twogrooms.com

INTERFAITH AND MULTIRACIAL FAMILIES

Association of Multiethnic Americans, Inc.
P.O. Box 341304
Los Angeles, CA 90034-1304
www.ameasite.org

Dovetail Institute for Interfaith Family Resources
775 Simon Greenwell Lane
Boston, KY 40107
800-530-1596

di-ifr@bardstown.com

Multiracial Americans of Southern California (MASC)
12228 Venice Blvd., Suite 452
Los Angeles, CA 90066

www.beliefnet.com

www.Chrismukkah.com

www.halfjew.com

www.interfaithclergy.network

www.InterfaithFamily.com

www.halfkorean.com

www.mixedfolks.com

Videos

Celebration of Age: 1997. *The Croning Ceremony*. Context Productions.
5525 North Via Entrada, Tucson, AZ 85718.

Common Threads: Stories from the Quilt. 1989 Telling Pictures, Inc.
And the NAMES Project Foundation.

Southern Comfort. 2001. Kate Davis documents the final year in the life of
transgender (female to male) Robert Eads. Next Wave Films.

INDEX